The Politics of Morality

Ohio University Press Polish and Polish-American Studies Series

Series Editor: John J. Bukowczyk

The Politics of Morality

*The Church, the State, and
Reproductive Rights in
Postsocialist Poland*

Joanna Mishtal

OHIO UNIVERSITY PRESS

ATHENS

Ohio University Press, Athens, Ohio 45701
ohioswallow.com
© 2015 by Ohio University Press
All rights reserved

To obtain permission to quote, reprint, or otherwise reproduce or distribute material from
Ohio University Press publications, please contact our rights and permissions department at
(740) 593-1154 or (740) 593-4536 (fax).

Printed in the United States of America
Ohio University Press books are printed on acid-free paper ⊗ ™
25 24 23 22 21 20 19 18 17 16 15   5 4 3 2 1

Library of Congress Cataloging-in-Publication Data
Mishtal, Joanna.
 The politics of morality : the church, the state, and reproductive rights in postsocialist
Poland / Joanna Mishtal.
    pages cm. — (Ohio University Press Polish and Polish-American studies series)
 Includes bibliographical references and index.
 ISBN 978-0-8214-2139-0 (hc : alk. paper) — ISBN 978-0-8214-2140-6 (pb : alk. paper) —
ISBN 978-0-8214-4517-4 (pdf)
 1. Women—Political activity—Poland. 2. Women's rights—Poland. 3. Church and state—
Poland. 4. Catholic Church—Political activity—Poland. 5. Reproductive rights—Poland.
6. Abortion—Poland. 7. Poland—Politics and government—1989– I. Title.
 HQ1236.5.P7M57 2015
 320.08209438—dc23
                     2015018324

Contents

Illustrations

Plates (following page 104)

Lech Wałęsa holding the historic Pope pen
The gate to the famous Gdańsk shipyard
A Catholic cross hanging in the Polish Parliament
The annual "wafer ritual" in the Polish Parliament
A street demonstration in front of the Polish Parliament
The annual manifa protest in Warsaw
Wanda Nowicka and Alicja Tysiąc
Corpus Christi street processions
Women on Waves
"What child? I don't have work!"

Figures

Graphs

Acknowledgments

The research and writing of this book have been quite challenging as I tried to make sense of the transformations taking place in my country of origin since I immigrated to the United States, and as I grapple with the prospects for its future. I owe a great debt to the many people who have supported my work, but especially all the research participants in Kraków, Warsaw, and Gdańsk who generously gave their time to this project and shared their insights and experiences with me. I am also grateful to Wanda Nowicka, Jola Konwa, and Bożena Jawień for facilitating my data collection in Warsaw and Kraków. My anthropological perspective was enriched by conversations with numerous Polish scholars, in particular Halina Grzymała-Moszczyńska, Ewa Hauser, Hanka Orla-Bukowska, and Joanna Regulska, who shared their insights and introduced me to other scholars and research participants. To everyone in Poland: dziękuję.

I have been fortunate to receive a number of grants and fellowships to support various phases of my work in Poland between 2000 and 2014. Research funding from the University of Colorado at Boulder included the Pre-dissertation Research Grant, the Graduate Fellowship, the Beverly Sears Grant, and the Dorothy Martin Doctoral Student Award. Research in 2002 was funded by the Fulbright Scholarship. The writing phase between 2004 and 2006 was supported by the American Council of Learned Societies Fellowship in East European Studies, the Thomas Edwin Devaney Fellowship awarded by the Center for Humanities and the Arts, University of Colorado at Boulder, and the Brown/Ricketts/Udick Grant awarded by the American Association of University Women. I also thank the Woodrow Wilson International Center for Scholars for funding my participation in the cross-disciplinary Junior Scholars' Training Seminar in 2004, where I spent four days with a group of distinguished Slavic Studies scholars who provided valuable comments on my work. The Charlotte Ellertson Post-doctoral Fellowship and Research Grant at Columbia University (2006 to

2008) generously funded my research conducted in Gdańsk. The University of Central Florida supported my research at the European Union in 2009 and 2010, and the International Research Exchanges Board (IREX) funded research in Warsaw in 2014. I greatly benefited from the Wenner-Gren Foundation Hunt Fellowship, which gave me six months of full-time writing of this book in 2011.

I feel extremely grateful for the extraordinary guidance I received from my doctoral adviser, colleague, and friend, Donna M. Goldstein. Donna has been instrumental in sparking my initial interest in anthropology and in my intellectual growth over the years. I greatly appreciate her visit during my fieldwork in Poland and her thoughtful reviews and critiques of the various chapters as well as the entire manuscript. I treasure her support and wisdom.

I am also indebted to Lonia A. Jakubowska (University College Utrecht), Janet Liebman Jacobs, Carole M. McGranahan, Paul Shankman, and Elizabeth Dunn. In particular, I thank Paul and Carole for their valuable comments on various aspects of earlier versions of this work. I have also greatly benefited from Lonia's generosity in meeting with me for a six-hour discussion in Warsaw during my early research, and subsequently the many stimulating and unfinished conversations with her, as well as with Anton Blok and Verena Blok, in Soest.

While at the Mailman School of Public Health at Columbia University, I was fortunate to work with Wendy Chavkin, who became my mentor and friend; she assisted me in developing my arguments and provided comments on the entire manuscript. I also acknowledge the Charlotte Ellertson Postdoctoral Fellowship community for their support and collegiality, especially Kelly Blanchard and Carole Joffe, and my colleagues in that community.

I have had the privilege of receiving feedback on various aspects and sections of this book from a number of exceptional colleagues, including Lorena Anton, Rachel Dannefer, Silvia De Zordo, Shana Harris, Michael H. Heim, Carla Jones, Padraic Kenney, Elizabeth Krause, Adriana Lamackova, Martha Lampland, Milena Marchesi, David Ost, Shana Penn, Michele Rivkin-Fish, Jane Schneider, Sydel Silverman, and Janine Wedel. In particular, I thank Michele Rivkin-Fish for her incisive reviews of several of my presentations and papers, from which this book benefited in significant ways. I also thank Silvia De Zordo for our wonderful collaborations, which have helped energize my thinking and writing. I owe special gratitude to Wendy Chavkin, Vince Darcangelo, Donna Goldstein, and Grace Hood, who read and commented on the entire manuscript, and propelled me forward with challenging feedback and encouraging words. I cherish their support, friendship, and intellectual companionship.

While at the University of Central Florida and in the final stages of manuscript writing, I received warm encouragement from my colleagues, in particular Stacy Barber, Roz Howard, Ty Matejowsky, Matt McIntyre, Beatriz Reyes-Foster, Maria Cristina Santana, Marla Toyne, and John Walker. I am grateful to Arlen Chase, the department chair, who supported my scholarship and writing in important ways.

Special thanks go to Elsa Fluss and Steve Wenglowsky for their painstaking editorial help on a number of key chapters and to Lauren Novak for help with transcription and general research assistance in Brussels. I also thank Morgen Warner and Rebecca Young for editing and formatting the list of references, Shana Harris and Kyra Harris for their assistance with photographs, and Luke Palmer and Namaste Reid for their technical support in many critical moments.

Many thanks go to my family in Częstochowa as well as friends for their support during the many years of researching and writing this book, in particular Apolonia Kondys, Sharon Conlin, Priscilla Craven, Shana Harris, Grace Hood, Sue Palmer, Magda Stawkowski, Tracy Sweely, and Carla Stanke. I also thank my friends and fellow graduate students, especially Carol Conzelman, Susan Erikson, Paulette Foss, David Hoffman, Ursula Lauper, and Jim Schechter. I extend my deep appreciation to Tom Flood for years of engaging conversations that helped me refine my arguments, as well as Stephen Serwin for uplifting comments and sharing my sense of the struggle that accompanies writing.

Finally, I thank the incisive anonymous reviewers for Ohio University Press as well as the director, Gillian Berchowitz, and the series editor, John Bukowczyk. I am particularly grateful to John for his sustained interest in my scholarship and extraordinary patience over the last few years. I also thank the editorial staff at Ohio University Press, including Nancy Basmajian and Ricky Huard, for working with me during the critical final phases of the project, and Teresa Jesionowski for her meticulous copyediting work. Additionally, I am grateful to Ewa Dąbrowska-Szulc, Joanna Erbel, Wojciech Surdziel, and Karolina Więckiewicz for sharing and donating their photographs for the book. Special thanks to artist Sébastien Thibault for his generosity in adapting and donating his illustration as the cover image for this book.

While many colleagues, friends, and anonymous reviewers contributed to the development of my ideas and arguments, I am solely responsible for any shortcomings or errors I may have made in this book. All translations from the Polish are mine, unless otherwise indicated.

Women's Rights and Democratization

The Polish Paradox

AMONG FORMER SOVIET-BLOC NATIONS, the Catholic Church has a powerful and wide footprint in democratic Poland. The story behind this involves the profound influence of the Polish Pope John Paul II that emboldened the church in Poland, together with the rise of the Solidarity oppositional movement, which captured international attention with the possibility of an overthrow. In 1989, after several years of struggle under the tyranny of martial law imposed by the state, Poland became one of the earliest East European sites where an oppositional movement successfully forced the regime's collapse. The incredible news caused international jubilation. But lurking behind the triumph of the Solidarity movement were the hidden dangers of a renewed political power of the church. Few in the media dared to voice a concern. After all, the focus was on the imminent end of Soviet communism and the Cold War, and the dawn of new rights and freedoms in the region. The severe restrictions on reproductive rights, including a ban on abortion, that ensued in Poland in the immediate aftermath of the regime's overthrow were overshadowed by the promising idea that Poland was "democratizing."

But what kind of democratization was it?

In this book, I explore the contentious politics of morality imposed by the church on the society since the 1989 transition to independence, and the contradictions of the Polish democratization process, which simultaneously brought new rights and freedoms while restricting others. Poland has been hailed for its role in the downfall of the state socialist regime, thus spurring democratization in the region, yet women enjoyed far greater protection of their rights before the fall of the regime. Poland is a place where the Catholic Church dominates politics and 89 percent of Poles proclaim Catholic affiliation yet only 40 percent practice regularly. Premarital sex, abortion, and contraception are widely practiced in direct defiance of the church. Poland is a place where the commitment to neoliberal economics has been widely praised by global capital interests; however, class stratification disproportionately affecting women has been on a dramatic rise. And finally, Poland is a place with a plummeting birthrate in spite of the restrictions on family planning. Ultimately, as the feminist scholar and activist Ann Snitow observed in 1993 in *The Nation*, in the Polish transition from communism to democracy: "The church wins, women lose" (Snitow 1993, 556).

But all was not lost. Since then, the struggles for reproductive rights have escalated in Poland and are reflected in a rise of an organized feminist movement that increasingly is opening new democratic channels to challenge traditional power structures and restrictive laws through the European Union courts. In addition, Polish women's individual everyday acts to exercise their will by resisting the restrictive laws reveal an undercurrent of ongoing struggles and contestations of the dominance of the church. In fact, Polish women's choice to severely limit births (Poland has one of the lowest birthrates in the world) is one of the great paradoxes in a system that restricts access to family planning and where the state and the church actively call on women to have more children. Yet even as the church has been losing social influence on the people, it continues to be powerful in politics both symbolically and in policymaking decisions. Moreover, the Vatican with its selection of conservative popes in Benedict XVI and Francis[1] has stayed the course on the prohibition of abortion and contraception, and continues to push for restrictive policies at state levels, especially in nations, like Poland, with a strong church presence. In this book, I trace and examine these struggles and contradictions, and show that the battle for reproductive rights, and abortion rights in particular, is not only far from over in Poland but is increasingly spilling into the international European arena.

This book is based on twenty-three months of anthropological research that I conducted in Kraków, Warsaw, and Gdańsk, Poland, between 2000 and 2014. As a Polish American who emigrated to the United States in 1981 as a tennis player on the girls' national team just before the political turmoil,

I held a unique perspective as a refugee whose exposure to North American scholarship and feminism has made me a keen "insider-outsider" observer of my culture of origin (Sherif 2001). Traditional anthropology used to assert the importance of being an outsider—being distanced from one's proposed culture of study. But more recently the discipline has recognized the advantage of training anthropologists with more complicated identities who themselves have experienced emigration, exile, and return. Although a "partial insider" researcher faces a challenge to avoid making assumptions or quick judgments in the field, anthropologists have also noted clear advantages as "insiders studying their own cultures offer new angles of vision and depth of understanding" (Clifford and Marcus 1986, 9). Indeed, during fieldwork, my dual identity was simultaneously challenging and a place of privilege as I constantly negotiated the boundaries between enjoying the familiarity of my home country and maintaining the scholarly distance of a researcher. In the end, my partial insider status and fluency in the Polish language were essential in facilitating my acceptance as a researcher.

The Accidental Refugee

I was born and grew up in the Catholic center of Poland, in the city of Częstochowa, the home of the Black Madonna icon and the Jasna Góra monastery, located in the south of the country. I completed elementary and part of high school in the public state socialist education system and concurrently attended religion classes at the local Catholic parish, as was typical for children of most Catholic families at that time. At the age of eight I began playing tennis with a wooden racquet and a single tennis ball, which I washed and dried daily. As my skills improved, I began to take part in individual and team tournament competitions, and by the age of thirteen I reached the number two ranking in the category of "junior girls" in Poland. Consequently, I was fortunate to be selected by the state to join the Polish National Junior Tennis Team, a spot I was able to maintain for three years, although my position on the team fluctuated. I qualified to travel abroad only occasionally as the government sent just one or maybe two girls to compete internationally, but in November 1981, our team of six players— three girls and three boys, ages fourteen to eighteen—was sent to compete in the Orange Bowl Junior World Tennis Championships in Miami Beach,

Florida. On December 13, only two weeks after our team's arrival in the United States, I learned that due to the escalating political unrest linked to the increased oppositional activism of the Solidarity movement, the communist state had imposed martial law. In our Florida hotel room, we watched images of Polish unrest repeatedly shown on US television in breaking news footage, but because we did not speak English none of us knew exactly what was going on, and, more important, what the implications were.[2] Discussing the matter with our coach was out of the question. We hardly knew him as he was not the national team coach. The rumor on the team had it that he was "handpicked" by the government to travel with us—despite his lack of English and minimal international travel experience—because as a married man with children he was the least likely among the coaches to defect and would therefore serve as a suitable chaperone to make sure we all came back as well. (In contrast, our actual national coach was single and fluent in English, and was therefore a more likely defector.)

But the martial law crackdown and the civil war–like situation there made it seem too dangerous to go back. Indeed, on the second day of the unrest, I received a phone call at the hotel from an old family friend in New York, Lucien, who asked me: "Do you understand what's happening in Poland?" Lucien immigrated to the United States from Poland after the war in the late 1940s. He urged me not to return with the team as scheduled in January, but to come live with his family until the political situation in Poland was sorted out. He also told me not to share my intention with anyone as that could compromise the plan, but to be prepared to categorically tell the coach that I was not returning when the time was right. Four weeks later, after completing competitions (in which I lost almost all of my matches), I flew back with the team from Florida to New York, where we had a layover en route to Warsaw. As planned, I called Lucien from one of JFK's public phones, for only ten cents. When I announced to the coach that I was not going back, he showed little emotion, as though he expected that one of the players might defect. He was less prepared to hear that another girl on the team had also made clandestine plans to stay in the United States. All three boys then declared they too were not going back, but only two of them had been able to make their own arrangements in other US cities where they knew someone. Lucien promptly came to the airport and collected me and the one boy who had nowhere else to go, to live with his family in Queens. In the end, the coach returned to Poland with only one of the six players (the youngest girl). I remember that he was upset but not surprised, which spoke to the intensity and gravity of the situation at home.

Unlike some of the older players and coaches, I never intended to leave Poland permanently, so I waited in Queens for the turmoil in Poland to sort itself out and an opportune moment to return home. I resisted suggestions from well-meaning Polish Americans that I should ask for asylum on political grounds, worrying that such action might make it impossible for me to return. I was unable to contact my family for several months as telephone lines were frozen, and later calls were monitored by a censor, but it was nevertheless clear that martial law would last for some time and the future was uncertain. With the support of the Polish community in New York, which was eager to help me both financially and emotionally and offer valuable advice, I made a decision to stay. It was a hard decision but one I knew I needed to make. Once I was able to freely speak to my family, I was relieved to hear that they supported my decision to stay in the United States and in fact had worried early on that I might return with the team in the midst of the crisis. My main concerns now were that I owned only a suitcase of tennis clothes, inappropriate for winter in New York, and spoke no English since, thus far, I had studied only the required Russian in school, and German as an elective because my father deemed it the most useful language for a Pole. I realized quickly that my German was not very helpful in the United States and began to study English intensively. I was fortunate to have tennis skills that allowed me to find work as a tennis instructor for the following decade, and this was crucial in enabling me to become independent and pursue a high school and then a college education. It took nine years before the situation was stable enough for me to return to Poland and see my family.

Similar to many of the participants in my research, when growing up in state socialist Poland I took it for granted that abortion and contraception were available, despite the strong presence of the Catholic Church even during the state socialist era. Although Poland lacked the full range of family planning options, controlling one's fertility was nevertheless standard and expected, and the birthrate in Poland gradually declined with greater access to hormonal contraceptives in the 1970s. From my perspective as a high school teenager, both knowledge about pregnancy prevention and the availability of abortion and contraception were important, as none of my friends among school or tennis peers wanted to become pregnant at an early age. Unintended pregnancies occasionally did happen among the teens or older siblings and cousins—everyone knew the word *wpadka,* literally an accident—and some pregnancies indeed ended in abortions. This was a discreet matter known only to one's closest friends. But publicly, there was no controversy and virtually no discussion about the issue. The church simply did not talk about abortion during the state socialist era, and the moralistic tone around reproduction was largely absent. The state was secular and implemented reproductive rights, which were formally part of the gender equality rhetoric.

Feminist Encounters

The formal ideology of equality manifested itself in a particular way in my early education when I was held back for a year from starting grade school because presumably I was a precocious child (based on a brief assessment by a school psychologist). The idea was that brighter kids do not need to enter school as early, and therefore holding them back a year could equalize the playing field for the incoming cohort of kids. Unfortunately the outcome was that when I finally started school at the age of seven, I was still unable to read or write, and I felt rather inadequate vis-à-vis other children. However, once I started my education, I experienced a strong sense of gender equality, both in the educational setting and in sports, where girls and boys were typically given a similar degree of attention, encouragement, and discipline from teachers and coaches. Later during my research in Poland, I found that similar experiences were often explained by participants in my study as stemming from the state socialist regime's approach to gender equality. This involved granting important women's rights, including reproductive rights, as well as equal rights to education and employment by the state.

The kind of "state feminism" experienced in Poland and other nations in the Soviet region starkly contrasted with the prolonged struggles for women's rights in North America. In the United States, the right to abortion was fought for for decades and hard-won only in 1973 with the *Roe v. Wade* Supreme Court case, seventeen years later than in Poland, where abortion rights were granted by the state socialist regime in 1956. Similarly, contraception was legal and state subsidized in Poland starting in the 1950s (Okólski 1983), but in the United States it was legalized only in 1969 via the

Griswold v. Connecticut Supreme Court ruling, which deemed family planning as a decision domain protected by the right to privacy. Since my exposure in the 1980s to the history of the North American feminist movement, I began to appreciate what it means to struggle for rights. I was particularly moved by Carole Joffe's *Doctors of Conscience: The Struggles to Provide Abortion Before and After Roe v. Wade* (1995) about the dedication and heroism of physicians who provided abortions clandestinely. These stories opened my eyes to women's vulnerability in a setting where abortion is illegal and to the unending struggle for this right.

Since I settled in the United States, I have observed reproductive rights gains here repeatedly challenged by the political right, with bills aiming to restrict access to abortion at the federal level as well as state by state.[3] Indeed, in the 1980s reproductive rights seemed far more stable in Poland. However, when the transition to Polish independence began in the early 1990s, I watched with both interest and trepidation how rapidly the church dismantled access to abortion, contraception, and sex education in Poland. I wondered, How could this be? After decades of access to these services, what kind of forces does it take to roll back long-standing rights? And where is the Polish feminist movement to resist these restrictions?

Just as the majority of the US public rejoiced about the fall of communism, I questioned the nature of the democratization process that was under way, and the effects of these changes on women's access to health care. It is from these questions that my research project emerged during the late 1990s, and later crystallized and came to fruition in the 2000s.

The Research Process

I approached my fieldwork with three distinct but interrelated research questions: (1) What are the effects of postsocialist democratization in Poland on reproductive rights, policies, and access to health care? (2) How are the categories of gender and reproduction used in the political agendas of the Catholic Church and the state? And (3) How do women experience these shifts, and what coping strategies do they employ to navigate the new system? This study is based on twenty-three months of ethnographic research between 2000 and 2014 in Kraków, Warsaw, and Gdańsk: three months in 2000, three months in 2001, twelve months in 2002, three months in 2007, and two months in 2014. During 2002, I conducted fieldwork as a Fulbright scholar affiliated with the Department of Social Anthropology at the Jagiellonian University.

My goal during my fieldwork was to bring together multiple voices and experiences of Polish women, doctors, and reproductive rights advocates, as well as the perspectives of the Catholic clergy and laypersons engaged in work on behalf of the church. I conducted participant-observation and unstructured and semistructured interviews with 123 women from varied socioeconomic backgrounds. Beginning with 13 independent "seeds" established during the preliminary research in 2000 through professional and informal aquiantances, I then utilized snowball sampling to expand my sample to include a mixture of women from different socioeconomic and educational backgrounds. In addition to conducting interviews (one to four with each participant), I also spent a significant amount of time in day-to-day activities with study participants in their homes and other social settings, including social outings, religious events and gatherings, horseback riding and pottery classes, and work-related gatherings. I spent a significant amount of time in 2002 in the social service offices, mainly in the Kraków neighborhood of Nowa Huta, but also in Podgórze, with the social workers, some of whom took me along on their daily rounds to visit their clients. I also spent time in the offices of reproductive rights nongovernmental organizations (NGOs). All of the above ethnographic and qualitative methods are uniquely suited to in-depth investigations of lived experiences, attitudes, and perspectives, allowing for subtleties and depth that is not always afforded by other methods (Bernard 1995). As mentioned earlier, my native background and my language skills were invaluable assets in collecting rich ethnographic material.

My interviews generated detailed narratives of life histories, memories of state socialism, reproductive desires and decisions, experiences with family planning and reproductive and sexual health care, and understandings and meanings of abortion policies, feminism, and women's activism around reproductive rights. I also interviewed twenty-six physicians specializing in obstetrics and gynecology and six family planning educators in three major health care facilities probing the meanings that health care providers attached to the rapid changes in reproductive policies, and the ways they experienced and coped with these changes. I interviewed women's rights advocates, and observed and participated in the activities of several NGOs:

the Federation for Women and Family Planning, Women's Foundation eFKa, Women's Rights Center, National Women's Information Center, Our Stork: The Association for Infertility Treatment and the Support of Adoption, and the Network of East–West Women. I chose to focus on these organizations because of the prominence of their work relevant to reproductive rights and policies. I spent most of my time at the Federation for Women and Family Planning, which is the only NGO wholly devoted to reproductive health and rights. I interviewed fifty-two feminist activists, both affiliated and unaffiliated with these organizations. I analyzed the organizations' internal and public documents, attended meetings, and traveled to national conferences where these groups debated their strategies. My analysis of the Catholic Church's perspectives and work around the politics of reproduction draws on interviews with the clergy, including priests in local parishes and monks affiliated with the Dominican and the Jesuit orders, as well as on interviews with Bishop Tadeusz Pieronek and the priest Stanisław Obirek, both well-known representatives of the episcopate in the Polish media.

The phase of my research that took place in 2007 complemented my earlier fieldwork (which focused on Kraków and Warsaw) in terms of methods and analytical approaches. I returned to Poland, this time to Gdańsk, to further explore the most perplexing finding of my earlier research—the rapidly declining birthrate among Polish women despite the severe restrictions on family planning. For this study, in addition to unstructured and semistructured interviews, I expanded my methods to include a quantitative health survey and broadened my theoretical approach with demographic analyses. Specifically, I explored how women made reproductive decisions in the postsocialist context of economic constraints, and I examined the influence of employment and income on reproductive desires and choices. I was also interested in the degree to which the church as an institution and one's personal sense of religiosity shape women's decisions about terminating a pregnancy, using contraception, and pursuing illegal abortions. Situating my fieldwork in four major health care clinics in Gdańsk, I interviewed 55 women of reproductive age and completed 418 health surveys. I complemented my analysis with a review of demographic scholarship related to the "low" and "lowest low" fertility nations. In 2014, I returned to Warsaw for another phase of research about the politics of reproduction, but this time I focused on the "in vitro" debate and the struggle of advocacy groups to secure regulation and state subsidies for infertility treatment against the opposition from the Catholic Church. During this project, I focused on the work of Our Stork, a nongovernmental organization, but I also continued to collect data with the Federation for Women and Family Planning. To analyze the qualitative material I employed thematic coding of the texts, either manually or using the NVivo and ATLAS ti software, and examined the narratives for repeating themes and thematic consistencies and discrepancies. The analysis of my 2007 health survey was performed by a biostatistician using SPSS software at the Mailman School of Public Health at Columbia University.

My research findings and the conclusions presented in this book are directly derived from over 1,800 pages of single-spaced narratives that were generated by the interviews that I conducted during my fieldwork. They were also triangulated with other sources of data including governmental publications, Polish church and Vatican documents, and statistical and survey data generated by the Polish state as well as the EU. Additionally, I kept careful field notes of all research activities and observations, which were valuable in contextualizing the qualitative narratives. All names of research participants are pseudonyms, unless noted otherwise in endnotes. Individuals whose real names are used agreed to be quoted as such. Likewise, pseudonyms are used for the names of clinics and other locations and street names in addresses where research was conducted. The human subject research protocol was approved by the Institutional Review Board at the University of Colorado at Boulder for the early phases and at Columbia University for the later phase.

Theorizing the Politics of Reproduction in Postsocialist Poland

The theoretical orientation of this book engages with several domains in anthropological and social science literatures, including scholarship on gender, reproduction, history and political economy, postsocialism, and democratization and transition politics, as well as on church-state governance. Specifically, this research makes a contribution at the theoretical intersection of two anthropological projects: (1) *agency and power*—how human agency may be shaped in diverse ways in different settings of power as women go through their lives finding ways of navigating and coping with new predicaments, and (2) *gender, health, and religion*—in particular, how gender, religious morality, and policy interact to affect access to health care and shape experiences related to the body and health.

Agency and Power

This study offers a historicized view of the central contradiction of post-socialist democratization in Poland—that it is an emerging democracy, on the one hand; and that there is a declining tolerance for reproductive rights, women's rights, and political or religious pluralism, on the other hand. This contradiction remains obscured in much of the postsocialist scholarship, as the feminist scholar Natasha Kolchevska argues (2005, 1–4) in her review of gender as an analytic category in Slavic studies scholarship, observing that research on East Europe tends to focus on economic transformations and nationalism.[4] My goal in this book is to problematize these metanarratives that tend to conflate democracy in this region with free market liberalism, the EU expansion, or the mushrooming of NGOs. I propose instead that the hallmark of the transition to postsocialism in Poland is a new type of church-state "gender regime" which swiftly instituted restrictions on reproductive rights since the fall of state socialism in 1989 (Connell 1990, 523; Mohanty 2003, 64).[5]

I therefore present an alternative understanding of Polish democratization refocused on reproductive politics, and I make a contribution to the theoretical debates on the significance of regime change and transition politics for feminist consciousness-raising and mobilization. Thus my analysis shows how political organization of reproduction is at the core of producing postsocialist Poland (Ginsburg and Rapp 1989, 1991, 1995). Specifically, my research is in direct dialogue with the work of Gail Kligman (Gal and Kligman 2000a, 2000b; Kligman 1998), Susan Gal (Gal 1994; Gal and Kligman 2000a, 2000b), Martha Lampland (1994, 1995), and Katherine Verdery (1993, 1996) in demonstrating the centrality of the governance of women's bodies in postsocialist politics and gender as an essential constitutive feature of the Polish democratization process. My analysis of the effects of the neoliberal economic transformations on access to health care engages with the work of Michele Rivkin-Fish (2005), who argued in her ethnography that women's health care in post-Soviet Russia has suffered due to the emergence of neoliberal "privatizing" and "individualizing" discourses in medicine. Similarly, I explore in the case of Poland the shrinking of social services and other structural support, and analyze the ways in which Polish women cope with these changes.

Although gender plays an important role in the politics of other East European nations, the situation in Poland is unique, owing mainly to the historical importance of the Polish Catholic Church. In other nations, the antifeminist discourses against the socialist states' reproductive and women's rights emerged after 1989 as tools used by political parties and the media to distance themselves from the communist past, but little change took place at the legislative level.[6] In Poland, however, unlike in any other nation in the region, these discourses were translated into concrete policies restricting reproductive rights, and these new circumstances are shaping Polish women's experiences of reproduction, sexuality, and health. Simultaneously, comparative studies show that Polish women suffer greater hardships as a result of neoliberal economics and gender-based discriminations in employment than women in other postsocialist nations (Domański 2002; Fodor et al. 2002). Polish women's experiences are therefore both unique and telling—they show how globalizing forces, combined with locally specific history and politics, are experienced in different ways across the postsocialist region. Therefore, this book also makes a contribution to the scholarship on political economy and globalization by shifting the lens from the broad effects of the postsocialist economic instabilities such as employment insecurity and currency devaluation as reasons for the plummeting birthrate, to the specific and decisive gendered effects of neoliberal structural transformations that differentially and disproportionately affect women.

Gender, Health, and Religion

This book examines the political and institutional aspects of religion and their effects on health by focusing on the relations of power, rather than on relations of religious meanings. Through this approach, my goal is to contribute a deeper understanding of the influence of religious institutions and state-church politics on women's health and access to health care—an area of research that remains understudied. In fact, the anthropologist Marcia Inhorn's (2006) comprehensive review of scholarship on women and health observes that there exists a relative dearth of studies examining the effects of religious institutions on health and well-being because studies that analyze religion tend to focus on questions of religiosity and faith, rather than the political side of religion. To this end, I utilize social theorist Michel Foucault's (1991a) concept of governmentality—the internalized, individual self-regulation or self-censorship resulting from the state's governance of individuals and populations—in the context of a religious regime (Bax 1991; Wolf 1991) to theorize the religious institutional mechanisms of disciplinary power shaping women's reproductive experiences in Poland.

The concept of governmentality is rarely used as an analytical framework in the context of religion in anthropological scholarship (typically it is applied to the state and neoliberalism). Yet examining religion and governmentality together is highly valuable in the context of Poland, when we consider Foucault's later work completed after 1976, and compiled by a scholar of religion and culture, Jeremy R. Carrette (1999, 2000) as well as explored by others (Chidester 1986; Garmany 2010). In particular, the concept of "political spirituality" identified by Carrette (2000)—a shift toward the political dimensions of the church that collapses the spiritual, the ethical, and the political—offers a useful theoretical lens for linking religious governmentality with the politics of gender in Poland. Thus, rather than conceptualizing governmentality within the context of the state apparatus alone, I theorize the church as the regime of disciplinary power enforcing religious morality and self-regulation of body conduct. I demonstrate how in the context of postsocialist democratization the church had been able to act as "a superb instrument of power for itself" (Foucault 1991b, 107) acting via religious rituals as well as legislative mechanisms. The focal element of governmentality—the attention to institutions creating constraining effects in specific ideological ways—is highly relevant to the ways in which the church functions as a disciplining and surveilling institution. In this book, I therefore highlight how religious governmentality's pervasive nature goes beyond distinct political moments, and I ultimately show how the spiritual, the ethical, and the political are collapsed into a single "trajectory of truth" in public discourses (Carrette 2000, 138).

Despite the utility of Foucault's conceptual framework, scholars have noted his gender-blind and implicitly masculinist constructions of power (Brodribb 1993; Carrette 2000; Soper 1993). I bring sharp awareness to his limitations in the analysis of gender as I carry such analysis both implicitly and explicitly beyond Foucault's understanding of power by examining how decisions about reproductive rights and policies affect women. Thus the story about the church-state politics of morality in postsocialist Poland is about both the "sexed body" and the "sexed doctrine" (Carrette 2000, 127). This book directly examines these mechanisms of religious power and analyzes the *gendered effects* they produce.

My Contribution

Building on these relevant concepts, my own analysis makes two contributions. First, I contribute the theoretical framework of *moral governance,* which expands the term "governance" used by scholars thus far, to explain how particular "moral" discussions and mechanisms have been used to enact individual surveillance and political intimidation to maintain legislative control over reproduction. I also show how moral governance is used in practice: how it manifests in specific processes and discourses used to shape policy changes, as well as in specific mechanisms of enforcement at the community and individual level.

Second, I contribute a case study of *unofficial biopolitics* in Poland. Specifically, my research shows that despite the powerful set of surveilling and controlling mechanisms in place after the fall of state socialism, this is not merely another case of Foucauldian biopolitics as a secular rationality of a liberal democracy promoted in the name of optimizing the state, but rather the nature of Polish biopolitics lies in its religious and moral governance promoted in the name of Catholic-nationalist state-building. However, it is one that does not fully succeed because women routinely resist the church's strictures through various unsanctioned, individualized practices. These resistances are revealed at the individual level in illicit practices and decisions related to contraception, but they also inform the prolonged demographic decline at the society level.

Organization

In the opening chapter, I trace historically the strategic negotiating between the church and the state in Poland beginning with state socialism and leading to the de facto merging of church and state after 1989. This chapter provides the basis for understanding the current political situation in which reproductive rights have been so curtailed. My goal is to illuminate for the reader why the church has been successful in implementing its agenda on morality after the collapse of the regime in 1989 and until the present moment.

In chapter 2, I investigate specific reproductive rights restrictions that were implemented, in particular the 1993 abortion ban, and show how such policies were put in place and how society acquiesced to these changes, despite decades of legal access to these services. Increasingly, the reproductive rights restrictions in Poland are becoming the subject of legal battles in the European Court of Human Rights where some Polish women, with the assistance of reproductive rights advocates, have taken their cases and won. Chapter 3 demonstrates that Polish feminist activism greatly intensified owing to the indignation and disbelief triggered by the abortion struggle in the early 1990s. I present a number of narratives showing how feminist consciousness awoke during this time. To this end, I draw on stories of current activists, in particular Wanda Nowicka, who at the time of my research was the president of the Federation for Women and Family Planning in Warsaw and is currently the vice marshal (deputy speaker) of the Lower House of the Polish Parliament, and Kazia Szczuka, a feminist author and historian. This chapter also shows that the challenges of feminist consolidation were acutely aggravated by the decisive power of the Catholic Church in postsocialist politics.

Whereas chapters 1 through 3 focus primarily on conflicts around policymaking and the role of organizations and institutions of the church, the state, and the women's movement, chapter 4 explores specific techniques of reproductive and sexual regulation targeted at the level of individuals. Here I demonstrate the unprecedented intensification of direct regulation of women's bodily conduct taking place through techniques of surveillance exercised by the clergy since the early 1990s, including such mechanisms as confession and the *Kolęda* house calls. This chapter offers a window into the ways in which these directives are implemented by priests and the effects they have on individual women who seek the services of the church for periodic absolution. Chapter 5 shows how in the face of intensified religious surveillance and restrictive reproductive and sexual health laws, many women defy the church's directives by making personal reinterpretations of its teachings and of their obligation to the church. This includes pursuing illegal procedures in the clandestine abortion underground. This chapter investigates the ways in which the underground functions and is used by women as a strategy to sidestep legal restrictions on abortion.

In chapter 6, I engage with the final conundrum: a rapidly declining fertility rate despite the restrictions on family planning. This chapter examines the effects of the neoliberal cuts on social services and the simultaneous rise in pronatalist and nationalist discourses blaming women for "refusing" to reproduce. The continued very low birthrate in Poland has been the source of intense anxiety for the state and the church, but with little genuine concern about women's reproductive experiences and dilemmas that are underpinning the low fertility.

I conclude the book by considering some of the implications of more than two decades of morality politics implemented in postsocialist Poland. The special status and recognition afforded to the Catholic Church in a liberal democratizing state is highly significant for women's rights, because the church traditionally chooses to intervene in those policies that mainly affect women, including reproductive rights, sexual rights, and family policy. The case of Poland highlights how conflict between religious-nationalist political agendas and women's rights undermines social and gender justice. I therefore ask broader questions about the role of women's rights in liberal democracies, and I look toward the future to consider the growing role of the European Union politics in shaping women's health and rights in Europe.

I ⦙⦙⦙ "The Church Was Helping Us Win Freedom"

Democratic Transition and the Return of God

ON AUGUST 31, 1980, the state socialist regime of Poland finally caved after thirty-three years of what some Poles refer to as the "occupation." Following a series of strikes and mounting social unrest, the regime agreed to sign a document establishing the legality of the first oppositional organization in Eastern Europe, the Solidarity Labor Union. The populist hero of this movement, Lech Wałęsa, was a shipyard electrician who had risen to leadership in Solidarity through years of highly visible political protest. The document he signed on behalf of Solidarity was indeed historic; as such, the event was captured by the worldwide media. In particular, one photo of him waving the pen he used to sign his organization into power was quickly broadcast internationally. The pen he waved that day held a small but visible image of Pope John Paul II encased in clear plastic. The historic photo of Wałęsa holding the "Pope pen" in front of a mass of supporters became a symbol celebrating Solidarity's victorious moment, which through history's eyes was but a prelude to the eventual total collapse of the regime nine years later in 1989. While the world rejoiced at the dawn of new democratic freedoms, hardly anyone suspected that the pope's image on that pen would foreshadow the rise of the Catholic Church in Poland, a power that would become instrumental in curtailing women's rights. In that moment the decades of women's reproductive rights began to unravel.

The Polish state socialist regime collapsed fully in 1989; around that time or shortly thereafter other Soviet regimes in the region crumbled. Amid the upheaval, the new, democratically elected Polish Parliament, working in tandem with the Catholic Church, proposed a ban on abortion as one of the most urgent legal changes of the day. The news shocked the nation. After all, Poland was in a state of economic and political chaos, as even basic goods and services were lacking. Not only that, Polish women had enjoyed liberal access to abortion for the previous thirty-three years and most of them did not even recall a time when abortion was illegal, so the sudden prospect of a ban on the service took many by surprise. One of the women I interviewed years later in 2002 summarized the moment this way: "It was as if people simply couldn't get their minds around the idea that such a thing is possible," and another added in the same conversation: "The reason that people didn't mobilize [against antiabortion rhetoric] was because there was an enormous trust of the church, because the church was helping us win freedom." This sense of confusion was marked by a sense betrayal by the church, which until now had been a beacon of hope, having played a critical role in Solidarity's oppositional struggle as the movement gathered momentum throughout the 1980s. Until this moment, the church had been viewed as a symbol of freedom, not repression.

This turn of events raised questions for anthropological and feminist observers. As I watched the events in Poland from afar, from the United States, I saw that to many of my friends and colleagues in the United States, the shift toward restricting reproductive rights after the fall of the socialist regime seemed counterintuitive mainly because it was communism, not democracy, that has been typically associated with limits on rights and freedoms. But to the friends, colleagues, and individuals I interviewed in Poland several years later during my fieldwork from 2000 to 2007, this shift, as extreme as it was, was also somewhat expected—they understood implicitly that the church would expect repayment for its strong support of the opposition movement by heeding the church agenda in the political and juridical decision making of the newly independent nation. This expectation was particularly true about issues that are central to the self-definition of the church as a moral authority regarding sexuality, reproduction, gender roles, and the family.

But how was the Catholic Church able to do this? How was the political ground prepared, and by whom, to launch newly liberated Poland toward an all-out "morality campaign" against abortion when empty grocery shelves and rations on food, shoes, and even toilet paper were the order of the day?

To answer these questions and to place the current situation in a context that begins to explain the apparent contradictions of a democratizing nation on the one hand and diminishing rights on the other, it is useful to trace historically how the church gradually consolidated its power under the socialist regime. A historical analysis of church-state relations will show that drastic reproductive policy changes in postsocialist law were the outcome of a long-standing quest by the church to regain political power after several decades of marginalization.

Catholic Nationalism in a Historical Perspective

Roman Catholicism has been the dominant religion among Poles for centuries. The conversion of Poland to Roman Catholicism in 966 CE by King Mieszko I was the beginning of a powerful symbolic link between Polish sovereign statehood and Roman Catholicism. Between the twelfth and eighteenth centuries, Poland was home to multiple religions, including Eastern Orthodox Ukrainians, Anabaptists, Unitarians, Lutherans, Calvinists, Armenian Apostolic adherents, Muslim Tartars, and Jewish Karaimes. Although Poland did not join the Crusades, it allowed the Inquisition to be carried out in the fifteenth and sixteenth centuries, and by the end of the eighteenth century, the Catholic Church began to fully assert its dominance (Peters 2005).

The kind of overt quest for political influence evident in today's politics in Poland began in 1918 during the interwar period when Catholicism was considered a state religion. The historian Neal Pease notes that the "church and State coexisted harmoniously in interwar Poland, exchanging benevolence for reciprocal benefits within a constitutional structure that stopped just short of proclaiming the Roman church as the established national confession" (Pease 1991, 422). Later, under state socialism, the church cultivated a memory of this era as a church-state model inherent in a Catholic nation like Poland (Szostkiewicz 1999). The struggle between the state socialist regime and the opposition ultimately provided the opportunity for the church to reaffirm its symbolic role as a beacon of national freedom.[1]

Historically, the Polish church was indeed the bearer of Polish national identity—patriotic religious discourse intensified under duress during periods of foreign occupation, in particular, by Prussia, Russia, and Austria from 1795 to 1918, and by the Nazi occupiers from 1939 to 1945. However, during the Nazi occupation of Poland, the Catholic Church was also found to have mixed responses to the occupier, which included cooperative arrangements and support of the Nazi campaign, including against Jews (Friedrich 2005, 733–39). Nevertheless, the efforts of the church in supporting national resistance during these times held the partitioned nation together in the popular imagination and later reinforced the church's political legitimacy as the "national religion."[2] Although a large number of non-Catholics continued to live in Poland until the end of World War II, they experienced persecution under the Catholic hegemony. By 1945 Poland became ethnically and religiously nearly homogeneous as a result of the deportation and extermination of the Jewish population and the shifting of the borders westward, which caused the loss of the Orthodox Ukrainian, Russian, and Byelorussian populations (Hetnal 1998). The annexed German population on the western side, many of whom did not identify as Catholic, soon was forced to move deeper into Germany. Thus post–World War II Poland was increasingly homogeneous in terms of religion.

References to the historical devotion of the church to Polish independence abound in public discourses but are especially striking for churchgoers—this nationalist sentiment was commonly mentioned during Sunday masses and holiday sermons I occasionally attended with friends and research participants in Kraków, Warsaw, and Gdańsk, and particularly during the many speeches broadcast when the pope visited Kraków in August 2002.[3] The ever-present nature of this religiopatriotic discourse is significant in the ways in which the church continues to be cast as the moral authority and a political leader.

Church-State Relations under State Socialism, 1947–89

Although the church presented itself in opposition to the state during the state socialist rule, the two players coexisted in a cooperative dynamic of "antagonistic interdependencies" (Wolf 1991, 5–6), recognizing each other's dependence on one another amid ongoing struggles to assert power. Theoretically, the two regimes—the socialist state and the church—have had three important elements in common. First, both developed strategies for nation-building and community-building, working toward inducing the population to live and think according to the principles of a particular ideology, be it Marxist or Catholic. Second, both were confronted with problems of internal dissent and external conflict creating ongoing difficulties. And third, both have had expansionist agendas working to spread their influence over larger territory and new sectors of society. These similarities in authoritarianism between the communist state and the Catholic Church are captured in the popular Polish expression that the "red" regime has been replaced by the "black" one, referring to priests' cassocks. The main difference between a state and a religious regime lies in their sources of power: the state controls the population through punitive means and taxation, whereas the church in Europe, which had lost its access to physical punishment in the seventeenth century, uses a kind of moral governance (Bax 1991, 11–13). Thus the status of the church as a moral authority was of utmost importance to the religious leaders, but now, as I will show, the church's power has been fused with state power.

Relative to other Soviet bloc nations, the Polish Catholic Church was simply too powerful to be effectively restrained; therefore it enjoyed a significant amount of freedom.[4] The uniquely high affiliation of Poles with Roman Catholicism (over 90 percent) forced the state to use tactics that were adapted to this power dynamic (Hetnal 1998, 504). Consequently, many policies implemented by the state were not unilateral but rather the outcome of negotiations with the Polish episcopate (Diskin 2001). The state also recognized that the continued visibility and importance of the church maintained a sense of stability among a populace coping with postwar chaos. Conversely, the church was dependent on the state for its survival in socialism.

The antagonistic character of the two institutions was rooted in their competing visions of secular modernity and Catholic traditionalism, with tensions displayed in both rhetorical and practical terms. From its inception, the secular Polish United Workers' Party (Polska Zjednoczona Partia Robotnicza, PZPR) set out to separate the church and state (Wasilewski and Wnuk-Lipiński 1995, 675), which had immediate implications for women's rights. As soon as the party took power in 1945, a decree was introduced that legalized divorce, denied the legality of Catholic marriage ceremonies, and required a civil marriage contract (Rosada and Gwóźdź 1955). That same year the religious oath that had been required of all civil employees was discontinued, and mandatory religious education in schools was partially eliminated, allowing atheist and non-Catholic students to be exempt from religion courses (Rosada and Gwóźdź 1955). A few years later abortion was decriminalized, and the state began to subsidize contraceptives.

In a frantic response to the state's measures, Pope Pius XII excommunicated all Catholics who were PZPR members, while Cardinal Stefan Wyszyński, speaking on behalf of the Polish episcopate, sharply criticized the regime (which had little effect as PZPR membership continued to grow). Polish bishops reacted with a call to boycott socialist political candidates in their Catholic weekly, *Tygodnik Powszechny*, on September 22, 1946: "Catholics cannot belong to any organizations or parties the principles of which are incompatible with Christian teachings. Catholics may vote only for those persons, electoral lists and programs that are not in opposition to Catholic teachings and morality."[5] On the local level of towns and villages, the clergy began to refuse sacraments to Catholics who were sympathetic to the socialist state. The state, however, saw the excommunications and the local hostilities instigated by the clergy as an opportunity to further curb the church's power and later that year instituted jail sentences for clergy who refused to provide sacraments to citizens based on political objections. By 1948 the PZPR party voted itself into all government offices, and the totalitarian nature of the state socialist party became clear.

The Secular Left

The lines of conflict during the 1950s were not drawn simply between the church and the state: for much of the socialist period the leftist intelligentsia—as distinct from the communist state—also favored secularization, angering the church. The role of the Left is best illuminated by tracing the opposition-to-the-regime activism of Adam Michnik, the leading intellectual dissident during communism. His secular Jewish roots and his political leadership shaped the way the Left conceptualized its relationship to the other two actors, the communist state and the church. Certainly, from the end of World War II the secular Left was perceived, especially in intellectual circles, in the same terms as the socialists: they were antifascist and in favor of a planned economy and agrarian reform. The overwhelming majority of leftist intelligentsia, including the Catholic Left,[6] placed significant hopes in state reforms aimed at separating the church from the state. In particular,

Michnik argued that distancing the church from politics would draw Poland out of its "social and cultural backwardness." Drawing on the French
thinker Jean-Marie Domenach, he called secularism "insurance created by
believers and nonbelievers alike against the seizure of the state by totalitarian philosophies" (Michnik 1993, 175, 18).[7]

Yet by the end of the 1950s the Left turned against the state socialists
in defense of individual rights. But why this change of heart if socialist
politics are typically critical of individualism? The political scientist
David Ost writes that historically the Polish Left understood socialism
as a liberal democracy, which explains why Michnik was more likely to
rely in his reasoning on John Stuart Mill and his "splendid booklet" than
on Marx and Engels (Michnik 1993, 144). The liberal nature of the Polish
Left is highly significant for present-day politics and accounts for the
lack of true leftist parties in the current political spectrum, an issue I
return to later.

Michnik and the Left now had two enemies: the state and the church.
To make matters worse Michnik agitated the episcopate by rationalizing
that "liberals are not concerned with God" but that instead liberalism is a
purely political matter—a curious position given the political role of the
church in Poland (Michnik 1993, 143).

The Concessions

Getting beyond the complex triangle of struggles between the church, the
Left, and the socialist state, the state began to see the usefulness of some
level of cooperation with the church. In fact, the church, primarily concerned about issues of taxes and religious education in public schools, readily agreed to negotiate with the regime after some initial resistance. By 1950
the church signed a modus vivendi with the state—a working agreement (or
a type of deal between contending parties) containing several compromises,
but including in particular, that the pope was to remain a strictly religious
rather than political authority for the Polish episcopate. In exchange, the
state allowed freedom of public worship, the continued operation of the
Catholic University in Lublin, and the reintroduction of religious education in public schools, though these were optional upon parental written
request and not everywhere available (Monticone 1986, 18).[8]

The modus vivendi benefited both sides: the clergy ceased to discuss criminal state activities such as illegal arrests and police frame-ups, and in exchange, the church was promised a degree of autonomy and, significantly, established itself as a force that the regime could not dismiss (Diskin 2001; Swatos 1994). Despite the new cooperative relations the new Constitution of 1952 spelled out the full separation of church and specified freedom *from* religion and the illegality of coercing anyone into participating in religious activities. The outraged Cardinal Wyszyński, speaking on behalf of the Polish episcopate, strongly criticized the Constitution but was promptly arrested and put in prison (and later in house arrest) for three years (Rosada and Gwóźdź 1955, 224–27).

The revelations of atrocities committed by Stalin that were revealed after his death in 1953 seriously undermined the legitimacy of Soviet communism and deeply disheartened socialists around the world.[9] After the brief reign of Georgy Malenkov following Stalin's death, the next Soviet leader, Nikita Khrushchev, denounced Stalin, but even so, oppositional movements against the Soviet Union rapidly formed in Poland and Hungary. As pressure on the state mounted, the PZPR selected a new leader, Władysław Gomułka, who was perceived by the Polish episcopate as a moderate. Indeed, Gomułka immediately released imprisoned Cardinal Wyszyński and established more cordial relations. Pacifying the church was important for the state in its struggle against the Left. Gomułka promptly began to repress the Left through political arrests and imprisonment, effectively taking control of post-Stalinist unrest and imposing the superficial sense of stability required by the Soviet Union, without the interference of the clergy (Monticone 1986, 35).

As the opposition from the Left grew, the state became increasingly willing to resort to violence. In January 1968 the authorities shut down a production of a play titled *Dziady* (*Forefathers' Eve*) that stirred patriotic emotion in a Warsaw theater when the audience, mostly students and faculty of Warsaw University, broke out into a demonstration as the play's dialogue mentioned the democratic struggle against Tsarist Russia.[10] Police materialized rapidly, and the demonstration was quickly dispersed. The next day students responded with open protests, which were followed by severe and violent clashes with the police. The riots ended in the arrest of hundreds in the opposition leftist movement, among them Michnik. These arrests were under the guise of an anti-Semitic cover—the state depicted protesters as Jewish radicals aiming to incapacitate Poland from within (Ekiert 1997, 318; Michnik 1993, 96).[11]

The stance of the church during the 1968 riots is telling and indicative of the semicooperative relations between the church and the regime throughout most of the state socialist period. During the riots the church stood silent as the government cracked down on the students and professors, casting the conflict as an internal struggle among socialists. Some of the clergy made vague pronouncements against the violence but not the anti-Semitism. Most, however, maintained silence. The passivity of the church during this time, in light of its previous rights rhetoric, suggests that the church refrained from supporting a secular group—a fact that Michnik and others recalled with bitter resentment, seeing "how morally defeated the church can become if it makes itself the supreme value and ignores the need for human solidarity, which the poor and oppressed have always expected Christianity to promote" (Michnik 1993, 102–3). While the Left experienced persecution by the regime, relations between the church and the state were calm due to concessions made the few years before. This sidelining of the church was in fact critical in helping the regime crack down on dissidents. Until the final decade of the regime the two actors were interdependent as each helped the other to survive, but each also harbored deep antagonisms, which were mainly kept in check, until much later.

Women's Experiences under State Socialism

Women's experiences during state socialism were complicated and contradictory. As the state socialist PZPR Party membership continued to grow, women were vastly underrepresented in its ranks as compared to men, and the male-dominated nature of the party membership suggested a systematic exclusion of female participation in politics (Hanley 2003, 1092). (Despite their small numbers in PZPR, women's representation in government was greater under the state socialist regime than it has been under the democratic rule since 1989.) Nevertheless, Marxist egalitarian principles drove many new policies regarding expanded access to education, health care, and employment, especially for women, thereby creating substantial improvements in the living standards of the population. Generous social service policies were established to relieve women of the burdens of caretaking and to facilitate their entry into paid employment. The state provided many households with basic appliances and opened a network of public child care centers—from infant care facilities to library-like places for teens. Welfare benefits were expanded to include cash provisions to supplement families' and single mothers' wages, purchase school books and supplies, and support the care of disabled children. The state also subsidized a chain of cafeterias called *Bar Mleczny* (literally, Milk Bars) offering inexpensive home-style meals that could be picked up in stackable containers on the way home from work (Mishtal 2009a). As a result of these policies, Polish women's full-time employment rose to 78 percent during state socialism (Fodor 2002, 371–72), and the state assumed the role of a "virtual husband," relieving women from considerable housework, while the actual husbands at home experienced little change in gender roles—women were still expected to manage the home and care for children, husbands, and elderly or sick relatives.

The separation of church and state also resulted in significant new reproductive health services and rights. The state unflinchingly liberalized reproductive rights in the first decade of its rule, despite vigorous opposition from the church. In 1956 the state legalized abortion for medical and socioeconomic reasons for pregnancies of up to fourteen weeks.[12] It made the procedure free of charge if performed in a public hospital (Fuszara 1991, 117). Despite the church's prohibition on abortion, Polish women rapidly took advantage of the new law, and in 1965 alone 158,000 women pursued safe and legal abortion in state hospitals. After this peak abortion rates began to decline, which coincided with an increase in biomedical contraceptive use. In fact, despite the opposition from the church, there was a sixfold rise in sales of the birth control pill from 1969 to 1979 (Okólski 1983). The state openly endorsed family planning and sex education and established subsidies for both. A law was passed requiring doctors to inform women who had just delivered a child or had an abortion about their contraceptive options, which included education about the newly available hormonal contraceptives. In addition, the national health care system began to cover 70 percent of the cost of prescription contraceptives (Mazur 1981, 196; Okólski 1983). Overall, state socialists made efforts to popularize biomedical contraceptive methods and made them financially accessible. Although the liberalization of reproductive rights was substantial, it omitted voluntary sterilization, which remains illegal to this day (Rutkiewicz 2001).

State socialist reproductive reforms reflected not only the secular ideology of the regime and exercised the first separation of church and state in

Poland's history, but they were also consistent with the socialist gender equity rhetoric (the policies also had the utilitarian effect of enlarging the labor pool). The regime's gender equity campaign, also known as "state feminism" (because rights for which women fought in the West were simply given out by the state without any struggle) sharply broke with the previously dominant discourse of the primacy of motherhood. The Polish state offered women greater reproductive and sexual autonomy, in addition to employment and education access, and in general, women made significant gains during this period. In interviews with several Polish scholars who have carried out retrospective analyses of women's status under state socialism and have drawn on their own experiences, the situation is recalled in the following way, as summarized by Mariola,[13] a gender studies scholar:

> Even though women were the overworked heroes of everyday life, at least they benefited from it [state socialism] and drew a moral and personal satisfaction. The sheer fact that women had their own money, whatever the money was, it was something. Women fared better than men in socialism which destroyed the man but not the woman—typically the man was less educated than the woman, and he couldn't support the family, so the socialist man was only so so [*byle jaki*]. The man lost all the previous advantages: before, he was the boss and the master [*pan i władca*] in the patriarchal peasant family, but then suddenly these things no longer existed. (Interview with Mariola, Warsaw, 2002)

Małgorzata Fuszara, a sociologist and one of the most prominent gender studies scholars based in Warsaw, explained the value of access to employment and education this way: "[The] equal rights of women were included in the [Polish] Constitution back then; many nations were struggling for such rights with little success, including in the US. There were elements that dealt with a variety of rights: from minor ones like the right to keep your maiden name after marriage to certain employment rights, although there were no gender-related quotas in Poland. But this varied in the region."

The experiences of Kazia Szczuka, a feminist author and historian, are emblematic of those women who valued these gains but who qualified this by expressing the doubts about the regime's top-down implementation:

> Communists operated on the assumption that emancipation is important and that women need access to the workplace. So in some sense, these feminist vignettes did exist. Communism gave us a feeling that there was equality, abortion was legal and so on. Later, we all became more ambivalent about it because, on the one hand, I think that truly many women with higher education got

jobs, thanks to that awful regime. We could perhaps argue that if there were no communism, women would also find access to the workplace, but nevertheless it did, indeed, happen much sooner as a directive of the state. (Interview with Szczuka, Warsaw, 2002)

Despite these benefits, independent feminist thought was systematically suppressed by the state as a precaution against antistate organizing and dissent. In the 1970s, international feminism brought attention to gender inequities and facilitated the emergence of women's movements around the globe, but this wave had little impact in Poland and elsewhere in this region. State socialist authorities throughout Eastern Europe met the emergence of Western, second-wave feminism with intolerance, claiming that the state was the only legitimate source of women's emancipation. Problems that the Polish regime cast as nonexistent, namely gender inequality and high fertility, were front and center in the 1967 Declaration on the Elimination of Discrimination against Women and at the First United Nations World Conference on Women in Mexico City in 1975, as well as events associated with the United Nations World Population Year in 1974.

Indeed, this rhetoric did not seem that far away from the truth—in addition to a number of new rights, fertility also began to gradually decline, and in any case it was not as high as in other parts of the world to begin with.[14] The international events did not mobilize Polish women; virtually no grassroots or elite mobilization occurred during these years. A number of women were part of the leftist intelligentsia, but the movement cared little about feminist causes. For those in the academic circles aware of the developments in the West, the lack of any media coverage conveyed an impression that women's problems in Poland were fundamentally different from those of their Western counterparts, as the socialist state cultivated the appearance of an East-West dichotomy. This notion persisted in state discourse until after the fall of the regime in 1989, when the evidence of the similarities of women's struggles, including the almost universal undervaluation of female labor, revealed the shared predicaments on both sides of the iron curtain.

The Radicalization of the Church

As a result of carefully planned political maneuvering by the church during the state socialist era, the church was finally able to reconstitute and consolidate its power in the late 1970s and throughout the last decade of the regime in the 1980s (Hann 1997, 2000; Weigel 1992). Under socialist rule the church became visibly active on behalf of the Solidarity labor union, but only after it was clear that the organization was a solid oppositional entity in the 1980s. In the early phase of Solidarity, the group consisted mainly of a heterogeneous coalition of activists. As Wałęsa became more prominent in the movement, the nature of the group began to shift toward a closer tie with the church.[15] Soon, Solidarity and Wałęsa flaunted the Catholic aspect of the union—symbolism in images of the pope, crucifixes on the gates of the Gdańsk shipyard, and Wałęsa's ubiquitous Black Madonna lapel pin all signified a deep ideological connection between the growing anticommunist workers movement and the church.[16]

The popularity of the church also grew among the wider public—affiliation with Catholicism reached its peak at 98 percent in the 1980s, and weekly mass attendance soared to an unprecedented 80 percent (although it has fallen back since to only 40 percent)[17] (Stark and Iannaccone 1996). During this period the fusion between the political and the spiritual was stark in the form of "political spirituality" in which religion was an overt political force (Carrette 2000, 139).

Despite the cozy church-state relations that existed until this time, the church increasingly positioned itself to appear progressive and was commonly viewed by the population at large as the protector of the people from the state. One of the veteran activists and a member of the Left, Hanka Lipowska-Teutsch, explained that during state socialism "the church provided that space to build resistance and national identity. It was an institution, not a religion, but an institution in which as a participant you felt that it was a stabilizing mechanism, a sort of alternative system. That was the subjective experience at the time" (interview with Lipowska-Teutsch, Kraków, 2002). Other activists explained that the church offered the only structure that provided freedom of action—some of the important mobilization and organization of the movement took place in churches and parish basements. The growing presence and involvement of the church in the opposition motivated a radical reversal of direction of the secular Left led by Michnik to embrace the church as an ally against the state.

At first glance, it seemed implausible that the Left should turn to the church. Michnik believed, however, that the church needed to be shown that it had nothing to fear from the leftists. As trusted as Michnik was in his judgment and leadership, many among the intelligentsia worried that the embrace of the church would send it toward increasingly greater power and bolster the fundamentalist hardliners within. Sure enough, as the church secured the support of both Solidarity and the intelligentsia, the Polish episcopate, led by Józef Glemp (after the death of Cardinal Wyszyński), began to shift in a fundamentalist direction. This was reflected by the even more vocal antiabortion and anticontraception rhetoric. The "radicalization" of the church was taking place as the episcopate increasingly envisioned a religious postsocialist state, intolerant of political or religious pluralism. Glemp argued that in a Catholic nation like Poland, "neutral" (secular) institutions are out of place because they are not "in tune with the national mood," and declared that the church cannot support the right of nonbelievers organizing their own institutions (Ost 1993, 20).[18]

Eventually Michnik declared he was wrong and urged the Left to distance itself from the church, but it was too late to slow down the momentum of the episcopate, which was propelled even further by the election of a Polish pope (Ekiert 1997, 319–20). The election of Karol Wojtyła as Pope John Paul II in 1978 was of great political significance, a fact that was cast by the Polish episcopate and the new pope in a historic and nationalist light, claiming divine intervention on behalf of the Polish nation.[19] The pope had a grandiose and unique vision for the country—he not only envisioned Polish nationalism and religious "purity" as a precursor to Polish emancipation from Soviet rule but also as the instrument of the liberation of Western European nations from secular downfall. Poland was depicted by the church as the "Christ of nations," given the nation's tragic history of occupation and suffering, which would be followed by national rebirth (Byrnes 1997, 438).[20] During his visit to Poland in 1979, the pope spoke about his own role in this process as a prophet of sorts: "Is it not Christ's will, is it not what the Holy Spirit dispenses, that this Polish Pope, this Slav Pope, should at this precise moment manifest the spiritual unity of Christian Europe?" (Paltrow 1986, 16).

Despite the pope's overgenerous assessment of Poland's influence in Europe, the Polish episcopate became wholly committed to his vision. In a great measure this became a rhetorical, and later a practical, avenue for the involvement of the church in political decision making. Of particular concern to Michnik and the Left was the use of civil rights rhetoric in the speeches and pronouncements released by the church to advance a religious agenda: "The general democratic demand for civil rights turns into a particular demand for the rights of Catholics, the struggle for social autonomy is reduced to a campaign aimed at guaranteeing the Catholic hierarchy a privileged influence on public life, and the conflict between the totalitarian state and a pluralistic society begins to be expressed as a dispute between an atheistic government and a Catholic nation" (Michnik 1993, 253–54).

The warning among the Left to withdraw support for the church came too late because the church was rapidly consolidating its power. The Polish episcopate and the pope provided significant and tangible support to the Solidarity movement—symbolically reflected by the pope pen that Wałęsa used to sign the legalization of the union in 1980[21]—and were deeply entrenched in the collective struggle against the regime and in exerting pressure on the collapsing socialist state. In 1981 the state imposed martial law for nineteen months in order to crush the opposition; the move was later rationalized by the head of the regime, General Wojciech Jaruzelski, as a patriotic maneuver to prevent the Soviet military from having to invade Poland to control the dissent. Even though not all arrested were released when martial law was lifted in 1983, the movement only gained in strength and the support of the population.

But women activists working within the movement were greatly worried as they observed that Solidarity's rhetoric subsumed women's concerns under the larger struggle against the state. Moreover, Solidarity's leadership was overwhelmingly male; the upper echelons devalued women within the movement by depicting their efforts and leadership in the organization as merely supportive, preparing food for clandestine meetings of the opposition, bringing sandwiches to the striking workers in the shipyard, but generally taking a secondary role in discussions (Penn 2005). Concerns about preserving women's rights during what looked like an impending regime transition were on the back burner at best, and cast as irrelevant and counterproductive at worst.

The feminist scholar Heidi Hartman laments that when feminism meets Marxism, feminist struggle is bound to be eclipsed by the larger class struggle that forms the basis of Marxist philosophy (Hartmann 2010). What is interesting in Poland, however, is that the formally Marxist state demonstrated that the conceptualization of women as workers did not preclude the implementation of important women's rights. Instead, it was the Solidarity movement, an anticommunist yet workers' organization, that marginalized women's rights.

The Concordat and the Merging of the Church and State

By the end of the decade the debt that Solidarity owed to the church was enormous, and the organization was eager to repay it. During the period spanning several years before the fall of the socialist regime in 1989 and the immediate postsocialist transition, the Catholic Church enjoyed a powerful and growing influence in key policy changes. Already by the mid-1980s the church engaged in a successful campaign to hang crucifixes in all public schools, and by 1989 in the upper and lower houses of the Parliament and most other governmental offices (Mucha 1989).

When the socialist state was collapsing in 1989, Catholic credentials played a significant role in the public imagery produced by aspiring politicians. The anthropologist Longina Jakubowska (1990, 12) describes how Catholic and nationalist symbolism were used to create a particular type of political drama in the newly liberated Poland:

> Bridging patriotism and Catholicism, martyrs were often priests. Priest Marek of the Bar Confederation of 1768, a rebellion against Russian rule, Saint Maksymilian Kolbe of Auschwitz, and Father Popiełuszko were among the long line of Polish clergy who died in the struggle for Polish sovereignty. The image of a martyr serves as a vehicle for collective and personal political advancement. The candidates for Parliament in the 1989 election campaign effectively capitalized on their history of persecution and internment. Dates of imprisonment, their own as well as their families and forefathers, membership in the formerly illegal organizations, and participation in the actions of resistance, became key elements in qualifying for office.

Wałęsa, a devout and public Catholic with a history of resistance, arrests, and internment, fit all the prerequisites, and by 1990 he was elected president for a five-year term. Tadeusz Mazowiecki became the first prime minister, and he too had deep Catholic roots that had a political character—he and others in his post-1989 cabinet (who became deputies of the Lower House of the Parliament) had been members of the Catholic-nationalist organizations cooperating with the regime since the 1950s, including Znak Association, PAX Association, and the Christian Social Association. This is another important site of continuity of the church-state relationship in Poland which shows that this relationship is deeply embedded in Polish history and did not just start after 1989. Instead, the postsocialist church-state structure drew on a long-standing history of alliance, and after 1989 it further reinforced itself, expanded, and became visible.

Working in tandem with the church, Wałęsa and Mazowiecki immediately created numerous legislative changes that were imbued with the Catholic agenda. For example, in 1991 Wałęsa instituted the conscience clause law that allowed providers to refuse legally permissible health services by citing conscience-based objections. Since then, the law has been widely used by orthodox Catholic doctors to restrict access to reproductive and sexual health services. In addition, clergy were able to secure state positions on ethics committees in the Ministries of Health and Education. Arguably the most important gain for the church was the Concordat—an international treaty signed in 1993 between the state, the Polish episcopate, and the Vatican, which explicitly gives the church a privileged political position in Poland.[22] No other European nation's concordat carries the same value for the Catholic Church.

The Polish Concordat not only provides extraordinary privileges for the church but also limits state power over church activities. In other words, the church can influence the state, but the state has no influence over the church. Specifically, it guarantees all "churches and other faith-based organizations" equal rights under the law, but declares: "The relations between the Republic of Poland and the Catholic Church are defined by an international treaty with the Holy See as well as [Polish] laws" (art. 25). Minority religions are told that they can pursue their own agreements with the state; however, only the Polish Autocephalous Orthodox Church has done so. The Concordat also stipulates that any regulation of church-state relations in Poland not covered by the Concordat can take place only through trilateral talks between the Polish state, the Polish episcopate, and the Vatican (art. 27). Given that it requires international diplomatic negotiations, this provision undermines the legislative power of the Parliament and limits the sovereignty of the Polish state within its own territory. Furthermore, any conflict that may arise between the church and the state regarding either the interpretation or implementation of the Concordat must be resolved by trilateral talks involving the Vatican (art. 28). Although the state is required to respect canonical law, the church is not explicitly required to respect state law (Daniel 1995, 408). The irony that it was the nationalists who gave away the power of the Polish state to the Vatican seemed to have been mostly unnoticed.

The church successfully waged a battle to disallow the use of the word "separation" in the constitutional description of church-state relations. Cardinal Glemp publicly referred to the principle of church-state separation as a "communist-inspired" system (*Economist* 1991, 51). The final constitutional wording that was adopted describes the state and the church as "autonomous" and "mutually independent." Religious education in public schools became mandatory from preschool to high school. According to the law, children who are not religious or are of a non-Catholic faith are supposed to have the option of attending ethics courses rather than religion classes, but in nearly all public schools across Poland, with the exception of a few in Warsaw, ethics courses are not offered owing to apparent financial constraints, while over 20,000 priests and nuns have been hired as civil servants to teach religion (Simpson 1996). In schools where ethics courses are not offered, students can simply not attend the religion courses and receive a failing grade, but this grade will permanently stay on the student's transcript. The presence of the Catholic clergy is also guaranteed in all state "care," "educational," or "foster" facilities such as penitentiaries, juvenile reform institutions, hospitals, and elderly care homes (art. 17). All of these institutions are obligated to offer Sunday masses and individual Catholic counseling carried out by clergy hired with public funds. Other denominations lack these privileges. The symbolism of the church-state union is particularly expressive each year in December when the Parliament hosts highly ranked Catholic priests, including cardinals, for the Catholic "wafer ritual" (*opłatek*) during which the wafer, symbolizing the body of Christ, is shared between the politicians and the clergy, and accompanied by wishes.

As this historical overview shows, the present outcome of the de facto merging of the church and state is a result of a long-term effort by the church to establish itself as a political actor, not just in relation to the state, but within the state structure itself. These long-term efforts also reflect the church's vision as a "missionary," both in Poland and Europe. The importance of theorizing state and religious regimes together in the European context has been argued by the anthropologists Mart Bax and Eric Wolf, who note that "religious regimes are also political constellations. This implies . . . the formulation of ideologies and the working out of tactics and strategies of how to fight and how to win confrontations, encounters, and collusions" (Bax 1991, 9–10; Wolf 1991). Likewise, the concept of a religious regime is dynamic and useful for thinking about the case of Poland where both the broader politico-economic influences as well as individual-level governance of the church are felt. This history helps explain not only how the church maneuvered during the state socialist regime to retain and later expand its power, but critically, how this long-term effort created "the right moment" to impose a politics of morality in the ensuing years. As the Polish gender scholar and sociologist Małgorzata Fuszara poignantly observed: "The church didn't talk about abortion before '89. The pope never talked about abortion in Poland. . . . He talked about it in the US and in Western Europe, but never in Poland. As soon as the political situation changed, the first projects were to restrict abortion. Clearly, the church was waiting for the right moment" (interview with Fuszara, Warsaw, 2002).

2 ⫸ Restricting Access to Reproductive Services

Religious Power and Moral Governance

WHEN IN THE YEAR 2000, Alicja Tysiąc, a single mother of two living in Warsaw on a welfare allowance of $179 per month, became pregnant, three doctors told her that a pregnancy could seriously damage her eyesight. Alicja already suffered from very poor vision—she was severely near-sighted, relying on thick glasses with a prescription of −20 diopters on both sides. The pregnancy posed the risk of a retinal hemorrhage and detachment, potentially causing blindness. Yet despite Alicja's repeated requests, none of the doctors was willing to authorize an abortion because they argued that retinal detachment, even if quite likely to occur, was not absolutely certain. After exhausting all avenues to obtain an abortion, Alicja carried the pregnancy to term. By the second month her vision deteriorated to −24 diopters, and following the delivery she suffered a retinal hemorrhage in both eyes. As a result she was left with vision reduced to less than five feet, and she has since been classified as legally blind and disabled. She now requires the assistance of a state health care worker with daily activities.

What happened in the years after the fall of state socialism that made even abortions to save a woman's health no longer accessible? Why were doctors, who performed abortion readily during the previous decades, so reluctant now to authorize it, even in dire situations like Alicja's? Answers to these questions are complicated and should be considered in the context of the rhetorical and political shift toward moral governance though pervasive "morality" discussions that ensued in Poland after 1989. They are defined for the most part by the growing involvement of the Catholic

Church in policymaking and its resurgence in the media and public life. In this chapter I examine how moral governance works in practice at the level of policy and how it seeps through to everyday practices in the medical community.

The Wave of Moralization

When the state socialist regime fell in 1989, the primary goal of the church's lobbying was to restrict access to abortion. Women quickly found that the security of their rights during the socialist era was predicated on a particular political rhetoric of gender equity granted in a top-down approach by the socialists, and they learned of their rights' fragility only when the church regained dominance after the power shift of 1989 (Mishtal 2009c). According to Wanda Nowicka, the director of the Federation for Women and Family Planning (and as of 2011 Member of the Polish Parliament), whom I interviewed a number of times when I spent countless hours in her organization's headquarters during my fieldwork, women's shock at the new proposals was profound. She recounted, "Many people, especially on the left, were simply unprepared to respond to the upsurge of the right-wing church machinery and the wave of moralization that came with it despite the whole debate, so it came as a shock" (interview with Wanda Nowicka, Warsaw, 2002).

Nowicka and other women activists in Warsaw and Kraków recalled that this "wave of moralization" was especially evident in the way that women were depicted in Catholic-nationalist discourses in the media and in the politics of the day. Priests and politicians were heard redefining Polish women's identities around traditional gender differences, casting their social roles primarily in relation to others as mothers and wives, and calling for a return to the kind of "femininity" that was presumably lost when women entered employment outside the home during the previous decades. The wave of moralization simultaneously rejected women's rights and embraced the rights discourses in other ways. The church spoke of the "rights of the family" and "marriage rights," and on the individual level it argued for women's "right to motherhood." This rhetoric also allowed for the rise of new subject positions, such as "fetal rights" and more recently "embryonic rights" (Morgan and Roberts 2012).[1]

The "fetal imperative" (Michaels and Morgan 1999) is a form of "euphemized violence"; as the anthropologists Faye Ginsburg and Rayna Rapp have argued (1995, 4), it denies that pregnancy has severe consequences for women's lives, body experiences, and that women are indeed at the center of reproduction.

The Myth of Family Demise

But for Catholic conservatives, eager to recast Poland along religious values in the early 1990s, after the ostensibly secular socialist era marked by the separation of church and state, this kind of rhetoric served as an important political tool to consolidate their authority as postsocialist moral leaders. The church, in particular Pope John Paul II and Cardinal Józef Glemp, whom the pope appointed, condemned what they saw as "family demise" that allegedly occurred as a result of the state socialist promotion of women's entry into paid employment.[2] In reality, however, family ties actually were strengthened during the state socialist era as kin connections (znajomości) became essential in creating networks of relatives and acquaintances to help procure goods and services during the times of economic shortages in the 1970s and 1980s (Wedel 1986; 1992).[3] The church's "family demise" and "moral decline" rhetoric was mainly echoed by the conservative and nationalist elements of the media and Wałęsa's administration, with little reflection in the wider society, which was generally more concerned with the economic hardships of the early 1990s than with the society's state of moral fitness.

Nevertheless, the myth of family demise served in the early 1990s as one of the postsocialist rhetorical tools in reviving the church's public and political role. The condemnation of "permissive sexual behavior" under socialism became another significant theme in this discourse. The evidence the church saw as particularly telling was the fact that women in Poland, and elsewhere in the region, readily used abortion and contraceptive services—this was both common knowledge and also reflected in the steadily declining birthrate since abortion became legal and the state endorsed and subsidized birth control. Referred to by the Vatican as the "culture of death" and "contraceptive mentality," the church greatly intensified its opposition to family planning after 1989. Simultaneously, in an effort to revitalize the notion of reproduction as constitutive of

womanhood, Pope John Paul II in his "Letter to Women" (1995b) introduced the expression "the feminine genius," arguing that women "fulfill
their deepest vocation" through motherhood, hence the "genius" of their
reproductive capacity:

> It is thus my hope, dear sisters, that you will reflect carefully on what it means
> to speak of the "genius of women," not only in order to be able to see in this
> phrase a specific part of God's plan which needs to be accepted and appreciated,
> but also in order to let this genius be more fully expressed in the life of society
> as a whole. . . . The church sees in Mary the highest expression of the "feminine
> genius" and she finds in her a source of constant inspiration. Mary called herself
> the "handmaid of the Lord" (Lk 1:38). Through obedience to the Word of God
> she accepted her lofty yet not easy vocation as wife and mother in the family of
> Nazareth. (John Paul II 1995b, 5–6)

This morality discourse was made ubiquitous by the many Catholic media
outlets where such topics have been aired pervasively since the early 1990s.
During the initial phase of the postsocialist transition, the Polish church
established the ownership of a number of television and radio channels, especially the ultra-conservative Radio Maryja, a national daily *Nasz Dziennik*, ten weeklies, eleven biweeklies, and seventy-eight monthly publications
(Kubik 2001, 157). In 1992 the episcopate successfully ushered through the
legislation a controversial blasphemy law requiring radio and television
programs to "respect religious feelings of their audiences and, in particular,
respect the system of Christian values" (Daniel 1995, 406). This law has had
a chilling effect on free speech in postsocialist Poland and has made it easy
to punish anticlerical sentiments. Indeed, Reporters Without Borders has
observed instances of Polish media censorship where journalists were fined
or threatened with jail time for speaking against the church. In general Poland ranks near the bottom of European nations with respect to journalists'
ability to speak and write freely.[4] Interestingly, it has been generally unacceptable to criticize democracy and free speech, except insofar as these are
disrespectful to the church.

This discourse of "familism" also surfaced in other post-Soviet nations
where the Catholic influence was not necessarily strong—a trend that has
been understood as a way to remasculinize the men whom state socialism
supposedly disempowered by facilitating female education and employment (Haney 2003; Haney and Pollard 2003; Rivkin-Fish 2005, 12–13).

Likewise, in Russia political discourses claiming that there is a crisis of masculine identity, and the need to revive Russian men's power over child-bearing, is driven by the state's pronatalist agenda to increase fertility (Rivkin-Fish 2010, 703). Similar familism rhetoric is used to justify calls for a return of the "male breadwinner" model. The status of Polish and Russian men as traditional breadwinners was diminished under socialism partly through the elimination of the so-called family wage as women began to work; thus the men experienced women's increased financial and body autonomy as their wives, sisters, and mothers generated their own income and enjoyed an increased control over their reproduction and sexuality (Goven 1993; Watson 1996). But despite women's public sphere advancements during state socialism, they were certainly not emancipated in the private realm where most of the care work rested squarely on their shoulders and the reality of gender relations in the family remained unchanged.[5] Nevertheless, after the regime fell, the familism campaign launched by conservative politicians and media served to "remasculinize" men in the public sphere by targeting women and calling for their retraction to the home.[6] Simultaneously, women's rights and feminists who openly defended them were being stigmatized as products of communism. The return to traditional gender differences in public discourse also aimed at increasing the social distance between men and women and creating the selective political empowerment of men who took charge of the public and political sphere in the crucial years of the transition to capitalism (Watson 1996).

After the wave of moralization, accompanied by the rise of masculinism and familialism rhetoric that swept the political and media scene in the immediate post-1989 moment, it became clear that the church was poised to implement its political agenda, but now in more tangible ways. Moral governance was now to become law.

The Struggle for Rights Begins

The project to criminalize abortion was considered extremely urgent by the church and the Solidarity-derived administration of Lech Wałęsa; the "protection of the unborn" resolution was only the second legislative change proposed by the new parliament after the fall of the socialist state in 1989. Not surprisingly, the episcopate saw abortion as symbolic of society's secularization and the limited influence of the church during the previous decades; therefore, discussions about the proposed resolution to ban abortion became the means of reestablishing the church's power. Solidarity's Women's Section strongly objected to the resolution. Perceiving a narrow religious agenda behind the proposal, they decided to poll the workers in several regional factories and their numbers showed that 80 percent or more was against criminalization of abortion. However, when they presented their results to the Union's leader, Marian Krzaklewski (Wałęsa relinquished his leadership after assuming Poland's presidency), he was annoyed by the women's opposition and responded by dissolving the Women's Section for partisan "politicking." Indeed, in the assessment of the gender scholar Shana Penn (2005, 288–90), who conducted ethnographic research with the Solidarity women, the group was "too far ahead of their time to survive," especially as it believed that political decisions in newly liberated Poland would now be shaped by and respond to public voice and opinion. Instead, women who opposed abortion restrictions were deemed by the male-dominated Solidarity management as lacking "proper moral spine."

Wałęsa and his government, owing a substantial debt to the church, were highly sympathetic to the church's agenda. Already in the early 1980s Wałęsa, as Solidarity's leader and working in tandem with the church, pushed for restrictions on abortion. The regime yielded under the growing pressure and implemented a legal allowance for doctors to refuse health services, citing objections based on conscience as well as a mandatory counseling requirement for abortions of first pregnancies (Mazur 1981, 197). These earliest restrictions, implemented without a referendum, discouraged many women from using state clinics. Whenever possible they turned to private offices for the procedure. In 1991, Wałęsa, now in the position of the first postsocialist president, eagerly implemented an executive order requiring women seeking abortions to get permissions from two gynecologists, a physician, and a psychologist, rather than from just one physician, as was the case until then. Although the new mandatory consultations were subsidized by the state, it took a considerable amount of effort and time to carry out all four visits before the fourteen-week time limit elapsed. Moreover, if any of the providers denied permission judging, for example, that the economic hardship presented as the reason for seeking abortion sounded unconvincing or was not sufficiently severe, the time that lapsed seeking further appointments made it difficult to complete the required visits in the allotted time, thus placing considerable limits on women's ability to access the care.

The Role of Religious Bioethics

To further penetrate secular arenas of society and establish Poland as a Catholic state, the church argued that religious bioethics ought to guide ethical decision making in general, and in medicine and education in particular. By collapsing ethics and morality, the church formed an effective political and structural link between religious values and reproduction and sexuality. As new bioethics committees began to form in the early 1990s within the structure of Wałęsa's government, the clergy with seminary education in the area of moral theology secured positions of bioethics experts on committees linked to the Ministry of Health and other state agencies. By medical law, each bioethics committee must include, in addition to health care providers, a member who is considered of "high moral authority," which often means that these seats are taken by Catholic clergy (article 29, medical practice decree from 12/5/1996) (Nesterowicz 2001, 335–36). Therefore the church enjoys a unique and influential presence in hospitals and major health care facilities, including educational and research institutions such as medical academies and university clinics. Moreover, the clergy also participate in state programs related to HIV/AIDS, drug use, and professional conduct for health care providers.[7] But why would input on bioethical issues from a Catholic priest be problematic? An analysis of why and how certain aspects of health (especially reproduction and sexuality) are cast as moral in Catholic bioethics and therefore become the main target for moral governance that relies on particular universal directives explains the concern.

When bioethics began as a branch of philosophy around the 1960s in the Western world, religious influences in the form of moral theology and theological analyses were always present (Callahan 1999). Serving as ethics committee members in hospitals and state health institutions became a new profession for Catholic priests with higher education, especially in nations without a clear separation between church and state. Supranationally, the Vatican voices its position through direct involvement in bioethics debates by releasing specific documents. It is highly significant that Pope John Paul II, revered in Poland, authored the encyclical *Evangelium Vitae* in 1995—the key foundational document for the present formulation of Catholic bioethics on family planning. His document is a follow-up to an earlier, equally significant bioethics document written by Pope Paul VI in 1968, "The Encyclical *Humanae Vitae*: On the Regulation of Birth," which explicates the moral and ethical prohibition of abortion even to save the woman's life as well as all forms of contraception, except for chastity (Paul VI 1968, 6, 9). John Paul II's follow-up document is five times longer, reiterates the total prohibition of abortion, and addresses "new threats," including specific contraceptive methods, in vitro fertilization, and end-of-life decisions (John Paul II 1995a). Also of particular interest for reproductive health is the Charter for Health Care Workers, released by the Holy See in 1995, which contains instructions for health care providers for ethical conduct regarding abortion, contraception, in vitro fertilization, and other services relevant to the church (Pontifical Council for Pastoral Assistance to Health Care Workers 1995). The former Pope Benedict XVI released the "Instruction Dignitas Personae on Certain Bioethical Questions," in which he stresses that the fundamental principle in medicine should be one that "expresses a great 'yes' to human life and must be at the center of ethical reflection" (Levada and Ladaria 2008, 1). The Vatican contends that bioethics consists of objective (read: moral) truths and that these must be upheld even against individual patients' wishes, which are understood as inherently subjective. Other minority positions are likewise dismissed. For instance, the involvement of the Catholic Church in an AIDS prevention campaign led to the marginalization of the voices of sexual minorities, as activists were eclipsed by the "moral authority" of the church (Owczarzak 2009).

This "objective truths" paradigm, present in Catholic bioethics but also in other bioethics models, has been criticized by the anthropologist Arthur Kleinman as a case akin to a Martian landing on Earth and facing an ethical dilemma in which missing are "the powerful constraints of real worlds" and "desperate choices in situations in which the concrete details of historical circumstances, social structural constraints like limited education and income, interpersonal pressure, and a calamity in the household or workplace are at the core of what a dire ethical dilemma is all about" (Kleinman 1995, 48–49). In the United States, women's health and feminist bioethics movements of the 1960s likewise criticized the abstract nature of objective/

masculinist ethics paradigms and called for situating ethics in the particulars of real life, and recent theorists call for the ethics of patient empowerment and self-trust in health care (Sherwin 2008). As problematic as an objective truths paradigm is in evaluating human dilemmas full of ambiguity and complexity, it raises particular concerns when it comes to reproductive health—an area where restricting access to abortion and contraception under the cloak of moral objectivity or bioethical righteousness has been the dominant way of approaching health care delivery under Catholic health policies elsewhere, for example in Ireland and Malta, both of which are nations with a long history of church-state merging. This is exemplified when Catholic physicians invoke conscientious objection to refuse care that women seek and which is legally permissible but do not offer referrals to find services elsewhere. Or when a Catholic hospital declines to provide emergency contraception to victims of rape admitted to its emergency room.[8] In other words, Catholic bioethics' primary principle of "protection of life" not only overlooks the suffering of women facing desperate choices, but theoretically stands a priori against serious consideration of their circumstances. The lived experience is deemed subjective and therefore subordinate to the objective truths paradigm. Thus, when in the early 1990s the influential role of the Catholic Church within the structure of the postsocialist Polish state and in the realm of health policymaking became apparent, it posed serious concerns about the future of reproductive rights. Soon these concerns began to materialize.

Conscientious Objection and New Restrictions on Education and Services

Shortly after Wałęsa's executive order in 1990 requiring women seeking abortions to get permission from four health care providers, he eliminated sex education from schools. Previously sex education was hardly adequate, but efforts were made to root whatever lectures and classes were offered in science. The state sponsored school workshops and lectures for teachers and students by commissioning instructors from the Society for Conscious Motherhood (Towarzystwo Świadomego Macierzyństwa), which later became the Society for Family Development, TRR (Towarzystwo Rozwoju Rodziny). In the 1970s TRR began to work directly with the Ministries of

Health and Education, and in the 1980s the group developed a sex education program that became part of the required curriculum (Mazur 1981, 5).
When Wałęsa became president, he withdrew the subsidies for TRR, and
since then the organization has struggled to survive, paralyzed by lack of
funding. Wałęsa's administration replaced it with "Preparation for Life in a
Family," courses based on Catholic ideology that teach heteronormative
gender roles, homosexuality as a lifestyle choice, abstinence before marriage, and the detrimental health effects of contraception. Evidence-based
sex education with information about sexually transmitted infections, pregnancy prevention, and teen relationships is currently missing. When this
curriculum change took place, no referendum was even considered because
Catholic bioethical consideration formally superseded public opinion. A
longitudinal national survey a few years later in 1997, conducted by the
Polish scholar Zbigniew Izdebski, showed that 88 percent of Poles favored
science-based sex education in schools, and by 2005 this number grew to 92
percent (Izdebski 2006, 130). Other surveys since then are showing the
same results, but no change is discussed, except briefly when nongovernmental groups call attention to yet another national survey. But consecutive
conservative administrations have argued that sex education is currently
taught in the required "Preparation for Life in a Family" curriculum; therefore, on paper the educational need appears satisfied. In fact, the same claim
was used to justify a rejection by the Polish Parliament of a comprehensive
sex education bill in April 2014—a move that appears consistent with the
idea of maintaining a status quo vis-à-vis the Catholic Church.

Conscientious Objection, from the Doctors' Perspectives

One of the most crucial developments in restricting family planning access
in the early 1990s was the implementation of the conscience clause. In
1991, the church, backed by the state, pressured the medical establishment
to modify their ethics regulations by mobilizing the Catholic factions
within the medical community. As a result, a group of Catholic physicians
called an emergency conference, the Extraordinary National Assembly of
Physicians, to discuss revisions to medical ethics. The Catholic organizers
pushed for two major restrictions: the conscience clause law and a new
code specifically targeting abortion, which stated that only life- or
health-threatening circumstances or a pregnancy resulting from a crime

could warrant termination. A substantial group of doctors at the assembly strongly opposed abortion restrictions, in particular because the proposed code was in direct violation of the Polish abortion law, which at that time still allowed socioeconomic hardship reasons for the procedure. In a gesture of protest against the "backdoor" maneuver to limit abortion, 40 delegates walked out of the assembly believing that they were halting the process, but effectively excluding themselves from the vote on the new code, which was forced by the organizers anyway. In the end, of the remaining delegates, 354 voted for the new code (severe abortion restrictions), 317 voted against; the code was passed (Szawarski 1992). Had the 40 protesting delegates stayed and voted, the new code would have failed—an outcome that would have been consistent with an opinion poll taken among doctors just five months earlier and reported by *Gazeta Wyborcza*, the largest Polish daily, which showed that 63 percent of doctors wanted the liberal abortion law maintained (cited in Szawarski 1992).

Since the new code mainly included the conscience clause, abortion for socioeconomic reasons continued to be legal, in theory (Nowicka 1994; Regulska 1998). Nevertheless, the dispute that followed between the Catholic Assembly and Poland's Civil Rights Ombudsmen, Ewa Łętowska and later Tadeusz Zieliński, about the way the vote was forced and the legitimacy of the new Medical Code of Ethics continued for a while, however with no change to the code (Rich 1992, 1221).

The new code triggered among Catholic physicians a surge of refusals of services in cases of abortion in public hospitals, prescription contraceptives, and emergency contraceptives (Nowicka 2008a, 34–35). The conscience clause policy, now widely known in everyday language simply as *klauzula,* or "the clause," in theory balances the rights of both sides: it protects the right of an individual doctor to decline a service, but it also protects the right of the patient to obtain lawful medical care. In reality, however, the clause is being used outside of the current legal limits: while it is designed for individual use, it facilitates the withholding of medical services on a systemic scale, and it has been used without providing referrals, thereby leaving patients (mainly women seeking family planning) without a viable alternative (Mishtal 2009b). Specifically, the clause dictates that:

A physician can withhold health care services which are not in agreement with his [*sic*] conscience (with the exception described in article 30). He has the obligation to indicate realistic possibilities of obtaining such health care services from another physician or in another health care facility, and he [*sic*] has the obligation to substantiate and document this fact in the medical documentation. The physician who is an employee also has the obligation to inform his [*sic*] superior in writing prior to declining the service. (Nesterowicz 2001, 340)

Although the clause is for use by individual doctors in specific cases, it quickly became a tool of denying care on a more systemic scale. In particular, the clause began to be used to refuse lawfully allowed abortions; this was evidenced by an enormous drop in legally performed procedures recorded by the Polish state, from 105,333 in 1988 to 11,640 in 1992.[9] Entire health care facilities began to withhold abortion services via directives imposed on gynecologists by the management. They did this without consulting with staff physicians or allowing individual doctors to decide whether to use the clause. The example of the Greater Kraków Obstetrical/Gynecological Clinic is emblematic of how the clause was used, as recalled by Dr. Dembski, one of the directors of the facility and a veteran gynecologist in Kraków, whom I interviewed about the events following the implementation of this law.

> DR. DEMBSKI: This building where we're talking right now on Szopena Street number 78, the Greater Kraków Ob/Gyn Clinic, was one of the first in Poland where we adopted a moratorium on abortion in accord with the new clause [policy]. So even before the law banning abortion was in place, in this building abortions for social reasons were no longer performed. That's because people who didn't want it done here began to have a voice.

> AUTHOR: You mean doctors?

> DR. DEMBSKI: Yes, of course, doctors, but also the society.

> AUTHOR: And that was before the abortion ban?

> DR. DEMBSKI: Yes, it was two or three years before, because we had the so-called moratorium and this was done in two or three hospitals besides ours in Kraków. And a number of clinics also decided to adopt a moratorium on abortion. (Interview with Dembski, Kraków, 2002)

Although Dr. Dembski identified as a devout Catholic, his perspective on conscientious objection in his public and private practice was complicated, and at times contradictory and at odds with the church's views. He opposed abortion when requested for socioeconomic reasons and argued that requiring doctors who object to providing abortions is akin to the "rape of conscience," but he believed that abortions for medical reasons if recommended by him are well justified. In fact he mainly objected to abortion being used as a "form of contraception." Likewise, sterilization is both illegal in Poland and prohibited by the church, but when I began to ask Dr. Dembski about it, he interrupted and said: "I know what you're trying to say. The arrangement is this: while I'm doing the C-section I can do this . . . with a given patient if it was her fifth pregnancy, eighth or maybe seventh pregnancy, right after the C-section that's when this procedure is done." He strongly opposed contraceptives, which he refused to provide at the public clinic because of "interference with procreation," and because "the social teachings of the church oppose pharmaceutical approaches." But simultaneously, he offered them privately and found conferences and retreats dedicated solely to learning about contraceptives and sponsored by Bayer Schering pharmaceutical company useful because the plenary speakers are physicians who are leaders in the field.[10]

Dr. Dembski's particular understanding of conscientious objection revealed a selective, individualized approach, both in terms of which health services should be objected to and whether the objection is in a public or private clinical setting. When asked about how he reconciles his Catholicism with some of his practices that contradict the church's teachings, he explained that "we all have to have our own identity. . . . It all depends on the conscience of each individual," but when confronted by the question of imposing an abortion moratorium on the entire facility, he believed that he had the right to represent the doctors working beneath him because that is what he believed the majority wanted. In particular, he condemned female doctors: "It's ugly for me to say, but even female doctors [*lekarki*] would allow themselves to provide abortions. I know them, many of them." He then argued that the moratorium makes sense because it facilitates more conscientious behavior on everyone's part, given that the rule "makes it impossible" to offer the procedure, suggesting that even doctors who are willing to provide abortion will benefit from the rule. Another doctor in the same facility who supported Dr. Dembski's moratorium believed that "a number of doctors here used abortion for financial profit, but the rest of us felt that our conscience was being violated because, truth be told, everyone who participated in abortions, or who assisted, be it a doctor or a nurse or an anesthesiologist, acted unethically." Thus, he argued that the moratorium is a way to ensure that the facility operates according to proper (i.e., Catholic) bioethical guidelines; thus the moratorium, an early version of a conscientious objection, became one of the mechanisms of moral governance wielded at the level of a medical community, rather than just policy.

Not all doctors agreed with this view, but even so, they rarely spoke against their superiors due to the highly hierarchical seniority-based structure of the Polish medical system, in particular in major public or university-affiliated clinics, such as this one. Some saw the law as a divisive wedge and an imposition of a particular morality on the wider medical community. As one doctor explained, "The conscience clause and the subsequent abortion law polarized the medical community because of the severity of the restrictions that were suddenly in place but also because the laws were ideologically driven." Another doctor noted that "in Kraków, the restrictions are especially ideology-based because the bishop and the clergy are especially vocal against contraception and abortion." Aside from the hierarchical nature of the Polish medical community, a more significant reason for lack of opposition to a moratorium was the fear of publicly opposing the church or "getting on the church radar." According to Dr. Zaremba, a gynecologist and obstetrician in the same facility, whose response reflects this type of concern, the fear of harassment from the clergy is in fact the main reason why she and others went along with the decision in the hospital. She said of doctors who decline to provide abortion due to conscience "certainly they're the minority," but the majority of doctors who decline the service do so because they are afraid. Therefore, doctors rarely speak against the management's unilateral decisions because on some level it protects them from exposing themselves as "abortion doctors"; here is how she described the situation:

> DR. ZAREMBA: Here [at the hospital] the most drastic situation is with abortions—gynecologists here refuse to do them due to fear; and that's the majority of gynecologists.
>
> AUTHOR: Fear of what?
>
> DR. ZAREMBA: Fear of the environment, fear of colleagues, fear of being given the label of a "scraper" [*skrobacz*].[11] If you

live in a smaller community like me, you fear that the neighborhood priest will find out and publicly curse my practice or he'll say something from the pulpit, like: "Don't go to this doctor!" It's not worth it for me financially; my private practice will suffer; it will cost me. Sometimes you see doctors having to shut down their offices in small towns and open elsewhere; they have to liquidate. That's what happens. There are entire hospitals where it [abortion] is no longer done. . . . In the early years of the right-wing state [Wałęsa] it was very severe, then when we got the leftist government [Kwaśniewski] and there was the usual change of seats, the priests moved slightly to the side, and currently they exert their influence more from the shadows, taking advantage of established connections. (Interview with Zaremba, Kraków, 2002)

Although Dr. Zaremba's hospital is near Kraków's center, and her private practice is in her home on the edge of the city several miles away, her concern of being targeted by the church in her home community for activities at the hospital is well founded. The church publicly disciplines physicians by urging parishioners to boycott providers of abortion and contraception. Doctors also recalled the well-known case of Dr. Wacław Dec, an ob/gyn in Łódź who was posthumously denied a Catholic funeral first by the local parish rector (*proboszcz*) of the parish that owns the cemetery, and then by the archbishop Władysław Ziółek, for publicly stating that in his hospital a woman can obtain an abortion if she is in need.[12] One of the doctors recalled the case and argued that physicians are feeling very threatened after Dr. Dec's case: "He was a professor at the Medical Academy and was providing abortions only in cases of documented genetic issues, where there was an indication of necessity. But after his death they denied him the right to a church burial, which of course was very traumatic and terribly stigmatizing for the whole family, you see?" The doctor urged me, "Please look into this case—there was a discussion whether the bishop had the right to do this," because she believed that the antichurch backlash that followed was significant but not enough to assuage doctors' fears.

Indeed, the media took sides according to their political leanings—Catholic outlets supported the bishop's decision, while *Gazeta Wyborcza*, a centrist national paper, in its article titled "He didn't kill," presented a case sympathetic to Dr. Dec. Other nonreligious media were also sympathetic. In general, public reaction was clearly against the bishop's decision; after all, for decades during state socialism physicians across Poland provided abortions and women sought them, but no one was excommunicated or denied a religious burial. Media reported that in a show of support, more than three thousand people from all over Poland, including health care providers, academics, coal miners, and military personnel, arrived to attended his funeral, which was a civil military ceremony instead of a Catholic one—a rare occurrence in Poland, given that almost all cemeteries belong to Catholic parishes. Following the incident, a street was named in the honor of Colonel Professor Wacław Dec in Łódź (Korzerawska 1997).

Despite the wave of public disapproval for disciplining physicians, the fear of the church's harassment is having a chilling effect on doctors who otherwise support the right to abortion or contraception; even legally permissible abortions are often performed clandestinely in private offices by the doctors who otherwise decline to perform them in hospitals. The systemic use of conscientious refusals to deny lawful abortion in public hospitals while performing services clandestinely has several implications. Doctors can earn far more in their private clinics, and they shield themselves from the potential, or perceived, harassment by the church, leaving women to endure the secrecy and stigma of a clandestine procedure for a large fee (De Zordo and Mishtal 2011). As Dr. Zaremba explained, the clause law serves as a way to protect oneself from the church's censure as it is less risky to perform abortions illegally in one's private office, because one's patients are unlikely to expose the doctor, than to perform abortion "on record" in a public hospital. As other doctors confirmed, Kraków was especially polarized ideologically, even around provision of contraceptives, because the doctors feared the local parish rectors, who have been traditionally very vocal against these practices.

This polarization is also manifesting in the ways in which patients approach doctors. For instance, Dr. Zaremba noticed that her new patients (if not referred by another patient) since the 1990s who are seeking contraceptives "don't talk about it right away; they first try to figure out if there's an ideological problem" before they broach the topic. Other doctors noted a similar trend. The general conclusion was that patients and doctors must sort themselves out according to the ideology of the doctor who might or might not be willing to offer family planning. However, as many providers

pointed out, low-income patients who must seek care in public clinics because they cannot afford to change doctors and pursue services in private
offices have to accept the assigned doctor, regardless of an ideological mis-
match or whether the health needs of the patient are met or not.

Religiosity and Medicine: The Case of Dr. Malina

Despite the popular media depictions of Poland as a monolithic nation of
devout Catholics, of the 90 percent who affiliate with Roman Catholicism,
only 40 percent declare themselves to be regularly practicing Catholics.[13]
Since ritual practice and religiosity do not always align, the practice of Catholicism might manifest in a variety of ways in different people. The use of
conscientious objection among physicians in their medical practice is one
such way; however, the degree of religiosity is reflected in how many different services the doctor objects to. The same doctor who objects to abortion
might see contraception as "the lesser of two evils," as Dr. Zaremba did,
while rigorist Catholic doctors might see contraception as also off limits in
their clinics. Although all forms of contraception (except sterilization) are
legal in Poland, and thus theoretically accessible, the church strongly opposes so-called "artificial" family planning, including hormonal contraceptives and IUDs. The Vatican argues that they act as abortifacients by
preventing a fertilized egg from attaching to the uterine wall, even though
science has shown that the mechanism of action is the prevention of fertilization instead, although this may not always be true for IUDs. Furthermore,
medicine defines pregnancy as both fertilization and implantation. The
clergy and church documents cite the following passage as evidence from
the encyclical *Evangelium Vitae*—the key Vatican document. The passage is
worth recounting here in its entirety because of its relevance to the church's
anticontraception campaign:

> But despite their differences of nature and moral gravity, contraception and
> abortion are often closely connected, as fruits of the same tree. It is true that in
> many cases contraception and even abortion are practised under the pressure of
> real-life difficulties, which nonetheless can never exonerate from striving to ob-
> serve God's law fully. Still, in very many other instances such practices are
> rooted in a hedonistic mentality unwilling to accept responsibility in matters of
> sexuality, and they imply a self-centered concept of freedom, which regards
> procreation as an obstacle to personal fulfilment. The life which could result

from a sexual encounter thus becomes an enemy to be avoided at all costs, and abortion becomes the only possible decisive response to failed contraception. The close connection which exists, in mentality, between the practice of contraception and that of abortion is becoming increasingly obvious. It is being demonstrated in an alarming way by the development of chemical products, intrauterine devices and vaccines which, distributed with the same ease as contraceptives, really act as abortifacients in the very early stages of the development of the life of the new human being. (John Paul II 1995a, 10–11)

The sole form of fertility control permitted by the church is periodic abstinence, popularly referred to in Poland as *kalendarzyk małżeński* or the little marriage calendar.[14] Consequently, orthodox Catholic gynecologists promote only this kind of family planning and cite conscientious objection against prescribing or recommending contraceptives, including condoms. Dr. Malina, an ob/gyn in his forties and practicing since the mid-1990s, who is one of the lead physicians in the Małopolska Pro-Family Health Clinic (the clinic treats both state-insured and private patients), illuminates how this approach to birth control is conceptualized as both beneficial to the woman and scientifically sound. The clinic is known for its Catholic approach to health care and its embrace of the tenets of the encyclical *Humanae Vitae* of Pope Paul VI on the Regulation of Birth released by the Vatican on July 25, 1968. When I arrived at the clinic, other signs of its religious character were evident: a crucifix hung prominently above the reception desk, and a Pope John Paul II calendar was affixed to the waiting room wall. As we began the interview, Dr. Malina was eager to discuss his approach to gynecology as the moral and ethical choice in today's reproductive medicine, which constantly lures patients with problematic offerings in the form of a variety of contraceptives as well as artificial fertilization techniques. But when I broached the topic of natural contraception—a term which in popular discourse is used interchangeably with the calendar—he was a bit irritated at my use of the term:

> DR. MALINA: Look, there's no such thing as natural contraception; that's the wrong word. We support methods of observing fertility which give the spouses a sense of when they are fertile. I don't at all give out contraceptives because I don't want to, in some sense, take on that responsibility. I'm a believing person [*jestem wierzący*]. I believe that contraception is wrong. Approaching it scientifically,

contraception totally upsets the woman's hormonal system.
While taking contraceptives, ten years later there's a greater
frequency of breast cancer and cancers of the reproductive
system, therefore it's a factor that impedes health.
Everything can happen: there might be epileptic attacks,
joint pain, migraines, water retention, mood disturbances,
agitation, aggression, hunger, sadness.

AUTHOR: Are you now talking about all contraceptives or just
hormonal ones?

DR. MALINA: Yes, hormonal, so pills or injections, but the same is
true about barrier methods and IUDs and these have the
effect of early miscarriage. . . . Additionally, the foreign
body in the womb causes a reaction—a lesion and a
discharge of mucus. It's as if you held something in your
mouth—with time a sore will form, there might be an
inflammation. Similar thing happens in the womb.

AUTHOR: What about condoms?

DR. MALINA: That's another issue: psychological fear. All
contraception solidifies the fear of the child in spouses
because people start using contraceptives to avoid
pregnancy. They fear the pregnancy and that it will destroy
their well-arranged lives. This fear gets transferred onto
the child. They fear, to put it simply, they begin to fear
the child. Throughout the long period of time when
they use contraception this mechanism solidifies in their
subconscious minds. We know from statistics that people
who use contraception are more likely to decide to get an
abortion because in their subconscious the association is:
child–enemy. The child becomes the source of fear; that's
the psychological consequence of contraception. That's
why we talk about the psychological term "contraceptive
conscience." (Interview with Malina, Kraków, 2002)

Dr. Malina particularly bemoaned the arrival of pharmaceutical marketing
prominent on the Internet and in the "women's press" since 1989, and found
it highly unethical that pharma companies sponsor medical conferences and

that physicians are willing to attend them. Based on his practice, these trends are increasing the accessibility of information about hormonal contraceptives, which he blames for having to invoke the conscience clause more often as his young patients are asking about specific pills. Dr. Malina angrily criticized this practice, saying that "teenage girls know now that there's contraception and they want to start using it earlier. Pharmaceutical companies that produce contraceptives—it's like a trade in narcotics! Contraceptives don't cure illnesses, right?!" According to Dr. Malina, women who stayed under his care agreed with the clinic's religio-medical approach, but interviews with several of his patients also revealed that some patients found other benefits in utilizing the clinic. For example, Ewa, a twenty-seven-year-old accountant who was a patient of Dr. Malina's did not share his religious views but was quite satisfied with the health care she received. When I met her at the clinic on the day when she reported for one of her pregnancy checkups, she suggested we talk in her apartment instead. The place was in a newly developed subdivision in the south of Kraków, and Ewa was very happy to have a visitor since she was prescribed bed rest due to an "endangered pregnancy" [*ciąża zagrożona*], which is a commonly used diagnosis in Poland for a variety of concerns, ranging from typically minor occurrences of first trimester like spotting to serious ones like signs of premature labor. Ewa was experiencing spotting and was taken off work altogether from the ninth week of her pregnancy. I was especially interested in Ewa's experience with Dr. Malina in the context of her family planning decisions; therefore, she chose to start the story from when she became his patient.

> EWA: My husband and I lived together for a year and a half before we got married. I took birth control pills then. But once we married, we moved into this apartment here, and that's when I changed doctors and began to go to Dr. Malina because he was conveniently located. He put me on the calendar [kalendarzyk] right away and took me off the pills.

> AUTHOR: Did you plan your pregnancy using the calendar then?

> EWA: No, this pregnancy is an accident [wpadka] as they say, and it happened almost right away. I tried to follow instructions with the calendar but my cycle wasn't very regular and I couldn't tell very easily when I was and wasn't fertile.

> Maybe I didn't try hard enough to learn. In any case, we
> wanted a child but not so soon; I really wanted us to buy
> our own condominium first.
>
> AUTHOR: Do you like the calendar or do you think you might
> switch back to the pill?
>
> EWA: I trust Dr. Malina. He is good because he's very gentle, not
> like some doctors. I'm opposed to contraceptives for health
> reasons. I'm not very religious so that's not a reason for me.
> My friends who use the pill feel fine and that's their choice.
> (Interview with Ewa, Kraków, 2002)

Ewa was a sort of "default" user of the calendar. She explained that she was
not opposed to the pill before she began her care under Dr. Malina, suggesting that she internalized the notion taught by the doctor that contraceptives
had harmful health effects. She saw the ineffectiveness of the calendar as the
failure of her own diligence and the fault of her body's irregular cycle, rather
than an inaccuracy of the method itself. She argued that the calendar method
is 99.5 percent effective—a statistic taught by Dr. Malina, but according to
the WHO, the method is 97.2 percent effective in so-called consistently
ideal use, and only 80.4 percent effective in actual use (Freundl, Sivin, and
Batár 2010, 119). Thus, what spoke to Ewa was the scientific rationalization
of the calendar, on the one hand, and concerns about the harmful effects of
the pill, on the other hand, rather than a religious and moral rationale for
using the calendar method. Significantly, nearly all of the women I interviewed put high premium on having a nice doctor who treats them with
respect and gentleness, rather than with an authoritarian insolence—an
issue at the forefront of many patient rights organizations and a common
problem that has been highlighted elsewhere in the post-Soviet region
(Rivkin-Fish 2005).

Though patients' motivations for using the clinic varied, providers and
the clinic's staff shared the religio-medical approach, according to Dr.
Malina. Dr. Górska, a gynecologist with ten years of experience who joined
the Małopolska clinic specifically because of the clinic's match with her religious views, explained that invoking the clause allows her to practice
medicine according to her own sense of religious commitment. She said,
"Here in our clinic we completely do not condone contraception because
those are the rules of how we provide care" (interview with Górska,

Kraków, 2002). She added that since "patients who believe [in God] choose against contraception," and since "sex education should be carried out by the church," not doctors, she was justified in declining to prescribe contraceptives even to those patients that requested them. She was aware that many women, some who initially came to the Małopolska clinic but left, circumvent this practice by pursuing other doctors willing to prescribe contraceptives, but she argued that these patients' accrual of charges from further doctors is not sufficient concern to allow contraceptive services in her own practice. In cities, women are likely to get referrals from friends or search until they find a sympathetic doctor willing to offer the service, which can be especially burdensome and costly for women in rural areas where there may be only one physician (Mishtal 2010). Dr. Górska also acknowledged that low-income women would not be able to do this at all.

Indeed, the women in this study who pursued care at their regional public clinics told me that they could not afford to pay for a visit with a different physician. Therefore, the stratification of access to reproductive health care becomes especially evident when patients get trapped in situations in which the regional doctor, similarly to the Małopolska clinic providers, is unwilling to prescribe contraceptives. In such situations, the use of the clause results in fewer family planning options for women, especially for low-income, rural, immigrant, and young women who have limited resources or know-how, which leads many to the less reliable method of periodic abstinence and withdrawal, or, at best, condoms.

It is worth noting that physicians in Poland have their own professional organization, the Polish Gynecological Association (Polskie Towarzystwo Ginekologiczne), which is a member of FIGO, the International Federation of Gynecology and Obstetrics, and which has taken reproductive health positions that the church disapproves of, including acceptance of infertility services and the associated pre-implantation diagnosis, as well as recommendations of modern contraceptive use. However, it is clear that the religious form of medical practice, as exemplified by doctors like Malina, stands in disagreement with the organization's positions. Therefore, the existence of the Polish Gynecological Association and its membership in the wider international medical community does not necessarily promise that international standards of care are being offered to women in Polish clinics. On the ground, doctors' religiosity might override professional guidelines for reproductive health care.[15]

The 1993 Ban on Abortion, and the New Church-Left Collaboration

The conscience clause law paved the way for the near-total abortion ban implemented in 1993. Strikingly, the limitations on abortion written into the Medical Code of Ethics are nearly identical in practically all circumstances. At the outset, the Polish episcopate lobbied the members of Parliament who belonged to the Polish Catholic and Social Association to draft and file the "Law on the Legal Protection for the Conceived Child." As I explain in detail in the next chapter, opponents of the ban, including women's groups, requested a nationwide referendum, and public opinion at the time was overwhelmingly against banning abortion and in favor of a national vote on this issue. But the church regime as a political power constellation was primarily legitimized by a religious understanding of an absolute morality (the objective truths paradigm), and what can and cannot be subjected to a popular vote; therefore, the Catholic bishops strongly opposed a referendum, arguing that God's law cannot be subject to a vote. Consequently, the Catholic conservative prime minister, Hanna Suchocka (not only a woman but the first woman prime minister in Poland), who later became the Polish ambassador to the Vatican, working in tandem with Wałęsa, overrode the Charter of Civil Rights as well as public opinion, and rejected the petition. In the end, a referendum was never held, and the ban on abortion was instituted by the government in 1993 (Nowakowska and Korzeniowska 2000; Zielińska 2000).

The new law only sharpened conflicts over abortion access, and in 1996 the Polish Parliament, temporarily with a left-leaning majority led by President Kwaśniewski, passed the Family Planning Act, which reversed the 1993 ban by permitting abortion for socioeconomic reasons. But a year later, parliamentary power shifted once again in favor of the Catholic-nationalist Solidarity Election Action (AWS), a coalition of right-wing Catholic organizations. Their political agenda, known as the "Profamily Program," opposed abortion, contraception, and sex education. The AWS took the liberalized abortion law to the Constitutional Tribunal which promptly returned it to its 1993 form, and as a way to prevent future attempts at loosening the law, socioeconomic reasons for abortion were now declared unconstitutional. Echoing the bishops' words, the tribunal justified its rejection of a nationwide referendum on the grounds that a moral issue may not be regulated by a popular vote (Zielińska 2000, 34). The position of the tribunal, consistent with the dominant rhetoric of the early 1990s when the initial restrictions were being implemented, made it clear that reproduction was now firmly established in the political rather than the health realm. The tribunal, embracing the absolute morality of the church, depicted all matters of reproduction and sexuality as proper objects of political regulation, rather than decisions that can be left to an individual's conscience or a citizens' vote.

The current law makes abortion illegal in all but three cases: when the woman's life or health is in danger, when a prenatal test shows a serious incurable fetal deformity, or when the pregnancy is the result of rape or incest and has been reported to the police and the pregnancy is less than twelve weeks. Because of potential complications, all terminations in the first two cases can only be carried out in a hospital. Since 1956 only 3 percent of all abortions had been performed for these reasons. Hence, 97 percent of abortions were likely to be driven underground (Johannisson et al. 1997). Even legally permissible abortions are difficult to obtain because conscientious objection is frequently declared by the directors of hospitals on behalf on the entire staff, or individual physicians refuse to offer lawful abortion without giving a viable referral to a nonobjecting colleague. Two well-known cases of such refusals are the cases of Alicja Tysiąc, and more recently, the Agata case. Agata was a fourteen-year-old girl who was raped and had become pregnant as a result, but the hospital in Lublin where she sought care declined to performed the procedure or offer a referral.

In 2003 the minister of health, Marek Balicki, himself a physician, publicly acknowledged the existence of this phenomenon and released a formal letter to the governors of all provinces in Poland urging that they "remind the public health care facilities providing gynecological and obstetrical services . . . about the unconditional obligation to adhere to the [abortion] law," which allows for three circumstances under which abortions are lawful. He noted that "it was disconcerting to see that women have difficulty in exercising their right to obtain abortions in those cases that are permitted by the law," that they lack "free access to information," and "free access to means of family planning." He also urged that the clause may not be applied "at will and in an informal fashion," but that it "refers exclusively to a specific physician in a specific case, and under no circumstances could be used by an entire clinic or hospital based on the idea of 'collective conscience' of the facility via a general directive of the head of the clinic" (Balicki 2003, 1). Balicki's statements notwithstanding, no obvious or tangible consequences to his action emerged, given his negligble power and means to enforce the law. Therefore, despite the exceptions that should theoretically allow therapeutic abortion, the Polish abortion law is the most restrictive in Europe, outside of Ireland, in that even in the three exceptional cases women can be denied care.[16]

Although the church was decisive in initiating and shaping the law, and bishops played a frontline role in policy discussions, the episcopate was ultimately displeased with the three exceptions contained in the final version of the bill—the church wished for a total ban, even in life-threatening cases. However, additional opinion polls showed that the exceptions were strongly favored by the population, the majority of which opposed restrictions on abortion to begin with (Nowakowska and Korzeniowska 2000, 219–25). At that time the church backed away from insisting on a total ban, but it has resumed its campaign again in recent years, especially since 2007, when the close church-state relations have been further solidified during the administration of the Lech and Jarosław Kaczyński twins. They were both of Solidarity's and Wałęsa's inner circle. Lech Kaczyński was president of Poland from 2005 to 2010, and Jarosław Kaczyński was prime minister from 2006 to 2007, making for a powerful team occupying both of the key political offices.

But since the church reestablished itself as a powerful political actor after the fall of state socialism and threatens to inflict damage to political candidates during election campaigns if they oppose its agenda, it has been able to wield significant political capital with parties and politicians from across ideological spectra, not only the right-leaning nationalists. Even some of the most left-wing politicians in Poland have caved under the pressure from the episcopate. A striking example is Leszek Miller, the prime minister from 2001 to 2004, who reigned with the support of the leftist president Aleksander Kwaśniewski. Kwaśniewski was a declared atheist—a rare and brazen position for a politician in Poland, where the very national identity has often been equated with Catholicism, especially in public discourses around the regime transition and since then by conservative politicians and the media. Kwaśniewski's and Miller's party, the Democratic Left Alliance (SLD) was at the time the only leftist alternative to the various conservative parties and popularly viewed as a welcome change after the reign of Wałęsa.[17] During his campaign, Miller explicitly promised to liberalize restrictive abortion laws and restore sex education in schools. But once elected, he reneged on the promises. Likewise, Minister of Health Balicki, who was a member of the SLD Party and served at the ministry under Miller, was in the minority in his public advocacy for reproductive rights, and thus had little power to enforce his position about curbing the overuse of the clause. Miller and Kwaśniewski primarily wanted to usher Poland to EU membership (thus preferring less attention on controversial abortion politics) for which they needed a favorable nationwide vote in the upcoming referendum. Rightist parties presented an obstacle in this effort as they aired a protectionist stance arguing that if Poland were to join the EU, it would become a second-class citizen and a source of cheap labor for Western Europe.[18]

Miller was far more intimidated by the church. The bishops threatened to mobilize the nation to vote against EU membership if Miller pursued liberalization of abortion. To appease the church the SLD abandoned the idea, declaring that "for the time being the current law is a compromise." The parliamentary marshall of SLD, Marek Borowski, responded that "the present [abortion] measure is simply bad," and reminded that leftist politicians typically stood "against such tough abortion laws and understand women's rights differently from groups linked to the church or those on the political right" (Traynor 2003, 1). But SLD's secretary-general, Marek Dyduch, defended Miller's compromise with the church by reassuring that "we are not giving up our campaign promises regarding reproductive rights. After the referendum, we will begin to liberalize the anti-abortion law, which we know will be unacceptable to the Catholic Church." The church immediately demanded a retraction, which was promptly offered. Dyduch's statement was further overridden by President Kwaśniewski, who declared, "We should take a different approach, in the direction of educating about sex, contraceptives and marital responsibility," adding that "the present abortion law works" (Penn 2003, 1). Miller also reneged on the promise to introduce sex education in schools, and went even further when he eliminated contraceptive health insurance coverage—a move that greatly pleased the church, which now backed away from the anti-EU rhetoric. In a brief interview that the rector of the Pontifical Academy of Theology in Kraków and a prominent church spokesman, Bishop Pieronek, granted to this research in 2002, Pieronek explained that "the SLD was no longer an obstacle" because the church could now "work with it" and the leftists "were no longer creating problems" for the "Catholic agenda" (interview with Pieronek, Kraków, 2002). Pieronek added that "in a nation like Poland the state must regulate issues of morality until such time when the population is able to take on such a responsibility and until such responsibility becomes encoded in people's minds," highlighting the paternalistic role of the Polish church in terms not unlike those of the socialist regime.

The interdependency of the church and Miller's administration provoked a reaction from feminist NGOs, which mobilized prominent Polish women to make an official statement. They submitted "The Hundred Women Letter" to the European Parliament in February 2002, which was published in a number of media outlets, and signed by prominent Polish professors, artists, businesswomen, politicians, journalists, and activists. The letter aimed to bring the attention of the EU and those agencies overseeing the European integration process to this political maneuvering:

> Behind the scenes of the integration of Poland and the European Union virtual commerce in women's rights is taking place. . . . The defense of life from conception is treated as an objective dogma; however, abortion for socioeconomic reasons is spoken about using quotation marks as if it is an ideological claim proposed by feminists who are trying to legalize murder. . . . Clearly, this is an ideological scare tactic. Consequently not only is political reform stifled but also any attempt at an open debate is met with aggressive rhetoric. (*Gazeta.pl,* February 4, 2002)

The letter provoked little reaction and was generally written off by the media, the EU, and the Polish state. Strong reaction came from the Catholic press, however. Bishop Pieronek himself weighed in by saying that the letter was a product of "feminist concrete [*beton*] that even hydrochloric acid could not melt" and that therefore little attention should be paid to it. The expression "concrete" (and its permutation "communist concrete") in popular slang describes someone who is ideologically rigid. The bishop's statement quickly became a media sound bite, but little criticism of the actual statement appeared in the press, except for the reaction from the social-democratic Labor Union Party—a marginal group and the only political party for separation of church and state—which demanded an apology from the bishop, but none was forthcoming (KAI 2002, 1).

By the time Poland successfully joined the EU in 2004, Miller practically worked for the church. At the request of the episcopate, during the

EU negotiations he secured the "exclusion clause"—an addition of a legally binding agreement to be included in Poland's Accession Treaty that guarantees the Polish state the sovereignty or "separateness" to set national policies regarding "public morality" (i.e., anything related to reproduction and sexuality), regardless of the larger European policy trends or pressures. The relevant part of the treaty reads (art. 39): "Declaration by the Government of the Republic of Poland concerning public morality: the Government of the Republic of Poland understands that nothing in the provisions of the Treaty on European Union, of the Treaties establishing the European Communities and the provision of treaties amending or supplementing those treaties prevents the Polish State in regulating questions of moral significance, as well as those related to the protection of human life" (Ivanica 2003, 27). This was a critical victory for the Polish church, and a blow to the reproductive rights groups.

Religious Power and Moral Governance

Miller's deal with the church on the backs of women was entirely unnecessary in order to succeed in the EU vote. After all, the populace was overwhelmingly in favor of joining the EU given the persistently high unemployment rate and the increasing inequalities produced by the neoliberal economic shift of the first postsocialist decade. Indeed, the EU seemed to promise economic improvements and the ability to work abroad, as well as a cultural opening of Poland to Western Europe after decades of social and political isolation. Furthermore, Pope John Paul II was a supporter of Poland's EU membership. Despite his criticism of the "moral corruption" of the West, he was in favor of a unified Europe, as long as Poland entered on its own terms, preserving its sovereignty on abortion laws. Thus, any genuine attempt by the Polish episcopate to sabotage the referendum would have been an act of insubordination, and therefore highly unlikely in the ideologically monolithic institution of the Catholic Church, but essentially inconceivable if opposition was to involve the Polish episcopate against the Polish pope.

In a situation like Poland's where the postsocialist state is weak as it grapples with major economic and political shifts, the agendas of more powerful players such as the church or international financial actors outweighs the concerns of the populace. It became apparent that the new leftist state run by the SLD would continue in the puppet role of the previous conservative administration vis-à-vis the church. Indeed, the few politicians who openly favored separation of church and state flocked to the SLD, but many more in the party were happy to accommodate the demands of the church, casting it as a form of a necessary and prudent compromise. The leftists operated on the assumption that the state lacks the robustness, and therefore the confidence, to ignore the demands of a powerhouse like the episcopate. But simultaneously the SLD failed to recognize the robustness that came with a major popular mandate. After all, the leftists, many of whom were communist party members in pre-1989 Poland, were elected precisely because the conservative Catholic-nationalist government of Wałęsa brought years of deteriorating conditions and high unemployment, reaching 30 percent in rural areas. But the church successfully created a kind of Catholic political habitus with intensification of its presence and rhetoric from the 1980s onward. By the end of the first postsocialist decade, the church's influence in shaping tangible laws was substantial, with highly consequential intrusions into health care policy (the abortion ban and the elimination of subsidized contraceptives), education (mandatory religion courses and the elimination of sex education), and the media (the law requiring deference to Christian values in programming).

However, the conscience clause in the new medical ethics law was of particular significance. From the perspective of the church, after the successful ban on abortion the next battle focused on restricting access to lawful therapeutic abortions and to contraception, which remained legal. Promoting the use of the clause was the next best thing: if a direct law could not ban all abortions and contraceptives remained legal, then a law obliging Catholic physicians to limit access was what was left. The responsibility was now placed on the authority of physicians—morally trusted, but also bound by medical laws. Many Catholic doctors followed the call, but the clause had a powerful intimidating effect on other physicians as well. The health care providers and reproductive rights activists in this research consistently estimated that approximately a third of doctors refuse to perform legal abortions in hospitals and decline to prescribe contraceptives. This was interpreted as too few or too many, depending on the doctor's religious leanings. Overall, however, doctors in this study, whether conservative or liberal, understood the clause as encouraging providers to let their religiosity play a role in decisions about which health services they ought to provide, regardless of the fact that these services are lawful.

It is useful to consider the controlling and disciplining effects inherent in the unregulated use of the clause by physicians as reflective of a form of religious governmentality of the female patient. The concept of governmentality and the analysis of power developed by Michel Foucault (1977, 1978, 1991a) help illuminate how disciplinary power is exercised through specific institutional mechanisms—in the Polish case, both the larger Catholic Church and the individual doctors, but also state institutions such as the Ministry of Health. Foucault observed in his historical analysis of eighteenth-century Europe that physical forms of control and repression of the population exercised by the sovereign transformed over time into much subtler forms of power with the arrival of liberal democracies in the nineteenth century and on. The discourses that were instrumental to the spread of liberal political orders spoke of rights and freedoms, and the end of physical repression. Foucault observed that social control through "subjectification"—the production of docile and conforming subjects—became the goal of the state. The docile subject would have felt compelled to self-censor voluntarily in order to conform to particular ideological norms and practices dictated by the dominant institutions. Thus, the focal element of understanding how moral governance works both as an overarching web of sanctions, even at the time of one's burial, but also as a form of control that is individually internalized and enforced through specific ideological mechanisms, is highly relevant to the ways in which the Polish church functions as a disciplining and surveilling body.

For the Polish Catholic Church as an institutional regime, the clause was a critical political tool to expand the confines of its centralized power by incorporating subtle forms of regulation through which the ubiquity of power becomes less visible as it is broadly dispersed via a wide range of processes and techniques of control, rather than being directly wielded by the clergy. The conscience clause functions at two levels. At the larger public level it acts as a surveillance mechanism deployed by the church to expose doctors' conduct; that is, the clause was legally implemented so that every doctor had a way to self-govern and act in a manner consistent with conforming Catholics by refusing to provide particular services. Formal declaration of objection is also a way for doctors to show religious allegiance. In contrast, doctors who provide all health care services can then be identified and disciplined by the local clergy with refusals for burials or other forms of public intimidation. On a more intimate level of doctor-patient relationship, the clause is deployed by (some) doctors to discipline women by refusing to provide the services the church disapproves of. Thus, the present-day religious regime in Poland relies heavily on doctors as "religious specialists" in the enforcement of a distinct religiously sanctioned morality in medicine (Bax 1991, 9). In particular, the conscience clause law and the doctors who invoke it operate as tools of coercive power that legitimize and reproduce the moral authority of the church by making the clause compulsory in some hospitals regardless of the desires of individual doctors, and by narrowing women's reproductive and health options to the absolute moral parameters set by the Vatican.

In the end, the church's moral governance aims to produce docile doctors and docile women. The opening story of Alicja Tysiąc who qualified for a therapeutic abortion to save her eyesight but was ultimately denied the procedure is emblematic of the effects of the morality politics that ensued during these years. Alicja's doctors who explicitly recommended abortion to her were simultaneously unwilling to give her a formal authorization for the procedure and preferred to wait for other colleagues to take the public risk as she bounced between doctors in pursuit of the letter, one she never received. This fear and radical shift in practices and access from the state socialist times when abortion was readily available, to the postsocialist present when doctors are now reluctant to authorize the procedure even in dire situations, attests to the power of the moralization wave that ensued after 1989 as a result of the renewed political power of the church. This multilevel infiltration of Catholic ideology into public and private spaces created an atmosphere hostile to not only reproductive rights and health care, but to women's rights more broadly, and feminism in particular. But this attack did not go unanswered.

3 ⫲ Women Respond

Feminist Consciousness-Raising and Activism

At the time of socialism seeking abortion services was normal, without the moral burden. Now it has become a sin. In fact, feminist activists try to bring attention to the fact that we lost the language with which to speak about abortion. We are no longer supposed to talk of terminating a pregnancy or abortion; we're supposed to talk of killing a life. The whole issue became weighted down by a moral burden and we can't seem to undo it.

—Interview with Magda, Warsaw, 2002

As THE POLITICAL INFLUENCE of the church in the postsocialist legislative changes in the 1990s led to the establishment of a new "gender order" enforced through radical curtailment of reproductive rights, and a rise in political rhetoric of moralization, the church and conservative politicians also relied on the idea that all things communist were a priori wrong and immoral. Abortion was severely restricted, and it became difficult to obtain, even when legally permissible, as was the situation with Alicja Tysiąc. It was clear that this radical shift in laws and political discourses had an immense effect on ordinary women's access to care. This constriction of rights and access was the direct impetus for an extensive illegal abortion underground, and drove women to pursue information about abortion and contraception on the Internet or through networks of trusted doctors and friends. Some women chose to travel abroad for abortions to the neighboring nations of Belarus or Lithuania and elsewhere. Women could not even rely on all doctors to offer accurate information about sexually transmitted infections (STIs), especially since rigorist Catholic providers expect patients to be sexually inactive until a monogamous marriage, at which time STIs are presumed to be not of concern. In this new gender order, restricting reproductive rights became a key public tool of the church and the conservative right to reassert their political dominance and revive the masculinism of a patriarchal society of the past. In response, a number of feminist organizations formed in Poland, as well as in other parts of Eastern Europe. The political scientist Peggy Watson (1993, 71) sees the emergence of feminist groups in the region since 1989 as a rise against male intellectuals in power and their exclusion of women in the postsocialist public space. She argues that marginalization of women also provided an opportunity for feminist mobilization in response to the institutionalization of traditional inequalities—a process that "is in fact predicated on the rescinding of a range of rights accorded to women under state socialism."

A number of women's rights NGOs emerged in Poland from the political transition of the early 1990s. These groups took up a variety of efforts, including counseling related to reproductive rights (rights to contraception, emergency contraception, information about family planning, abortion in specific circumstances, and patients' rights in general), as well as legal and psychological counseling related to divorce, domestic violence, rape, and unemployment. To understand how the activist community conceptualized what was happening and the kind of goals they set out as they began to organize during this period, I took up extensive fieldwork with several organizations. The nascent women's movement was based around a few core NGOs and unaffiliated activists who often held academic or media positions. At the time of my fieldwork, I found claims that 90 to 200 NGOs promoting women's rights in Poland existed (Ghodsee 2004; McMahon 2002, 41) significantly exaggerated. Since I began my fieldwork, the number of active women's rights groups has increased, but as of 2014 it is still rather small, despite the high numbers posted on a variety of NGO lists.[1] The majority is severely underfunded—when I made my first visit to the location of one of the largest groups in Kraków, I found that their electricity had been shut off for nonpayment, a recurring problem.[2] As the group's founder, Monika, and I pulled up our chairs close to the brightness of the window for our first conversation, she explained that none of the staff is paid. Most groups in fact are extremely small, usually with a staff of two to five volunteers.[3] In Monika's organization, she and another colleague, Hanka Lipowska-Teutsch, performed nearly all of the services offered at the center, including counseling and fund-raising. With time they succeeded in recruiting an unemployment counselor, three attorneys, and a group of young activists who accompany the center's clients to the courthouse, all on a voluntary basis. Many of the organizations, however, have no fixed location, no office of any kind, and meet privately in one of the volunteer's apartments. Without a phone number or a post office box, these groups are difficult to reach and can be found only through word of mouth. I focused my research on the three most visible and active NGOs: the Federation for Women and Family Planning in Warsaw, the Women's Foundation eFKa in Kraków, and the Center for Women's Rights in Kraków.[4]

As I developed relationships with the women in the three groups, I was referred further to a number of unaffiliated women and men active in the movement in both cities, and the circle of activists I got to know began to grow wider. I wanted to focus on the experiences and perspectives of those groups and individuals that were most closely involved in the reproductive rights effort, therefore the Federation, which is the only organization in Poland solely devoted to reproductive and sexual rights, became my main research focus. The Federation's location—not far from the center of Warsaw and on the edge of a residential neighborhood—makes it readily accessible by tram from the Central Train Station. The office of the organization, in addition to providing the work space for the staff, houses a small library of feminist literature, educational materials and posters used in public events and campaigns, and a meticulous collection of newspaper clippings that track abortion news from the early 1990s until the present. Judging by its paid staff and the presence of some of their staff at international conferences and events at the EU, it appeared as though the Federation enjoyed a better financial footing than other groups I was familiar with. Wanda Nowicka, whom I got to know well, was the most engaged reproductive rights advocate at the time of my fieldwork, both in

Poland and in international meetings and events, where she sought to forge links with activists from other countries. A classicist by education with a graduate degree from the University of Warsaw and postgraduate education in law and medical ethics, she was the Federation's founding president. She also cofounded the ASTRA Network—Central and Eastern European Women's Network for Sexual and Reproductive Health and Rights—that links a large group of reproductive rights activists throughout the post-Soviet region.

During the 1980s and early 1990s, Nowicka first worked at the National Library of Science and later in Warsaw high schools teaching Latin, Greek, and English. When we first met in 2000, she recounted that the Federation began as a coalition of five smaller groups and several motivated activists, all of whom shared the goal of maintaining reproductive rights in postsocialist Poland. The pivotal organization in the coalition was the Association for State Neutrality, Neutrum, created by Nowicka and a group of her friends in response to the strong visibility of the church in post-1989 politics. They became alarmed when the church was successful in ushering in mandatory religious education in public schools through the legislature, and they worried about the possibility of a religious state. As Nowicka explained: "First there was religion in schools, later the church got involved in abortion, but the entire activism of our group started from worries about church-state relations" (interview with Wanda Nowicka, Warsaw, 2002). When the five organizations merged to form the Federation, reproduction was at the center of their agenda. Nowicka found it impossible to continue to split her time between social and political organizing and teaching high school, and chose to devote herself fully to advocacy work on behalf of women's rights. Public tension around the issue of abortion, and significant public resistance to the possibility of restrictions evident in the national opinion polls became a powerful motivation for Nowicka and other activists to unite into a larger, more effective structure. Although much of my fieldwork took place with the Federation because of its focus on reproductive rights, all three organizations (including the Kraków-based groups, the Center for Women's Rights, and eFKa), as well as numerous unaffiliated advocates, welcomed my research, and I was grateful for the many interviews and hours spent in their offices gathering information, perusing materials, and participating in their activities and events.

The Initial Shock

The events and experiences of the early 1990s caught many women by surprise. The narratives offered by women during my fieldwork at the NGOs as well as many ordinary women I interviewed in Kraków, Warsaw, and Gdańsk that were not part of the feminist movement show that although the rights women gained under state socialism via top-down directives had not always been fully appreciated, many women valued these gains, assuming and hoping that their rights would remain unchanged. Not surprisingly, the severity of the first version of the abortion bill—allowing abortions to save the life, but not the health, of a woman—triggered widespread public opposition, which quickly forced its modification to include the health protection clause. Wanda Nowicka noted that although "this version elicited an enormous public resistance, later what followed was weariness and also a sense of hopelessness because it became clear that the whole political machinery was rolling forward."

Despite the general public apathy at the time as economic conditions were deteriorating due to the "shock therapy" cuts in public jobs and services instituted by the postsocialist administration, Wanda and activists across Poland escalated their efforts to protect abortion rights as the situation began to heat up.[5] Under the Polish Charter of Civil Rights, a bill must be put to a nationwide vote if 500,000 signatures in favor of a referendum are collected. At the height of the debate, the activists formed the Committee to Create a Referendum and collected 1.3 million signatures—well surpassing the minimum needed to put the issue to a vote. Almost duplicating the situation from 1991 when Solidarity's Women's Section polled regional factories to show that 80 percent were against restricting abortion, here too women's organizations believed in the democratic process of people's right to petition the government, given that nationwide surveys at that time showed that 82 percent of people polled were opposed to a total ban on abortion and 60 percent were for legal access with no or minimal restrictions. Moreover, a poll showed that 74 percent of Poles wanted the opportunity to vote on the proposed law (Nowakowska and Korzeniowska 2000, 219–25; Simpson 1994). But Solidarity's Prime Minister Suchocka, who later became the Polish ambassador to the Vatican, rejected the petition for referendum, stating that "issues of morality" are not subject to a popular vote. Wanda recalled this moment:

We gathered the signatures everywhere—on the streets, in stores—we got hundreds of thousands of signatures, and at that point, I think, people still believed that something could be done and that these signatures would mean something. Later, it turned out that the parliament wasn't at all perturbed by this, and that's how this sense of powerlessness came about—this sense that there's nothing we can do anymore. And that I think was significant. On the other hand, the indifference of the majority of Polish society that was against the ban but didn't follow the debate closely is significant too. It was as if people simply couldn't get their minds around the idea that an abortion ban could happen, that such a thing was possible. Many people were simply unprepared despite the whole debate, so it came as a shock. But the shock wasn't severe enough to start a revolution over it either. (Interview with Wanda Nowicka, Warsaw, 2002).

Kazia Szczuka, another prominent activist in Warsaw who supported Nowicka's efforts, recalled how this sense of shock also had an immobilizing effect: "I was so surprised by the proposal [to ban abortion] that I didn't want to think about it; I didn't believe it; I pushed it out of my mind." Renata,[6] an activist in Kraków, in contrast, recalled how imminent the ban on abortion felt once Suchocka rejected the signatures, and explained the futility of the protests: "When the anti-abortion law was about to take effect in 1993, there was a lot of activity; people protested; there were open letters to the authorities. But it was too late; it had no effect" (interview with Renata, Kraków, 2002). Nowicka recalled that as the abortion rights protests organized by women's rights groups became known, a counterprotest was generated as a "river of people" organized by parishes across Poland was bused to Warsaw to support the abortion ban.

Doctors stayed conspicuously outside this struggle and did little to stop the policy restrictions of the early 1990s (De Zordo and Mishtal 2011). Instead, they began to offer abortion clandestinely for a high fee in private offices, launching an extensive abortion underground, a topic I take up in a later chapter. Typically doctors wanted to stay out of the conflict, worrying about potential harassment by the clergy and preferring to focus on their medical practice instead. But this lack of political engagement among physicians should also be understood within the complexity of historical disenfranchisement of doctors, postsocialist neoliberal cuts in health care and wages, and the lack of political unity within the medical community itself as physicians' organizations had been banned under communism in an effort to prevent professional solidarity among the well-educated.[7] The lack of an alliance between physicians and advocacy organizations accentuated the challenges faced by women's groups, who fought the battle publicly (De Zordo and Mishtal 2011).

Still, the escalating threat to abortion access was the central force that galvanized women's groups. The Polish sociologist Małgorzata Fuszara declared in 1991 that "mobilization of the Polish women's movement seems to me to be the outstanding achievement of the parliamentary campaign to ban abortion" (Fuszara 1991,128).[8] But the movement, mainly consisting of educated middle-class women such as Nowicka and Monika, was rather meager in the face of a well-organized church. Moreover, the movement fragmented into separate issues (in part because of the foreign funding for NGOs that encouraged more specific agendas)—while some groups focused on reproductive rights, others became involved in other causes such as domestic violence, and the rights of immigrant women, especially. Yet this fragmentation also reflects a style of advocacy that is akin to the "Western package" of feminist ideas, and is broadly understood; one activist explained, "For us, feminism isn't just a type of intellectual discourse, but rather we'd like to offer broad antidiscrimination support; we'd like to bring in the voices from the widest possible range of groups; in other words, anyone who is suffering from the hierarchical structure of the world, so to speak, is within our sphere of interest" (interview with Edyta, Kraków, 2002). Indeed, outreach offered by feminist organizations in Poland includes support to Roma, Chechen, and Armenian women, as well as generally cooperative relations with the gay and lesbian communities. In fact, the largest Polish LGBT organization, Campaign Against Homophobia (KPH—Kampania Przeciw Homofobii), feminist groups, and public advocates such as Nowicka and Szczuka have in recent years been visible in the Polish media and public life as groups that share a common interest in advocating against discrimination.[9]

At the time of the abortion debate in 1993, despite considerable efforts to organize the broader public, women's groups were unable to force a referendum on abortion. The Charter of Civil Rights that was newly developed after the fall of the regime turned out to hold little value against Suchocka's position that abortion was a matter for moral governance, and therefore not subject to debate. Thus, the abortion bill banning 97 percent abortions became law in 1993 (David and Titkow 1994; Johannisson et al. 1997; Titkow 1999).

What Happened? Making Sense of Setbacks

The women in the feminist movement I spoke to understood these early, yet defining, challenges and defeats as resulting from the historical trajectories of the Polish church and state merging, women's political inexperience, and discursive disadvantages that impeded the mobilization of a women's movement in the early 1990s. State feminism of the socialist era was seen as a double-edged sword—on the one hand, many valuable rights were handed down to women by the regime, and on the other hand, these top-down gains contributed to women's political passivity after 1989.[10] The regime's long-term suppression of independent feminist thought—and all political thought for that matter—also explained the shock that women experienced when their rights were being rolled back after 1989, and the slow start of those who attempted to organize the opposition. Their disbelief was also mixed with a sense betrayal by the church, which until now had represented freedom after a decade of church support for the Solidarity opposition movement. Most women found themselves blindsided by the regressive proposals, unable to believe that abortion could be banned after decades of legal access. Many also did not take seriously the possibility of mandatory religious education in schools until after it was too late.

Understandings of the historical roots of Polish feminism and its influence during the turmoil of the early 1990s varied. Traces of feminist thought appeared in nineteenth-century Polish literature, shortly after the French Revolution sparked European feminism, and some activists I interviewed were highly aware of that legacy. According to Sławomira Walczewska (2000, 92–95), the founder of the eFKa group in Kraków, Polish feminist thought permeated the works by Maria Konopnicka, Eliza Orzeszkowa, and Zofia Nałkowska, written in the 1800s and 1900s, which contested the "gender contract of the noble knighthood," wherein a female caretaker and a male protector constituted the idealized gender roles.[11] Walczewska believed that the long-standing history of Polish feminism is marginalized and neglected in popular and academic discourses, but other activists argued that this legacy is rather negligible because it did not mobilize a struggle for rights and remained a literary phenomenon available mainly to the privileged. Julia, an activist and a gender studies scholar, explained:

The traces of feminism in the writings by Orzeszkowa and Konopnicka were minimal. There was no feminist movement in Poland, and these authors weren't fighting for equal rights. What I mean is that there was no process of building [feminist] consciousness, and no process of transforming men. In Western Europe this process took two hundred years. Of course people suffered, women suffered, but simultaneously gender attitudes were changing, so when equal rights came, both men and women were ready because they already perceived one another in a different light. However, we, the patriarchal peasant society, were handed down equal rights from the communists, but we were not prepared. (Interview with Julia, Warsaw, 2002)

Julia further argued that because "Poland was a backward, peasant nation" before socialism, the population was not sufficiently mature in political terms to appreciate the state feminist programs that came forth:

Poland and other East European nations, except perhaps for Hungary and Czechoslovakia, were simply agricultural and incredibly backward [*niezwykle zacofanymi*]. After all, prewar Poland was 60 percent rural—these were real peasants, not some farmers. On top of this, the Polish elites had been murdered, if not by one [aggressor] then by another; therefore, in reality we faced socialism and the postwar rebuilding of the nation as a peasant society. And, by the power of a decree, and overnight, women were given the right to work, the right to a voice, everything, and this despite the fact that they never fought for these things. The remnants of feminism in the writings of Orzeszkowa and Konopnicka—this was simply laughable [*śmiech na sali*, literally: laughter in the auditorium] and had no bearing on the rights that Polish women were granted. (Interview with Julia, Warsaw, 2002)

While the form of state feminism implemented by the socialist government indeed increased women's autonomy, it was also perceived by some as easy emancipation that lulled women into political immobility because it worked to prevent the development of grassroots feminist thought by suppressing the flow of information about Western women's rights developments. Julia recalled, for example, that the 1967 Declaration on the Elimination of Discrimination against Women and the First United Nations World Conference on Women in Mexico City in 1975, as well as events associated with the United Nations World Population Year in 1974, all went virtually unnoticed by the state media; Julia and her academic friends were only aware of these developments because of their contacts with scholars abroad.

"Us vs. Them" Rhetoric

But efforts to stifle feminist mobilization were not confined to the socialist regime. As I described in the preceding chapter, the opposition movement, Solidarity, continued this trend in the 1980s when its leadership dissolved Solidarity's Women's Section, when the group began to mobilize and speak against the early proposals to restrict abortion rights. The potential benefits from an alliance between the nascent women's movement and the already robust and established labor movement could have been many, but the Catholic nature of Solidarity certainly precluded reproductive rights as a common cause.

Historically, benefits of links between labor and women's movements have been shown in the Scandinavian and Latin American contexts. During times of political transitions, women's rights made the greatest inroads when labor and feminist movements shared political agendas and collaborated as allies, rather than when they worked independently or in antagonistic ways.[12] For instance, during the Brazilian political transition from 1985 to 1988, the resistance to the military rule relied on new oppositional discourses that mobilized women to join the fight. Sonia Alvarez, a scholar of Brazil, observed (1990, 223) that the opposition's elites were "reaching down into civil society for new allies, . . . courting the female electorate as never before, [and] expanding the structure of political opportunities for women." She demonstrated that an important element of political legitimacy for the new Brazilian elites became their support of women's causes, which facilitated the consolidation of the Brazilian women's movement.[13]

In Poland, however, the oppositional discourse subsumed women's rights under the general workers' rights category (Bernhard 1993; Long 1996; Penn 2005; Rueschemeyer 1998; Staniszkis 1984). The Solidarity trade union leaders were overwhelmingly men, while women were perceived to play a limited supportive role (Laba 1991).[14] The movement deployed the rhetoric of women as mothers and martyrs, and consigned women activists to work in the shadows of their male counterparts; as the historian Padraic Kenney observed, "Women made the sandwiches while men made politics" (2002, 67).[15] The women in the union generally aimed for the higher goal of the movement, namely building a unified resistance to the regime, and many dismissed women's concerns as marginal. In fact, the emerging Solidarity elites had little reason to court the female electorate, which was already squarely on their side given the rigid "us vs. them" dichotomy that dominated the oppositional discourse. Jolanta, one of the activists in Warsaw and a member of Solidarity during the 1980s explains: "Many people didn't have the awareness back then that the polarization of 'they' and 'us' was going to change later. In the oppositional circles it was clear that 'they' meant communists, and 'we' meant Solidarity. It's true that Solidarity had its flaws—it was antifeminist, occasionally, but we didn't want to acknowledge that; it was a bit too clerical but again we treated that as folklore" (interview with Jolanta, Warsaw, 2002).

Jolanta added that in the postsocialist permutation of this rhetoric, feminists were considered to be associated with communists, and therefore clumped into the "they" side of the polarization. The emerging women's groups did not fare well under the Solidarity-derived post-1989 government, despite Solidarity's own status as a new social movement. In addition to reproductive rights restrictions, the post-1989 period was marked by both a woman-unfriendly administration and workplace. The massive layoffs that followed in the early 1990s were marked by a disproportionate dismissal of women. Female workers who were members of the Solidarity trade union were not protected to any greater extent than women without such membership, as the political scientist David Ost (2005) demonstrates. Specifically, he found (2005, 145) that union leaders, rather than protecting women from unfair layoffs, were actually eager to have them fired, and felt that the companies "employed too many women and that women ought to be laid off before men." Ost observed that sexist attitudes among Solidarity's managers were disguised in nongendered terms when the union leaders made "recommendations for lopsided layoffs" by arguing that women had less technical training than men and were therefore unskilled workers.[16] But overwhelmingly the general population supported the opposition against the regime and welcomed the postsocialist administration run by Solidarity-derived members. The anti-regime sentiment was so strong in fact that once freedom was attained, the norm became to unquestionably embrace the new system, regardless of whether the new situation brought relief or hardship. The old regime was so discredited that once it fell, life simply had to be better, come what may. In this particular social and political climate, women's rights groups who spoke for maintaining socialist reproductive policies or voiced criticism of layoffs were quickly labeled communist and discredited, which stifled the movement's wider appeal.

Other women activists explained the slow reaction to the reproductive rights restrictions as the legacy of a historical lack of women's organizing in

Poland as compared to men's organizing, and a peculiar relationship between women and the state. Walczewska of the eFKa organization in
Kraków argued that "in a historical and social sense, we don't have the experience of [organizing] and the education of self-mobilization that the men
have had. Women, if at all, created rather small and closed forms of organizations such as the family, clubs for friends, and such." Hanka Lipowska-
Teutsch, another activist from Kraków, affiliated with the Center for
Women's Rights, explained that she felt a sense of weakness and helpless-
ness vis-à-vis the larger system, and sees that for many ordinary women this
feeling prevents them from acting on their own behalf:

> In Brazil, historically speaking, I believe that political unrest happens often and
> that the people in power feel that they are in a state of flux, but in Poland once
> you're sitting in a position, that's where you'll sit. We have the appropriate
> metaphor of "hanging onto a stool" [*siedzić na stołku*]—when a politician who
> is elected for four years doesn't at all experience it that way, because he figures
> that once he finishes being a member of the Parliament then he'll become a
> bank director, and so on. . . . I feel that sense of weakness in our civil society in
> Poland. (Interview with Hanka Lipowska-Teutsch, Kraków, 2002)

Likewise, Nowicka described that during the early years of mobilizing
participants from a wide variety of circles, she found that "the women
whom I spoke with articulated a strong skepticism toward the socialist and
the postsocialist states alike, along with a sense of hopelessness about their
ability to influence politics in a state that has shown itself to care more
about its alliance with the church than about women's rights or public opinion." This sentiment is not confined to women, or to the turmoil of the
early 1990s. Poland has one of the lowest voter turnouts in Europe at less
than 50 percent in 2012, which suggests that the population as a whole is
rather cynical about its ability to influence the political process (Kostadinova 2003).[17] But most salient, there was a lack of recognition of the importance of women's rights.

A Slow Start

Given these historical trajectories and the lack of political experience with
mobilization, feminist consciousness awoke later in a reaction to political
changes—a slow and ineffective start in the face of a quickly moving

church-state machinery to restrict reproductive rights. Nowicka explained her own trajectory this way:

> My feminist consciousness developed only in the beginning of the 1990s be-cause in my home where I grew up my mother had a professional career in the seventies, and gender discrimination wasn't felt. Now women have the aware-ness in retrospect that we lacked true equality back then, but nevertheless, we had the impression that equality was there, that we can work, for example. There were women who had professional careers. And clearly, it was different as compared to the West where women had to fight for their rights. Here, we were, so to speak, given these things. I realized that we lacked equality only in 1990 when the issue of abortion began. That's when we realized that the rights we've been given can also be taken away, suddenly and easily. In this moment the lack of gender equality in Poland became very evident, it became very visi-ble, and that's when I had to reevaluate my entire worldview. During socialism, I wasn't a self-aware feminist: I was a person who was realizing her life in a feminist manner; however, it was all happening without the consciousness. I realized that I'm a conscious feminist only later, in 1990. (Interview with Wanda Nowicka, Warsaw, 2002)

Many activists argued that the security of women's rights during the social-ist era in Poland was predicated on a particular political rhetoric, and women learned of the fragility of their rights only when the Catholic-nationalist gender discourse became the dominant rhetoric after the power shift of 1989. Nowicka concluded that equality could be achieved only through a struggle, "a process of fighting for each right," the way "feminism devel-oped in the West." Others related similar awakenings. Kazia Szczuka, who was one of the early activists and currently occupies a prominent place in Polish media, explained how her consciousness developed:

> SzczuKA: . . . before that point, I had no awareness.
>
> AUTHOR: Why? How do you see it?
>
> SzczuKA: Communism gave us a feeling that there was equality; abortion was legal and so on. During my youth, everything revolved around a paradigm of independence, meaning that, all of us together were fighting against the evil communism, so vignettes that were feminist or gender-related simply didn't exist. Certainly my friends and I were quite liberated, so to speak. The conservative style that we see today didn't

exist yet. It wasn't there. Everybody that didn't like the communists—and that was the majority, especially among young people—was able to conduct an absolutely liberated lifestyle, without any questions about whether premarital sex was allowed or anything of this kind. It was clear that, yes, it was allowed, and so was abortion. When I look back, the only gender problem I see back then is the small number of women who held state power.

AUTHOR: Was there no feminist rhetoric in communism then?

SZCZUKA: Look, communists operated on the assumption that emancipation is important and that women need access to the workplace. So in some sense, these feminist vignettes did exist. Later, we all became more ambivalent about it because, on the one hand, I think that truly many women with higher education got jobs, thanks to that awful regime. We could perhaps argue that if there was no communism women would also find access to the workplace, but nevertheless it did, indeed, happen much sooner as a directive of the state. And this gain wasn't ever appreciated fully. On the other hand, the communist system strongly censored, denied, and questioned Western feminism, the whole Second Wave. In other words, communist equality meant that women continued to work at home, continued to be responsible for the family and so on; there was no change in mentality and women didn't participate in state power. In reality there were no legal protections in place for women. It was a very patriarchally structured state. (Interview with Kazia Szczuka, Warsaw, 2002)

Szczuka draws a clear distinction between the sexually more "liberated" communist period and the "conservative style" that ensued after 1989. She recalled that when the church began calling for an abortion ban, most women were caught off guard, refusing to believe that regressive policies would materialize. Nevertheless, women from her academic circles at the university and from other educational institutions began to mobilize and formed a robust feminist elite that continues to have a visible presence in public policy debates and the media. Over time Szczuka became visible in the media as a prochoice activist and for equal status of men and women, as well as an advocate for the rights of gays and lesbians, activities that made her a regular target of the conservative and religious media. In 2004 Szczuka published a book titled *The Silence of the Lambs,* in which she offers an analysis of why Polish women have had so little influence on the changes in reproductive rights after 1989, and concludes that the pervasive silence about experiences with abortion has been the key contributing factor in the low level of mobilization during the political transition period.

The Lost Language

In addition to the pervasive rhetorical paralysis that Szczuka identifies, the language about abortion was lost to the morality discourse imposed by powerful conservative and Catholic political voices. The redefinition of women's identities around traditional gender differences dominated the rhetoric of the early 1990s and served as a political tool of Catholic conservatives to consolidate their authority as "moral" leaders. The juxtaposition of these powerful and authorized discursive formations framing reproduction as a Catholic and patriotic imperative, and abortion and contraception as grave transgressions that have no place in Poland, with the increasing forms of opposition against the church raises the question, What can be said publicly to contest these religious assumptions? To what extent can women, journalists, or health care providers be allowed to offer critiques publicly about them?

The women in the feminist movement I spoke to understood these early, defining challenges in terms of specific discursive disadvantages. In particular, they recalled a sense of having lost the language with which to speak about reproductive rights during this time; as Renata, one of the activists in Kraków explained, before 1989 "abortion wasn't weighted down by the language of morality, that it's the killing of the unborn. Before, it was a normal thing, part of everyday life. Since then it became a sin." Kinga Dunin, a prominent feminist journalist, recalled this shift:

> In the '80s the language with which we talked about abortion was taken away from us. It became "life is sacred" and "killing is bad." So if I'm agreeing that abortion is bad because I'm killing, then every argument in favor of abortion access doesn't work, because: If it's bad, then why do it? This weakness also results from the lack of political culture, the inability to think in the categories of

a liberal state, in which if I think it's bad and you think it's good then we need the kind of law that allows me to do what I want and you to do what you want. Therefore, discussion about abortion shouldn't be about morality but about how to organize a state that represents people with a variety of perspectives. The morality discourse was imposed by the church, and it looks like we got pulled into this discourse; we don't have the courage to question it anymore. We missed the moment when we could. (Interview with Kinga Dunin, Warsaw, 2002)

The colonization of language turned out to be one of the most powerful tools of moral governance, which had significant damaging effects on the ability of women's groups to challenge the church-state momentum. The shift toward the language of morality provided the church an important discursive shield against critiques of any legislative changes that could be subsumed under the general rubric of public morality. Dunin argued that abortion and contraception—both "relatively neutral terms" under state socialism—were successfully "redefined as murder, while the popular expression for abortion *skrobanka* [literally, little scraping] is now treated as a form of brutal colloquialism and outside acceptable norms." As the redefinition of public discourse into moral categories took root, the church pressed for further legislative changes. Sex education in schools was also deemed nondebatable and was eliminated in an internal move by the state. Several years later health insurance coverage for contraceptives would also be cut in a similar fashion. State subsidies for TRR's sex education program were soon withdrawn, and access to family planning was pitted against the "rights of the unborn."[18] Dunin and Renata lamented that perhaps it was difficult for the nascent feminist movement to know how to deal with the church's campaign after communism collapsed: "It was the beginning, we were just learning, so we let ourselves be pulled into a discussion at the moral level: is this a child or no, does it have a soul or does it not have a soul, in which week does it acquire a soul? All this was completely idiotic because we let ourselves be entangled in the kind of moral discourse, the kind of philosophy of life that nobody has the courage to question." Feminist scholars have argued that in the US setting the avoidance of direct engagement with the "fetal subject" has allowed a backlash against women's body integrity in nationalistic debates (Michaels and Morgan 1999, 2). Likewise, in the Polish context, as Dunin, Renata, and others observed, the early phase of the movement was a time of slow reaction and engagement, as activists were only beginning to develop responses and their own language.

The Stigmatization of Feminism

During the transition years in the early 1990s, identifying as a women's rights activist was risky and potentially stigmatizing in a political climate that was hostile to women's causes, or even gender analysis. Ann Snitow, an American gender scholar and feminist activist who has been an important link between the Polish and American feminist communities and traveled to Poland numerous times during this period to support local activists, observed (1993) that the ubiquitous public antifeminist imagery and stereotypes played a significant role in making the nascent Polish women's movement unappealing to a wider audience. Likewise, the Polish feminist scholar Agnieszka Graff (2001) observes that the antifeminist and antiwoman climate compelled even prominent female politicians to represent themselves as "feminine" and "motherly" first, and as competent public figures second. Even women students at the University of Łódź were found to hold stigmatizing views about feminists reproduced in the media; however, their perspective changed dramatically after the students had an opportunity to take a gender studies course in which they debated and discussed issues of concern to women and feminist vignettes in general (Oleksy 2000).

The media played a significant role in the stigmatization of feminists. Wanda Nowicka, of the Federation for Women and Family Planning, was a frequent guest on television shows that discussed reproductive rights; her presence is typically juxtaposed with strong Catholic anti-abortion participants,[19] leading to an antagonistic exchange of views—and thus both sides appear quite extreme. Indeed, the majority of women I interviewed who were outside of the movement told me that their familiarity with the activists was mainly through these media appearances and said they perceived feminism as an ideology that appeared "extreme" or "aggressive," echoing the stereotypes of the NGOs promoted by the church and much of the Polish media in general.

In fact, feminism has been mocked, discredited, and marginalized in public discourse. Eliza, an activist with the Women's Foundation eFKa organization in Kraków, recalled an incident related to the publication of their quarterly *Zadra* (literally, means a thorn or a splinter), which publishes articles of interest to women and women's rights in general (akin to *Ms. Magazine* in the United States).[20] The words a "feminist publication" are featured inconspicuously on the cover of *Zadra*, and are written in a rather small font. As Eliza related, the group's magazine faced de facto censorship in the city of Białystok in one of the Empik bookstores, the largest bookstore chain in Poland. Eliza recalled an experience that was quite disturbing for the activists in eFKa that edit and publish *Zadra*: "The local manager of the Empik bookstore in Białystok apparently decided to hide the magazine and keep the issues in the back of the store. People wrote to me that when she [the bookstore manager] was asked about *Zadra* she replied that she does not intend to sell such a publication. When they pressured her, she finally brought an issue out from the back [of the store]. It's a type of censorship" (interview with Eliza, Kraków, 2002). The Polish gender scholar Bożena Chołuj interpreted (1997, 17) these antifeminist sentiments in the following way: "What we have in Poland is the existence of antifeminism without ever there having been feminism in the first place. The few active feminist voices don't yet amount to a movement; it's a drop in the bucket, in which the rule of the propatriarchal stereotypes is very strong, while the traditionalism that's represented by political parties shows that an objectifying attitude toward women is still a legitimate way of defining one's political position."

The public antifeminism that Chołuj described explains why many activists I interviewed typically chose not to advertise their feminist orientation in their workplaces (almost all had regular day jobs in addition to advocacy work) believing that such association would be detrimental. Monika, for example, who worked alongside social workers and psychologists, revealed she was quite cautious about referring to herself as a feminist at the workplace or even in conversations outside of work: "A label of a feminist translates into alienation, both personal and professional. What I mean is that women who, in some way, openly shift to the feminist side experience the 'Hegelian bite': it's as though she becomes infected with a virus that she should be ashamed of; she can never be cleansed of the disease of being a feminist in the eyes of others."

She elaborated that her feminist consciousness is like a "Hegelian bite" (*ukąszenie heglowskie*, borrowing from Czesław Miłosz)[21] in the sense that it is a conviction that a morally better world with greater equality is possible, and that the sense of alienation and stigma that comes with being a feminist in Poland is a historical necessity and an unavoidable price to pay for that vision. It is in their struggle against these antifeminist sentiments that the activists drew the most support from Western feminisms and Western aid for Polish NGOs. Monika continued:

If not for the gains that feminists made in the West, nobody would even listen to us here. Look at the structural changes that feminist activism in the West produced: various policies preventing discrimination, changes in European laws, international human rights conventions—these are various norms and practices that exist now in the West. Without this capital the Polish feminist movement would have no chance because of the aggression against it, the ill will, the attempts to diagnose and exclude our movement as a form of deviancy. All this would take away any chances of our functioning. So the political capital of the German or French or the American women's movements is very important for us. (Interview with Monika, Kraków, 2002)

Others similarly reflected that they drew on Western feminist ideas as a result of experiences with colleagues from academic circles abroad, especially Germany, Sweden, France, Austria, and the United States.[22] Monika went on to explain that the message of feminist movements in the West that is particularly valuable in the Polish context is that "women across societies are second-class citizens and that they are not happy in that position, even if the gendered hierarchies of power manifest themselves differently" in different settings. Without this transnational political capital, Monika argued, feminists in Poland would have been accused of trying to convince otherwise satisfied women that "they should be disgruntled and that they should fight for something they're not interested in fighting for."[23] Thus, activists in Poland were able to draw on the upsurge of global feminist work, aligning their movement with transnational causes, in particular efforts to cast women's rights as human rights. The human rights approach has been critically useful for Nowicka and the Federation, especially when the group takes causes to the European Union theater (a strategy trend that would intensify later in the 2000s).

Women's groups have had to battle critiques from the Catholic Church, often facing direct challenges. Studies in Poland, Hungary, and the Czech Republic showed that feminism was portrayed in the political and church discourse as discouraging motherhood (Goven 2000; Grzybowski 1998; Siemińska 1994). In Poland, the church tries to tackle the increased visibility of feminism via mandatory middle school religion classes. During the time of my fieldwork, a review of required textbooks for religion classes—approved by the Ministry of Education and the Polish episcopate—revealed a section titled "A Woman: The Real and False Feminism," authored by Jesuit priests (Jezuici 1998, 91). The following excerpt reveals an effort to recast the issue in terms of biological imperatives: "Feminists lament their femininity—they reject it and would prefer to be more like men. However, a man cannot be the only model of humanity because God created a man and a woman. . . . A feminist is a scholar, an activist, and a politician. She rejects not only motherhood but the entire womanly specificity. Physically and spiritually a woman always has to give life. Her deepest purpose is to be a mother."[24] Some scholars of Poland assert that this view of feminism as in conflict with motherhood has also been promoted by Solidarity's politics, and the patriarchal nature of the post-1989 Catholic-nationalist state, and that such forces have been powerful deterrents to feminist consciousness building in Poland (Oleksy 2000, 2004; Watson 1993). Others added that the strong focus on the family promoted by the church has been a significant barrier to the growth of solidarity among women (Marody 1993). The Polish church also condemned the "evils of liberal pedagogy" and feminism as ideologies that promote individualism and egotism, thereby driving women to reject the self-sacrificing *Matka Polka* (Polish Mother) identity in favor of careers (Bartnik 2010). The Polish episcopate's concerns about the influence of feminism and the departure from biologically based gender roles were reflected on a transnational level when then Cardinal Ratzinger, who later became Pope Benedict XVI, released a letter to the bishops urging a local effort against the influence of "radical" feminism that claims gender to be culturally constructed and "viewed as mere effects of historical and cultural conditioning" (Ratzinger 2004, 1).

Some women I spoke to outside of the movement rejected feminism because they knew little about it or perceived it as an ideology. Skepticism toward "ideological thinking" was often expressed as an aversion stemming from what was understood as a failed ideology of state socialism. Studies of the perceptions of feminism in Eastern Europe find that Western feminism is often rejected because it seems like another foreign ideology (Šiklová 1993, 1997). The women I interviewed who expressed "a fear of getting into an ideology too deeply" also preferred to use "pragmatism" as a guiding principle rather than what they perceived as feminism's "rigid set of beliefs." Some described feminism as a departure from "healthy mainstream rationality" predicated on fitting within the dominant norms that protect against ostracism. At best, some women viewed feminism as an interesting intellectual endeavor, but dissociated from the reality of everyday living. Similar fears and reservations prevented women from associating themselves with any political group. Some were simply unsure of the movement's nature: "I don't understand, for example, whether or not it's a struggle; it's probably a struggle against the stereotype of a woman, right?" replied a high school–educated twenty-three-year-old artist in Kraków (interviewed in 2002) when I asked her whether she was familiar with any of the feminist groups in her area. These sentiments, uncertainties, and confusions were quite common among women in my fieldwork who were not directly linked to the feminist movement, including the working-class and the underemployed women whom I met through the social services offices in Kraków, most of whom had never heard of NGOs. And none was familiar with the feminist magazine *Zadra* published by the eFKa group, despite its accessible and popular writing style and availability in major chain bookstores. However, many women also believed that the negative portrayals of feminist activists in the media are exaggerated and should be taken with a grain of salt, even if their activism takes place "out there."

Although the negative discourses about women's rights groups and feminism in general fuel the stigma and the marginalization of the Polish movement, the groups have been receiving significant foreign funding support. The sponsorship by Western donors, for which the groups vigorously compete with one another, is critical in sustaining their work and survival at the basic level of operation. As each organization manages on a tiny budget drawn from numerous funders, the groups are not beholden to any funder's particular agenda. As I inquired about the degree of the influence of Western donors in my conversations with activists, Viktoria (of the Federation) countered with, "No. This absolutely doesn't exist. First of all, the Federation was never financed in a significant measure by one [foreign] foundation, and because of that we're able to maintain autonomy. If a donor's money is only a percent of the budget, then its influence will be limited. We are an independent institution." Some of the women allowed that there might be motivation to suggest the kind of projects that the donors would most likely fund, but ultimately argued that the political agendas are firmly set from below. Monika (of the Center for Women's Rights) explained that in any case funders' agendas are often defined broadly: "The goals of the sponsors are more general in nature—that we adhere to our role in the defense of human rights and proceed according to the standards of operating a civil society organization—that's something we aimed to do from the start." Agata, from the Federation, concurred: "It is here where we come up with our ideas, where we create our activism. However, we do cooperate with international agencies dealing with rights such as the UN, and we try to use their ideas but, still, it has nothing to do with money; we simply believe that they have an important strategy" (interview with Agata, Warsaw, 2002).

What was worrisome to the activists was a sort of professionalization of their movement rather than a growth of the movement from the grassroots up—a phenomenon that scholars have termed "NGOization."[25] In the context of post-Soviet Russia, Julie Hemment (2004, 2007) has observed similar challenges, where more funding is offered to new NGOs than to supporting the work of existing groups, and donors typically prefer advocacy along specific themes, making the groups constantly adapt to the requirements of the funders as well as compete with one another, rather than focusing on their own, locally defined priorities.[26] Monika argued that unlike in the United States where grassroots mobilization took place before the professionalization of the NGOs, in Poland "the problem is that, before we were able to see a genuine social change, the money from the foreign sponsors, mainly from the US, had already arrived." She argued that because "the revolution on the grassroots level has been partially blocked" owing to the negative portrayal of feminists, "this rapid professionalization is difficult for us, and perhaps that's our distinct context in which we'll have to raise feminist consciousness." The profound difficulties the movement experienced in preventing the criminalization of abortion and the challenges it faced in feminist consciousness raising in other social strata raised questions about how to advocate effectively with very limited resources in a highly charged political environment.

Feminist Strategies and Projects

In the summer of 2002 the activists with whom I had been doing research invited me to come along to a nationwide conference in Warsaw which they organized for women's NGOs. The key debate among the activists was whether to work strictly in the capacity of watchdogs vis-à-vis the state, or to engage with the state by seeking public offices as a way to influence policies from within. Opinions were divided: Nowicka was strongly in favor of using political parties to advance NGOs' causes, but Hanka Lipowska-Teutsch strongly disagreed with Nowicka's approach and worried that their causes might be co-opted. Still, most activists saw the state as susceptible to pressure from political elites, but the group wondered whether feminist leadership would be perceived as a viable political elite to be reckoned with. The challenge of this strategy stemmed from the fact that the population as a whole holds a rather negative view of the state and politicians (and might equate the feminist elite with the same)—such disgruntlement has been generated by the political opportunism, corruption, and accumulation of wealth among the political elite in both the socialist and the postsocialist eras. Skyrocketing unemployment rates, hovering between 17 and 18 percent for some years during the 2000s, fueled criticisms of economic mismanagement; and references to politicians as "a bunch of thieves" (*banda złodzieji*) were not uncommon in everyday conversations. The activists had no better opinion of the state—they equated it, with the exception of few individual politicians, with the agenda of the Catholic nationalist right, as even centrist politicians such as Leszek Miller were seemingly held hostage by threats that the church would dictate election outcomes by urging church members to vote for particular parties and politicians.

In general, however, the relationship of women to the state has been quite complicated in this region. In East Germany and in Poland, for instance, women's entry into the labor force during state socialism was not perceived by women as the solution to gender inequality, as women continued to experience inequalities in the family, and therefore ultimately viewed state-initiated solutions with skepticism (Borneman 1998; Gal 1994, 1996; Łobodzińska 1995; Rosenberg 1991; Titkow 1998). In contrast, in the former West Germany the state delegated the power to men indirectly through tax, property, and family laws, thereby allowing greater benefits in employment to men than to women. Consequently, West German women actually turned to the state to augment their power vis-à-vis the men and as a way to work toward equal status (Gal 1996).

Some Polish activists argued that since the state in its current composition, wherein even the leftist parties pander to the church, is unlikely to allow referenda on issues it deems "moral," only engagement of feminist leaders from within the state can provide the opportunity to influence policy. Wanda Nowicka, who occupied a prominent place at the NGO conference owing to the visibility of her work at the Federation, was a strong proponent of this method; she in fact had run for office in the 2000s hoping to work from within the state's structure toward the liberalization of the abortion policy. In October 2011, Nowicka was finally elected to the parliament, running as a member of Palikot's Movement—a new political party established by the politician and businessman Janusz Palikot in February 2011 with a leftist and anticlerical platform, which openly promotes reproductive and sexual rights, and the separation of church and state.[27] Palikot's Movement secured a surprisingly impressive 41 (out of 460) parliamentary seats. The *New York Times* quickly declared that the new party's election day success signals that Poland is departing from the devout Catholicism and conservatism of the past (Kulish 2011), although it is still unclear whether the success of Palikot's Movement indicates a new openness toward some liberal social causes or merely represents disgruntlement with the status quo. It is also unclear at this point to what extent Nowicka's reproductive rights agenda will influence the parliamentary debate schedule. In 2013, Nowicka became an independent member of the parliament (albeit with close links to the Palikot group), which could potentially garner a broader public appeal for her proposals. Meanwhile, the feminist groups have been working to provide services at the grassroots level and advocate for women's rights both locally and at the EU.

Although the women's rights movement, and reproductive rights activism in particular, is still rather small and stigmatized, the need for groups' services has been enormous and growing. The ongoing work taken up by most of the NGOs includes counseling services about legal rights and helping women across the socioeconomic spectrum with issues of health care access, divorce, domestic violence, sexual violence, housing rights, and unemployment. Legal protection and counseling about immigrant rights, especially for Roma women, is also in great demand. Monika, the founder of the Center for Women's Rights in Kraków, bemoaned having a psychology degree rather than one in law because she saw the greatest need to be advising women in legal matters and assisting them during legal proceedings in the courts. The Federation offers a variety of services but focuses on reproductive health and rights. One of the most critical services has been what is known as the "telephone of trust" (*telefon zaufania*)—run in the evenings, it is staffed by volunteer physicians, lawyers, psychologists, and sex education counselors. The hotline is used by women and girls of all ages, but in recent years about a third of inquiries are from men who are calling with family planning concerns. According to the activists I interviewed at the Federation, because of abstinence-only sex education in schools and misleading information about contraception, calls have ranged from basic questions about the effectiveness of condoms and whether HIV can be transmitted by sharing a glass with an infected person, to crisis situations involving rape, unprotected sex, or unintended pregnancy. Callers look for information about accessing abortion in the limited cases in which they are legal under the law, emergency contraception, and counseling about contraceptive options available in Poland. Increasingly callers contact the hotline to report an incident in which a doctor refused to prescribe contraceptives or give a referral for prenatal testing citing objections based on conscience. These callers typically seek clarification of their rights and a referral to another physician, as well as advice on whether or not to report the doctor to a regulatory body. In some of these cases the Federation seeks assistance from the Ombudsman for Patients' Rights. The Federation organizes public outreach campaigns, including street protests known as *manifa* (manifestation) held in downtown Warsaw and other large cities, which were reported by the local and national media, and mock tribunals, organized in collaboration with the Center for Reproductive Law and Policy (a US advocacy group), in which women talked about unwanted pregnancy and difficulties in obtaining contraceptives and prenatal tests.[28] Manifa protests have been held every year in March since 2000 in conjunction with International Women's Day. These protests garner significant support and crowds. The original slogan "Democracy without Women Is Half a Democracy" has expanded to other themes, including, "Nurseries, Not Churches," and most recently "We're Cutting the Umbilical Cord," urging a break with the Catholic Church. The latter theme continued in the 2014 manifa, with posters depicting images of surgical scissors symbolically cutting the church and state in two. The Warsaw protest is organized by the March 8th Agreement—a group of activists, mainly volunteers, affiliated with the Federation for Women and Family Planning. Despite the dedication to hold the annual protest, the signs from the 2014 event ("We're More Pissed Than a Year Ago") remind everyone that little has changed as a result of the demands made by the feminist groups, and the status quo regarding reproductive rights structured by the critical early postsocialist years remains.

Local Projects: Sex Education and "Social Schizophrenia"

Although contraceptives are not covered by health insurance and some doctors refuse to prescribe them, contraception is not illegal in Poland.

However, the focus on abstinence in lieu of evidence-based sex education contributes to a rather low level of knowledge about pregnancy and STI prevention. The limits on school-based sex education in the 1990s coincided with a rise in teen pregnancies, despite the fact that the total fertility rate actually declined markedly during this time (Makara-Studzińska, Kołodziej, and Turek 2005).[29] The pervasive shame model of sexuality rooted in the Catholic denial of body pleasure, especially teen sexuality, leads some physicians and women alike to avoid family planning information during medical visits until there is a health problem. One of the doctors I interviewed in Kraków summed up the situation this way: "Sex education in Poland is peer education—that's where the girls learn about contraception and about sex in general. The topic is just too embarrassing to bring up by either side. As a physician, I don't want to offend my patient by asking about contraception. I leave some brochures in my waiting room, and if she asks, then we'll talk." In light of these patchy opportunities for counseling at doctors' offices and the lack of sex education in schools, public awareness actions make up an important aspect of the work conducted by the Federation and the Center for Women's Rights. To address the niche of sex education for teens the Federation runs the "Ponton" (Lifesaver) campaign with a dedicated hotline on Fridays for teens seeking sex education information, and an extensive website, a blog, and a multitude of public events to disseminate sex education information to this population. During school vacations the organization dedicates a special "vacation hotline"—this service is used quite extensively by teens seeking information about how to prevent pregnancy and numerous other topics related to health and relationships.

One of the more successful, yet frustrating, public actions was a campaign carried out by the Center for Women's Rights in Kraków in 2001 and directed toward high school youth. The group wanted to respond to some of the misinformation that the students receive on the topic of sex education and decided to distribute simple sex education flyers in the Kraków school system. In preparation they researched several sex education programs in other European nations and concluded that Holland has the best and most effective approach. Here is how Edyta, one of the main organizers of the project, described their experience:

> EDYTA: The sex education campaign was an unbelievable experience!
> We compared foreign sex education programs, and it seemed
> that the best one is in Holland: they start very early and

emphasize responsibility, and that decisions about sex must be serious because the consequences are serious. So when one is deciding [to have sex] one would also have the awareness of the consequences and the ways of avoiding those consequences. Their campaign was very objective, not at all weighted down ideologically. So we prepared a great flyer, and we worked very hard to make it very objective and accurate. We printed out the flyer in numbers that were outright dramatic for our Polish conditions: 25,000 flyers! And this is what happened next. It seemed to us that we had an overwhelming number of arguments in support of this action; if nothing else, the number of teenage pregnancies was growing exponentially! Many studies were showing that the situation was becoming tragic. Clearly, we had to act. We couldn't sit and wait until the next girl in the second or third year of high school got pregnant because that would completely change her ability to decide about her life. So we went to the Board of Trustees of the school system. It was a group of women who at that time were in charge of whether such flyers would be allowed to be distributed. So the problem was this: we went armed with all these public health data saying that something must be done, however, they rejected us because they didn't like our flyer!

AUTHOR: What didn't they like?

EDYTA: They didn't like that it was on the topic of contraception! The flyer basically said: "Remember that a decision to have sex can change your life; therefore, be prepared." We also secured a number of free services from the local clinics [that were mentioned on the flyer], including free sex education counseling with a gynecologist, although a number of gynecologists did not want to provide any information on contraception, even if paid. In any case, the whole thing ended tragically: after two hours of discussion it seemed to me that the board would have to give permission, given the facts. That was not the case. As it turned out, they started to object that the flyer didn't include "natural methods," and that the only way the board would agree to their distribution was if we got written permission from every parent. So they didn't say "no" formally, but in reality there was no way for us to get permission from 25,000 parents!

AUTHOR: Where were you hoping to have the flyers distributed?

EDYTA: In the hallways of the schools. Now, students in their last year are legal adults, eighteen years old, not minors.

AUTHOR: Why would you need to get their parents' permission then?

EDYTA: Because there is a state policy that says that in regard to the sole matter of sex education the parents must make the decisions even if their child is eighteen years old. So an eighteen-year-old has no right to learn about contraceptives. You can look up this policy; it was handed down by the Ministry of Education; the Board was citing it during our meeting.

AUTHOR: So you were unable to use the flyers?

EDYTA: We were! We decided to contact the local radio station—Radio Kraków—and told them the story. They offered to air a call-in show to let us have a discussion about the situation with sex education in Poland. Of course, the main guests on the show were people who opposed sex education, but since we also participated we took advantage and advertised our flyers. We generated enormous interest that way! People were coming to the station during the show asking for flyers. The interest continued after the show; some students came and took extras to distribute in their classes. In the end, all 25,000 flyers were taken and distributed! I think that the interest was generated by the board not allowing the flyers; forbidden fruit always tastes better. (Interview with Edyta, Kraków, 2002)

One of the greatest frustrations this campaign brought out for Edyta (and other activists concurred) has been the repeated bumping up against *auto-cenzura* or the Catholic normative autocensorship or self-surveillance to which many Poles adhere when in public view. Edyta's irritation came from "the fact that despite the church's strong opposition to the use of contraceptives, including condoms, they are in fact widely used!" Indeed, the majority of Poles who identify as Catholic use contraceptives—after all, contraception is not illegal, and many doctors are indeed willing to prescribe contraceptives—and say that religion has little influence on their reproductive and contraceptive decisions. Only a small minority has been found to use the church-sanctioned periodic abstinence (Izdebski 2006, 124; Mishtal and Dannefer 2010); this method has been declining in use (Mishtal 2009a, 612). Nationally representative surveys between 1997 and 2005 show that Poles overwhelmingly favor sex education in schools—in 2005, 92 percent of the population was in favor, and 81 percent explicitly wanted teaching about contraceptive methods outside of abstinence (Izdebski 2006, 130). Edyta and others involved in the flyer project were convinced that surely at least some people on the School Board who opposed their flyers used contraception themselves—after all, nearly all were married, and most had no more than two children. What kind of social capital can be gained by adhering to religious norms in these public interactions? Activists called it a "social schizophrenia" that creates a duplicitous system in which the symbolic power of the church is maintained even by Poles who otherwise snub religious rules, as couples continue "to choose Catholic weddings and other rituals which fuel the whole machinery." They find it discouraging to know that the population often seeks to conform to the dominant official discourses, and thereby maintain a sort of politics of duplicity (Kligman 1998) wherein the majority favors access to contraception and sex education, but is reluctant to support such causes openly. This issue is certainly perceived as one of the key obstacles for the movement's advocacy work.

The Case of Agata

The Federation has assisted numerous women who have contacted them after having been refused lawful reproductive health care by doctors and facilities citing objections based on conscience. According to Nowicka and the survey with doctors conducted by the group, physicians who choose not to perform legally permissible abortions typically also fail to refer women to other facilities, leaving them without recourse, despite the legal obligation to provide a realistic possibility for the procedure elsewhere. The doctors that participated in the two studies reported that such practices exist to a great extent in the public clinical settings where they work.

Since the implementation of the conscience clause policy in 1992, the Federation has been contacted for advice by numerous women who have experienced refusals of care, and the group has gotten involved in a number of well-known cases. The case of a fourteen-year-old girl, known as Agata— who was raped by a classmate and not offered emergency contraception at the hospital, and after becoming pregnant pursued abortion in a local hospital—is one of the most recent examples that illustrates the situation (Nowicka 2008b). After obtaining documentation from the prosecutor certifying the crime, Agata and her mother, Anna, requested an abortion in a Lublin hospital. However, the hospital's director, Jacek Solarz, declared that the doctors in his facility did not perform the procedure, nor would they provide referrals. Agata's mother immediately contacted Nowicka and the Federation, and the organization promptly appealed on Agata's behalf to the Minister of Health, the Bureau of Patient's Rights, and Prime Minister Donald Tusk. But Dr. Solarz responded only by saying, "We have not been looking thus far for another hospital. I'm not afraid of legal sanctions because ethics is above the law" (Szlachetka and Pochrzest 2008). Instead of giving a viable referral as the law requires, Dr. Solarz required Agata to see a regional consultant linked to the hospital, who likewise declared his opposition, pressured Agata against abortion, and refused to refer her.

Agata was made to stay several days at another hospital, where she was told her case would be addressed when the vacationing director returned. While she waited, the hospital violated confidentiality and asked a priest, Krzysztof Podstawka, the director of the "House of a Single Mother"[30] shelter for pregnant women, to come to Agata's hospital room to persuade her not to have an abortion and to threaten her mother, Anna, with legal action to deprive her of parental rights if she resisted. When Agata and Anna resisted, the hospital director invoked "conscientious objection" for the entire facility. Agata and her mother alerted the Federation about the situation, but Podstawka quickly moved to obtain a court order, depriving Anna of parental rights. Agata was taken to Child Protection Services in Lublin while Anna desperately tried to reverse the court order. Concerned that Agata would be kept at the hospital as a way to let the time limit for abortion pass, Nowicka contacted Prime Minister Donald Tusk and sent out a national appeal to hospitals to agree to offer Agata an abortion elsewhere. No hospital responded, but one gynecologist offered to perform the procedure clandestinely.

Finally, the Minister of Health designated a Gdańsk hospital, 500 kilometers from Lublin, to perform the procedure, which was ultimately carried out semiclandestinely: the name of the facility was never revealed and Agata's abortion has not been recorded by the Ministry of Health, given that the ministry's 2008 Report shows that no abortions were performed that were registered as due to rape (Klimkowska 2013). In the end, physicians and hospitals involved in this case failed to follow even the narrowly defined abortion law (De Zordo and Mishtal 2011). Conservative media praised the priest's militancy, but the Polish *Newsweek* saw the case as "Antiabortion Terrorism" (Maziarski 2008). Reproductive rights advocates were decisive in calling attention to Agata's plight, assisting the daughter and mother along the way, and intervening with the prime minister. The power of hospital superiors to object to lawful abortions in a system-wide manner presents a challenge to sympathetic providers willing to offer care, but fearing the highly hierarchical system of Polish medicine leaves patients with little support outside of the assistance offered by the NGOs. The systemic "conscientious objection" and the public obedience to the church it implies, presents a rationalization for political passivity for physicians unwilling to publicly engage in the issue, even while many provide abortions clandestinely. This "social schizophrenia," as Edyta bemoaned, makes advocacy work difficult and frustrating.

Making Waves in Władysławowo

Besides directly responding to women and couples who seek help from the Federation, the group pursues media campaigns to keep alive public discussions of the restrictions on reproductive rights. In 2003 they invited the Dutch organization Women on Waves (WoW) to sail to Poland to draw attention to the Polish abortion ban. The Dutch gynecologist Rebecca Gomperts (the founder of WoW) and crew sailed in international waters near nations where abortion is illegal (thus far Ireland, Poland, Portugal, Spain, and Morocco), to help local activists bring attention to the issue of unsafe abortions. The *Langenort* is essentially a floating reproductive health facility—the crew primarily provides contraceptives and sex education. It can also offer mifepristone, a pharmaceutical early abortion, which is lawful outside of the territorial waters of countries where abortion is banned because the ship is under the legal jurisdiction of the Netherlands when in international waters. These efforts are primarily media events to raise awareness, and previous trips typically drew enormous public interest both locally and internationally.[31]

Once the *Langenort* docked on June 20, 2003, at the Władysławowo harbor, near Gdańsk in northern Poland on the Baltic Sea, the Federation's activists began to escort women aboard the ship through a group of protesters hurling eggs and tomato juice. The protesters who attempted to block the way were captured on a BBC World News video clip, which shows predominantly men shoving and pushing the women, calling them Nazis and Bolsheviks, some praying the rosary. But many others in the crowd supported the ship's visit. The ship's crew held a workshop aboard to train activists as sex educators, thereby also calling attention to the lack of sex education in Polish schools. The event brought enormous media attention to the abortion and sex education issues. Nowicka organized a press conference with Dr. Gomperts in the local city hall and a visual exhibit promoting abortion rights, which was attended by national media outlets. The bishop of Gdańsk urged the mayor of Władysławowo to cancel the press conference, but the mayor resisted. Nowicka was able to convince the police to block the entry into the press conference of two members of parliament from the League of Polish Families, a Catholic conservative party, knowing they intended to disrupt the event. According to WoW and the Federation, hundreds of Polish women called the ship's hotline asking for services during the visit, and the few who made it aboard for abortion services were offered follow-up medical care arranged by the Federation after the *Langenort*'s departure. The activists perceived the visit as a great success "in bringing attention to the Polish society of the need for legal abortion. . . . For more than two weeks abortion was the main topic in all newspapers, television and radio."[32]

A few months later in September they called attention to the findings of the Center for Public Opinion Research showing an increase in abortion rights support: 61 percent of those polled were in favor of relaxing the abortion ban—a 12 percent increase from the previous poll conducted just a year before (Derczyński 2003, 1–5). The national polling bureau concluded that the *Langenort*'s visit likely contributed to the swaying of public opinion in the prochoice direction. Despite this increase, during the two decades since

1993, the percentage of Poles in favor of less restrictive abortion law has overall declined; as of 2011, 47 percent support abortion rights, and 46 percent are against (Hipsz 2011, 4). Some of the activists I asked attributed this decline in support for abortion rights to mandatory religious education in schools and the Preparation for Life in a Family curriculum.

One strategy is to connect with the international field of policy and activism. Besides national campaigns such as the WoW visit, Wanda Nowicka, Edyta, and other activists in this research emphasized the importance of solidarity with women's struggles elsewhere around the world. They often reminded me that the Federation is actually a member of the ASTRA network—the regional supranational NGO network for Central and Eastern Europe—"advocating in a collective voice," and that involvement in women's rights campaigns on a transnational level connects Polish women's struggle with struggles elsewhere.[33] Indeed, their aim is to create coalitional politics around concrete political aims by supporting reproductive health and women's rights causes as the basis for common interest (rather than claiming common experiences or identities)—an approach that has been recognized as a productive strategy of transnational feminism (Butler 1990; Mohanty 2003).

For example, women's groups and several unaffiliated activists joined the rally outside of the Nigerian embassy in Warsaw in 2002 to protest a Nigerian court sentence of Amina Lawal to death by stoning for a pregnancy out of wedlock that she said resulted from rape. The demonstration was small, but the activists stayed for hours outside the front gate in an attempt to speak to the embassy officials. This effort connected with numerous protests against this ruling simultaneously in other parts of the world. The Federation has also been involved in supporting women's reproductive health projects through UNICEF programs in Africa to reduce unsafe abortions, neonatal tetanus, and other causes. The group's main web page proudly claims, "We help women in Africa," in a section that lists many such projects, but their presence is strongest in the East European region and Russia where the collaborative work with ASTRA results in an ongoing stream of news and case reports about reproductive health and rights issues, as well as specific actions aiming at providing services on the ground or targeting the attention of media and politicians in various locations. In Poland, struggling against a church that is hostile to women's rights issues and a state that is unwilling to listen, the groups maintain flexible strategies to take advantage of unforeseen political openings locally and to bring complaints before international institutions. Questions of how to apply political pressure are discussed; Nowicka and others believe that the human rights framework is most useful for their advocacy work, and increasingly the groups have been using this approach, especially since Poland became a member state of the EU in 2004.

The Cases of Alicja Tysiąc and Agata—The Stories' Endings

The story of Alicja Tysiąc is perhaps most widely known, not only in Poland but in Europe, as a case brought to the European Court of Human Rights (ECHR) in 2007 with the assistance of the Federation and other groups.[34] Tysiąc became disabled as a result of being unable to access abortion under the health-saving exception of the current law. She became legally blind due to the retinal hemorrhage she suffered as the pregnancy advanced, and subsequently she received a Class I disability rating, which is defined as being unable to work and live independently, and permanently needing the assistance of another person. With the help of the Federation, Tysiąc took the case against Poland to the ECHR. Before looking for justice in international courts, Tysiąc filed criminal charges against the head of gynecology and obstetrics of the Warsaw hospital, but her case was dismissed by the district prosecutor. The explanation she was offered was that there was no certainty that the pregnancy would cause her loss of vision, but this reasoning contradicted the Polish law which allows abortion to be performed in cases in which there is a mere possibility of a danger to health. To help Tysiąc through the intimidating and costly court system and arrange for pro bono legal counsel, the Federation both mobilized local legal help and reached out to international groups for assistance. Nowicka was able to mobilize the International Legal Program run by the Center for Reproductive Rights (CRR), a New York City–based NGO, which submitted an amicus brief to the ECHR. The involvement of the CRR was crucial as the group has extensive experience advocating for reproductive rights in a variety of legal and cultural contexts, as well as at the United Nations and in regional human rights forums.

As a result of these efforts, the ECHR's decided by a 6-to-1 vote that Tysiąc's human rights had been violated according to article 8 of the European Convention on Human Rights (to which Poland is a signatory), the right to the protection of private life, and she received 25,000 euros (approximately 34,000 USD) in damages. Significantly, the verdict declared that Poland failed to provide a legal mechanism through which a woman could exercise her right to abortion within the current law. The activists at the Federation were jubilant and energized. Press conferences, newspaper articles, and multiple interviews with Nowicka and Tysiąc followed. Prime Minister Kaczyński immediately declared that he would appeal because "if we don't appeal, we would have to change our law that protects life."[35] Despite Kaczyński's degree in law, his was an erroneous interpretation of the verdict, which only called for a viable mechanism to exercise the rights afforded by the laws that were already in place. But in effect, the verdict also called for more careful regulation of the use of the conscience clause when lawful services are denied, in particular to restrict its use to individual rather than systemic use—the same concern that the minister of health, Marek Balicki, sounded back in 2003 when he released the letter to the mayors of all provinces urging that the conscience clause should not be applied "at will" (Balicki 2003, 1). Kaczyński's take on the verdict as a threat to the Polish abortion law fueled other negative reactions against Tysiąc from the church and the conservatives.[36] His appeal, launched in June, was rejected in September.

Likewise, Agata and her mother also sued Poland at the European Court of Human Rights in 2010. They were aided through the process by the Federation and its lawyers. In October 2012, the ECHR declared that their human rights were violated and ordered Poland to pay 45,000 euros for nonspecuniary damages in addition to 16,000 euros for expenses they accrued as a result of the case. The court judged that Poland violated three articles: Article 8—the right to privacy, when the plaintiffs were denied access to lawful abortion and the hospitals breached confidentiality of her personal information, article 5, §1—right to liberty and security, and article 3—prohibition of inhuman or degrading treatment.[37]

While the Department for the Execution of Judgments of the ECHR is obligated to ensure that the verdict is effective, in reality few mechanisms exist to enforce the verdict. If Poland were to fail to comply with the judgment to implement legal means for recourse in situations of religious refusals of care, theoretically it could lose its voting rights in the EU. But this extreme case scenario is unlikely to happen. As of 2014, the Polish state created a policy known as "The Right to Object" as recourse for women like Alicja who seek abortion under the current law but are refused service. However, the committee that decides "The Right to Object" cases has up to thirty days to made a decision on a petition. Since abortion cases are highly time-sensitive, a delay of even a week or two can disqualify a woman from being eligible for the procedure within the current time limit of less than twelve weeks of pregnancy. This loophole makes the recourse virtually unusable, and indeed according to the attorney at the Federation for Women and Family Planning, Karolina Więckiewicz, very few women who find themselves in Alicja's situation opt to pursue this avenue. Meanwhile, from the perspective of the Department for the Execution of Judgments of the ECHR, Poland ostensibly complied with the verdict and the obligation to create a mechanism of recourse. The proof that the mechanism is not functional and that the committee's decision should be required within seven days, rests on the shoulders of feminist advocates who have to show that the new policy fails in a systemic, rather than in an individual, way—another challenge that will likely require long-term preparation and effort (interview with Więckiewicz, Warsaw, 2014).

Moreover, Poland enjoys the protection of the Polish EU Accession Treaty signed in 2004 when Poland entered the EU, which specifically stipulates the "separateness" of the Polish position on abortion and ensures that no EU treaties would hamper the Polish government in regulating issues of "morality" (Traynor 2003, 1). When I asked Nowicka why the Tysiąc victory is so critical for the feminist movement if in reality there is little hope for any change in the Polish abortion law, she explained that the local political channels are no longer viable targets of advocacy. The "ossified position," as she called it, of Polish politicians and the media against interfering with the church's agenda makes international advocacy strategies far more promising. Moreover, the international media attention that focused on the compelling case of Tysiąc had an energizing effect on the Polish feminist community, and the recent verdict in favor of Agata and her mother likewise have been received with enthusiasm in the Polish and international reproductive rights advocacy circles.

But the effect of these cases on access to abortion is still unclear. Two years after the Tysiąc verdict, in 2009, the Committee on Economic, Social and Cultural Rights—an agency that monitors the compliance of states with the UN Convention on Economic Social and Cultural Rights—expressed its concern that "alarming numbers" of Polish women "resort to clandestine, and often unsafe, abortion because of refusal of physicians and clinics to perform the legal operations on the basis of conscientious objection." This statement, similar in message to the Tysiąc verdict from 2007, again called on the Polish state to create a policy for "enforcing the legislation on abortion and implementing a mechanism of timely and systematic referral."[38] This time the Prime Minister Tusk responded and created the office of Patients' Rights Ombudsman, the first of its kind in Poland. The new office proceeded to finally implement the Tysiąc verdict by adding article 31 to the patients' rights law, which grants "the right to oppose a physician's opinion or decision" and the right to a timely review of the grievance by a medical committee in less than thirty days (Kozłowska 2011, 1). The first on the "sample list" of issues (posted by the ombudsman) that can be challenged using this law is any disagreement regarding the right to abortion, prenatal tests, and family planning. Over 40,000 cases of grievances have been submitted during the first year of the ombudsman's existence.[39] In the case of Agata and her mother, the Polish Ministry of Foreign Affairs declared in February of 2013 that it will not appeal the ECHR verdict on the grounds that it indeed has no legal basis for an appeal.[40]

Despite these key victories in the cases of Alicja Tysiąc and Agata, the Polish women's movement, galvanized when reproductive rights became threatened by the rise of Wałęsa's postsocialist administration, finds itself working in very difficult conditions dominated by an unreceptive state, an antagonistic church, and a media legally bound to adhere to Christian values. Unlike in Slovenia where feminist groups had a say within the structure of the government, and unlike Bulgaria where the church is politically weak, in Poland Nowicka and her colleagues stood entirely outside the state, in part by choice but more so as a necessity in a postsocialist administration that became tightly intertwined with the episcopate. In this climate, the movement was unable to prevent the ban on abortion in 1993 or the subsequent restrictions on insurance funding for contraceptives. It has been unable to reinstate sex education in schools, despite wide popular support for this measure. Likewise, it has not been able to force any legislation that would help women exercise their current limited right to abortion. But the movement has been able to accomplish a kind of feminist consciousness-raising that had not been possible during the state socialist era when women were generally lulled by the availability of certain reproductive rights, especially abortion.

I have just described how the religious morality agenda manifests itself overtly at the policy level and has fueled an ongoing political struggle as explained by these feminist advocates. Moreover, the colonization of language was one of the more critical tools with which moral governance was being executed, as well as an arena of challenge, if not outright setback, for the efforts of the nascent women's movement in Poland. In addition, the church also works on a more concealed, individual level, face-to-face with a priest in the confessional, a topic that I explore next.

Lech Wałęsa holding up the now historic pope pen during a celebration of the thirty-year anniversary of Solidarity, on August 31, 2010. *Photo credit: Wojciech Surdziel*

The gate to the famous Gdańsk shipyard is now decorated with images of the Polish pope, John Paul II, along with signs commemorating the Solidarity opposition movement. *Photo credit: Joanna Mishtal*

A Catholic cross hanging in the Polish Parliament. *Photo credit: Krzysztof Białoskórski*

The annual "wafer ritual" in the Polish Parliament. *Photo credit: Krzysztof Białoskórski*

A street demonstration in front of the Polish Parliament. One of the strategies of activists to bring attention to the widespread nature of abortion in Poland has been to motivate women to stop their silence about having had an abortion. Here the sign reads, "I made a choice. I terminated a pregnancy. Who are you to judge me?" Warsaw, 2006. *Photo credit: Ewa Dąbrowska-Szulc*

The annual *manifa* protest in Warsaw organized by women's rights groups. The sign reads: "We're cutting the umbilical cord," demanding a separation of the Polish Catholic Church from politics. Warsaw, March 2012. *Photo credit: Joanna Erbel*

Wanda Nowicka (*seated left*) and Alicja Tysiąc (*seated right*) during the press conference held at the Federation for Women and Family Planning after the European Court of Human Rights verdict in favor of Tysiąc in 2007. *Photo credit: The Polish Federation for Women and Family Planning*

The church continues a strong public presence with rituals such as the Corpus Christi street processions that take place in June in virtually every city, town, and village in Poland. Some in the audience express deference by kneeling on the sidewalk. Sopot, June 2007. *Photo credit: Joanna Mishtal*

The *Langenort* and the activists of Women on Waves in the Władysławowo harbor in June 2003. The sign on the ship reads in Polish: "Legal abortion is a right of women." *Photo credit: The Polish Federation for Women and Family Planning*

While originally organized because of the restrictions on reproductive rights, abortion rights in particular, street protests now also include critiques of the nationalist rhetoric calling on Polish women to have more children while the state offers little in terms of protection of women's employment rights. The sign on the torso reads: "What child? I don't have work!" *Photo credit: Porozumienie Kobiet 8 Marca*

4 ⫾ Confessions, *Kolęda* Rituals, and Other Surveillance

IT IS IN DIRECT dealings with the clergy and the parish that some of the most intensely experienced moral governance of the faithful takes place. Indeed, the resurgence of the influence of the church in the postsocialist period since 1989 meant not only the shaping of transition politics, influencing reforms and imparting a religious agenda to new policies as discussed earlier, but it also included an unprecedented intensification of direct regulation of women's reproductive and sexual behavior. This regulation of conduct takes place through direct surveillance techniques exercised by the clergy during routine religious rituals, including confessions, Christmas home visits by the clergy, and mandatory premarital courses and workshops.

The rituals themselves are not new—monthly confessions, for example, have historically been so commonplace that a missed month would typically warrant an explanation at the start of the subsequent confession. What emerged in my research as new, however, are the ways in which after the fall of the state socialist regime confessions and the home visits by the clergy are increasingly used as opportunities for surveillance of women's reproductive behaviors. These direct forms of intervention are carried out when the clergy and the faithful come into face-to-face contact during the variety of Catholic rituals observed in Poland. This form of scrutiny is fundamentally different as it works in a more immediate and intimate manner than policy mechanisms discussed in the preceding chapters.

Catholicism is the dominant religious affiliation in Poland. Nevertheless, the number of Poles identifying as Catholics has been dropping, according to the Public Opinion Research Center report released in 2009 (Boguszewski 2009). Catholic identification fell from a high of 96 percent in the early 1990s (which followed closely the all-time high in affiliation from the Solidarity years in the 1980s) to 86.7 percent in 2012 (Statistical Yearbook 2013, 16). In terms of religiosity, weekly mass attendance was highest in the 1980s and reached an unprecedented 80 percent during the years of the Solidarity movement consolidation against the socialist regime (Stark and Iannaccone 1996). Since then, the number of regularly practicing Catholics has been steadily dropping. The church's own statistics for 2012 on weekly church attendance show that only 40 percent of Poles attend Sunday masses, revealing a major discrepancy between the 86.7 percent religious affiliation and the actual level of religious practice.[1] These church data also show that whereas the number of Sunday mass attendees (termed *dominicantes* in church data) has been dropping, the percent of those attendees who take communion during Sunday masses (*communicantes*) has been increasing, which means that those who are staying in the church are the more dedicated practitioners to begin with, and those who are leaving have already been skipping communion during masses. In other words, the religiosity trend in Poland shows an overall shrinking of the numbers of practicing Catholics into a concentrated smaller and smaller group, but one of a more devout nature.[2] Overall about 30 percent of declared Catholics practice only occasionally, perhaps on major holidays. Poles living in rural areas tend to be more regular practicing Catholics than those living in cities, which is not surprising since in smaller communities the need to conform might be felt more strongly, and furthermore the church might have a greater ability for a more personalized presence, as compared with urban areas.

Consequently, an important question to consider in terms of direct forms of moral governance are: To what extent do the mechanisms of surveillance of women's bodily conduct have the ability to reach the population they are targeting? Since a third of the Catholics do not practice regularly, are they relatively immune to the church's pressures? To answer these questions it is useful to consider the ways in which the Catholic Church itself addresses the problem of relatively low mass attendance. To deal with this predicament, the church has a number of ways to reach those in the Catholic population who fail to attend services regularly or at all.

Many of these ways rely on the fact that the overwhelming majority of Poles, including sporadic churchgoers, desire a Catholic wedding in addition to a civil ceremony. Since the ratification of the Concordat—a trilateral treaty between the Polish state, the Vatican, and the Polish Catholic Church discussed earlier—Catholic marriages hold the legal status of civil ceremonies. This important legitimatization of Catholic marriages by the state gave added authority to Catholic ceremonies, and since then, many couples opt for the religious ceremony only. Another way to reach the population of sporadic churchgoers and nonchurchgoers who still identify as Catholics has been via mandatory premarital courses. These courses provide an avenue for the clergy to directly intervene in couples' sexual and reproductive behaviors and plans, a topic that I examine in detail later in this chapter.

Women appear to be reached more than men by the regulatory mechanisms of the church. The analysis of Polish religiosity based on sex reveals that although religiosity has been gradually declining for both groups, 54 percent of women practice regularly whereas only 41 percent of men do so (CBOS 2009, 9). This 13 percentage-point edge for women is observed across different age groups, and is especially more pronounced for older age groups. It suggests that women are not only the primary target group of this regulation of conduct, but they also expose themselves to such regulation more than men do. In addition, I found that the overwhelming majority of women I interviewed experienced direct questioning of their sexual and reproductive behavior and decisions by the clergy during certain Catholic rituals, but their partners were rarely subjected to the same scrutiny.

My investigation of the church's surveillance and its regulation of behaviors through disciplinary measures and norms engages with the concept of governmentality developed by Foucault (1991a). Foucault argued that overt power in Europe became concealed around the eighteenth century and was transformed into such subtle forms of regulatory "modern" power as surveillance, discipline, and bringing about normalization of behaviors. Foucault's argument is best summarized by Mitchell Dean (1999, 2), who explicates that "the term *governmentality* seeks to distinguish the particular mentalities, arts and regimes of government and administration . . . while the term *government* is used for any calculated direction of human conduct. . . . Foucault redefined 'government' . . . as the 'conduct of conduct,' i.e., as any more or less calculated means of the direction of how we be-have." In other words, governmentality is a method of controlling the populace and ultimately aims to replace overt regulation with hidden modes of rule as well as inculcating desire and need on the part of individuals to self-censor behaviors in order to bring them in line with the dominant norms. The focal element in Foucault's notion of governmentality that is useful for the context of Poland is his attention to how institutions aim to create constraining effects on behavior that are aligned with specific ideolo-gies—a point that is salient in the examination of the church as a disciplining and surveilling institution.

Although sexuality played a critical role in Foucault's investigation of the ways in which disciplinary power and surveillance are exercised, he fails to include gender as an analytical category; therefore much of femi-nist scholarship has debated the extent to which his analysis could be use-ful for examining women's experiences (e.g., Allen 1996; Brush 2003, 34–37; Fraser 1989; Hartsock 1990; Deveaux 1996, 213–17; and Soper 1993). Since Foucault's scholarship continues to be illuminating, espe-cially in analyzing institutional power, in this chapter I build on these feminist critiques by expanding the concept of governmentality to inves-tigate specific institutional disciplinary mechanisms and also by applying the analysis to the ways in which such methods have a gender-specific target and effect. The ritual of confession serves as the key site where these gendered effects are visible.

Confession, the Sacrament of Penance

Women I interviewed in my research reported that one of the Catholic rituals in which the intensification of surveillance of reproductive and sexual con-duct is most evident is confession. At the start of every confession one must tell the priest (also referred to as the confessor) the exact date when she or he completed the last confession; this way the priest is able to follow up with a question in the event that the person failed to confess for more than a month. The typical rubric that children learn in religion classes ahead of their First Communion and that penitents are expected to follow when con-fessing is:

PENITENT: Blessed be Jesus Christ.

Niech będzie pochawalony Jezus Chrystus.

PRIEST: Forever and ever, amen.

Na wieki wieków, amen.

PENITENT: In the name of the Father and the Son and the Holy Spirit, amen. The last time I went to confession was _____. I completed penance, I did not forget or conceal sins. I offended God with the following sins _____.

W imię Ojca i Syna i Ducha Świętego, amen. Ostatni raz u spowiedzi byłem/ am _____. Pokutę odprawiłam, grzechu nie zapomniałem/am ani nie zataiłem/am. Obraziłem/am Pana Boga nastepującymi grzechami

[The penitent now lists the sins]

I cannot remember any more sins, but I sincerely regret all of them and promise improvement. I ask for penance and absolution.

Więcej grzechów nie pamiętam, ale za wszystkie serdecznie żałuje i postanawiam poprawę. Proszę o rozgrzeszenie i pokutę.

Referring to the last confession establishes a sense of regularity and continuity of the ritual. Once the priest specifies the penance and gives absolution, he knocks three times on the confessional to signal that the confession has been completed: the penitent can now kiss the priest's stole (the scarf-like vestment worn by the priest when he administers sacraments, and which he hangs partially outside the confessional for easy access), and walk to the pew to carry out the penance, and wait for communion. This structured self-disclosure is a central aspect of the larger system of religious governance. Foucault observed that "Christianity is a confession," and as such it carries "obligation[s] of truth" in two different ways. First, Christianity requires that decisions made by the religious authorities are accepted as truth, including which set of propositions are true or untrue, and which books are sources of permanent truth. Second, it requires an obligation of truth about oneself: "every Christian has the duty to know who he [*sic*] is, what is happening to him. He has to know the faults he may have committed," and furthermore a Christian is "obliged to say these things to other people . . . and hence to bear witness against himself [*sic*]" (Carrette 1999, 169–70). These two sets of obligations are connected to each other because in order to access the truth of the faith, life, or love, the purification of the soul is necessary, which can be achieved only through confession and absolution.

According to Canon Law, Catholics are required to confess once a year, and this is the usual frequency of confessions in many countries with Catholic populations, including the United States, although the actual behaviors vary based on individual religiosity and the time of the year (*Catechism of the Catholic Church* 1993, secs. 1423–42). In Poland, however, Catholics are formally expected to confess every month. Children who attend catechism classes, which were traditionally offered at local parishes but are now also in public schools, are taught to confess monthly starting with First Communion at the age of eight or nine. Having confessed allows the penitent to then take communion: the priest places a small wafer, symbolizing the body of Christ, on their tongues. Individuals who have not been to confession for a few months or who have sinned since their last confession are theoretically not permitted to take communion because their souls are not sufficiently cleansed to accept the body of Christ in the form of the wafer. In contrast, US worshipers are encouraged to take communion during Sunday Mass even though they may not have been to a confession for a year or more. In Poland, the belief in the necessity of purifying the soul before accepting the communion wafer acts as a mechanism that motivates more frequent confession. This is one of the more significant differences in terms of what is expected of Catholics in Poland, as compared to Catholics in the United States, for example, or elsewhere; it has important implications for how surveillance of behaviors can be exercised more frequently in a stricter religious setting where assessment of behavior face-to-face (even if through a screen) with a priest is more frequent.

The relative strictness of Polish Catholicism is also evident in the conservative style of communion. Churches in many Catholic nations around the world have adopted the more recent method of "communion in the hand" permitted by the Holy See in 1969 as a response to a request from French bishops (Paul VI 1969). Since then, this perhaps less reverent method of communion was adopted in many nations, including strongly Catholic Ireland and Italy. Poland, in contrast, firmly rejected this possibility, and the Polish church continues to require that the faithful receive the communion wafer on the tongue while kneeling. (This religious strictness can be seen among the Polish diaspora in the United States, in particular in cities with large Polish communities and churches such as Los Angeles, Brooklyn, and Chicago. Similarly to my own reaction as a new immigrant, many newly arrived Poles I encountered in my early years in New York and Los Angeles preferred the familiarity of the strict customs of Polish Catholicism to the more relaxed ways of the US Catholic churches.)

In my research, women who were regular churchgoers explained that they considered the Sunday mass attendance, regular confessions, and communion as basic rituals in their Catholic practice. Women who described themselves as moderate or not very religious, but who nevertheless carried out basic religious rituals, explained that they tried to attend Sunday mass at least a couple of times a month, and went to confession and communion about every other month on average. During major holidays such as Christmas and Easter, the practice of rituals increases dramatically, even among those who are sporadic churchgoers, who often only follow the momentum of the family attending services together. In fact, the rate of confessions during the Easter holiday surges to 83 percent of the entire population of Poland.[3]

The clergy are expected to take advantage of this direct and private contact during the sacrament of confession to question the penitents about their behaviors and to follow up when appropriate with corrective teachings about what constitutes a "true family." This goal of corrective teaching was first highlighted by Pope John Paul II in his reaction to what he believed to be the secularization of Europe and the demise of the family in a letter he released on November 22, 1981. The letter, titled *Familiaris Consortio* and addressed to the clergy and the faithful, argues that "the corruption of the idea and the experience of freedom" in the Western world manifests itself in "a disturbing degradation of some fundamental values: a mistaken theoretical and practical concept of the independence of the spouses in relation to each other; . . . the growing number of divorces; the scourge of abortion; the ever more frequent recourse to sterilization; the appearance of a truly contraceptive mentality" (John Paul II 1981, 4). In addition to secularizing and modernizing trends, the Pope also perceived poverty as a demoralizing force, arguing that "large sections of humanity live in conditions of extreme poverty, in which promiscuity, lack of housing, the irregular nature and instability of relationships and the extreme lack of education make it impossible in practice to speak of a true family" (John Paul II 1981, 63). The pope calls on the clergy to provide corrective teachings on family values, but does not specify confession to be one of the main avenues through which this was to be accomplished. Subsequently, the pope working in tandem with his office of the Pontifical Council for the Family, released numerous letters and documents directed to the Catholic clergy to take up the topic of the family.[4] Many of these letters were directed to the Polish episcopate or individual archdioceses and dioceses in Poland, some of which were generated in association with the nine visits of the pope to Poland between 1979 and 2002. In light of the perceived moral decay in Western Europe and decades of state socialist secular policies in Eastern Europe, Poland, as the "Christ of nations" had a special role in the eyes of John Paul II as an exemplar of Christian rebirth. This reevangelization was to take place through a renewed focus on reproduction and sexuality, and in this campaign women were at the center of attention.

How to Confess Women?—A Manual for the Clergy

According to my research with the clergy and with the women who identify as practicing Catholics, confessions in Poland began to include specific questions probing reproductive and sexual conduct beginning in the early 1990s. However, a significant intensification of this line of questioning took place in the late 1990s, most likely as a result of a confessors' manual released by the Vatican in 1997. It was developed in part to address a need raised by the Second Vatican Council to formulate more precisely how to handle improper sexual and reproductive behavior among the faithful, a topic which until this time was mainly left to the good faith of the people. The manual was released on February 12, 1997, by the Pontifical Council for the Family at the direction of Pope John Paul II, under the decidedly chaste title *Vademecum for Confessors concerning Some Aspects of the Morality of Conjugal Life* (Trujillo and Hellín 1997). This document, designed as an instructional handbook for priests (hence, the title "vademecum"—a handbook or guidebook in Latin), has been identified by the US Conference of Catholic Bishops as one of the major church documents and "a standard guide."[5] The Catholic media have also widely referred to this as a definitive guide for confessors, including in Poland.[6]

The manual urges the clergy "to [implement] these teachings in pastoral practice" and to use these "clear and certain guidelines, to which the ministers of the Sacrament of Reconciliation can refer in their dialogue with souls."[7] Thus, the manual is "addressed specifically to confessors and seeks to offer some practical guidelines for the confession and absolution of the faithful in matters of conjugal chastity," and is designed to "overcome possible discrepancies and uncertainties in the practice of confessors." Pope John Paul II aimed therefore to both clarify and also harmonize the approach of priests to this topic.

The manual focuses on sins resulting from the use of hormonal contraceptives such as birth control pills and intrauterine devices, making women of reproductive age the target population for surveillance and corrective teachings. The clergy are counseled "to recall firm points of reference which make it possible to deal pastorally . . . with new methods of contraception" during confessions.[8] The church teaches the concept that sexuality and procreation are inseparable: any act of sexual intercourse devoid of the potential for pregnancy constitutes a sin.[9] In the context of Poland, the church claims that it was the period of state socialism that dissociated sexuality from procreation through liberal abortion laws, sexual education in schools, and a general "moral permissiveness" that is reflected in state-sanctioned fertility control. Thus, what the *Vademecum* refers to as "the new evangelization of the family" is an effort to recover the link between sex and procreation, a goal that is of paramount importance to the church.[10] According to the manual, the faithful must be reeducated to accept that this link is "willed by God and unable to be broken by man [sic] on his [sic] own initiative, between the two meanings of the conjugal act: the unitive meaning and the procreative meaning."[11] Therefore, on the topic of modern contraception the manual teaches the following:

> The church has always taught the intrinsic evil of contraception, that is, of every marital act intentionally rendered unfruitful. This teaching is to be held as definitive and irreformable. Contraception is gravely opposed to marital chastity; it is contrary to the good of the transmission of life (the procreative aspect of matrimony), and to the reciprocal self-giving of the spouses (the unitive aspect of matrimony); it harms true love and denies the sovereign role of God in the transmission of human life. . . . A specific and more serious moral evil is present in the use of means which have an abortive effect, impeding the implantation of the embryo which has just been fertilized or even causing its expulsion in an early stage of pregnancy.[12]

Thus, the document argues that contraception is a dual sin: it delinks sex and reproduction, but also induces abortion by preventing an already fertilized egg from attaching to the uterine wall. The latter statement is inconsistent with science and the position of the World Health Organization, which show that hormonal contraceptives block ovulation and/or prevent the sperm from reaching the egg; therefore, fertilization is prevented altogether.[13] Nevertheless, the church teaches that fertilization does take place. Therefore, hormonal methods of contraception are depicted as abortive, and a grave sin.[14] The clergy are instructed to ask whether a woman is using any contraceptive methods by proceeding with "a prudent reserve in inquiring into these sins, . . . [and] by encouragement to the penitents so that they may be able to reach sufficient repentance and accuse themselves fully of grave sins."[15] Thus, disciplining women about the use of contraceptives has been an important aspect of confession. The priests are "bound to admonish penitents regarding objectively grave transgressions," and the penitents are told to "re-examine and correct their behaviour."[16] In reality, however, women realize that for the most part they can continue to use contraception as long as they confess to using such methods. They find that, while the priests reprimand them for such conduct and tell them to discontinue the use of such methods, they nevertheless receive absolution. It is also commonly known that following an abortion a woman can receive an absolution through confession, although most women choose not to confess abortions, according to the priests I spoke with. The manual instructs the priests in these cases as follows: "Regarding absolution for the sin of abortion, . . . if repentance is sincere and it is difficult to send the penitent to the competent authority to whom the absolution of the censure is reserved, every confessor can absolve according to can. 1357 [Canon Law 1357], suggesting an adequate penitential act."[17] Such penitential acts typically involve some combination of different prayers, including the Hail Mary, the Our Father, and the like. Praying the rosary is often reserved for more severe penance, one requiring more time and reflection.

The Story of Disciplining Maya

The manual dictates that "frequent relapse into sins of contraception does not in itself constitute a motive for denying absolution; absolution cannot be imparted, however, in the absence of sufficient repentance or of the resolution not to fall again into sin."[18] As a result, women who use IUDs, which are inserted by a physician inside the uterus and last for a period of five to ten years, theoretically should not receive absolution because they cannot give the priest the "resolution not to fall again into sin."[19] The following story of Maya, a twenty-seven-year-old homemaker in Kraków, formerly an elementary school teacher, and her experience with the priest in her local parish when she decided to confess that she was using an IUD serves as an example of confessional disciplining from the perspective of the penitent. Maya recounted the story as follows:

MAYA: My husband was an alcoholic, but that wasn't enough, he also beat me; I had constant headaches from his abuse. He insisted he wanted a son and so I had five pregnancies one after another. And the pregnancies were such that a couple of times I got pregnant just a few months after I gave birth, and that's how I gave birth to five girls. . . . It was like this: one was at my breast, one was a year old, another was two years old, and again I'm pregnant. My sister-in-law came to visit and she said: "Girl, start taking some kind of contraceptives!" I told her: "No, because the church doesn't give permission." I went to confession and told my priest I'm considering some kind of contraceptives; he knew the situation in my house. . . . He said he's not giving permission for me to use any kind of abortive agents. . . . But soon I got pregnant again but I miscarried, so then I went to the doctor for an IUD.

AUTHOR: You, yourself, decided to go?

MAYA: Well, my sister-in-law came back, this time with my brother, and the three of us went to the doctor, and I got an IUD put in. But when I went to my next confession and told the priest about it he cursed me out of the church [*wyklął mnie z kościoła*]. I admitted to this, I admitted to him, and he said that I can come back once I have it [the IUD] removed. . . . So I went to my sister-in-law and my brother and cried, and I told them the priest said I have to have it removed. So they gave me money again for the gynecologist (because my husband wasn't giving me any money), and the gynecologist removed it. So then I went to the priest and told him I was all right and the priest gave

> me the absolution, only then he did. . . . Some time later my
> husband left me; he vandalized the house and left.

AUTHOR: Did you get a divorce?

MAYA: No, he just left, and nobody knows where he is. I can't
get married again anyway because I won't be able to get
absolution. . . . The priest told me that if I were to move in
with a man again, the two of us would have to come to the
church and each sign a declaration that we would live like
brother and sister; in other words, the separateness of beds
[*oddzielność od łoża*]. And then everything would be fine.
(Interview with Maya, Kraków, 2002)

Maya's seeking of absolution through self-imposed confession encapsulates
the confessional character of Catholic self-government. Maya explained to
me that receiving absolution was essential and that she believed that her
priest, given that he was aware of her difficult situation at home, would be
sympathetic to her predicament. Indeed, the reaction of her priest seemed
somewhat harsh, even from the perspective of other priests I interviewed. I
used Maya's story with a number of clergy with whom I had conversations
about the use of contraceptives among the parishioners. Although some of
them agreed with the approach of Maya's priest, others said they would
have preferred not to withhold absolution, but instead establish a dialogue
about her behavior, which they could continue until she removed the IUD.
One of the priests summarized these kinds of situations as follows: "I tell
them: 'Remember only one thing, you will regret your sins very deeply.'"

The story of Maya demonstrates what Foucault (1991a) described as governmentality—the voluntary self-disciplining or self-censorship when she
felt compelled to confess to the priest about using contraceptives. In the
"confessional" mode of governmentality prevalent in the West (Carrette
2000; Foucault 1991b), the women subjects, constructed as the "gatekeepers"
of public morality and Polish nationhood, are to confess within a power relationship to an authority (a priest, a doctor) who has the power to punish or
forgive in the "best interest" of the subject. Much of this self-government is
driven by the need to obtain absolution. The church, in fact, has been successful in making many of its followers internalize the idea that absolution is
critical to an individual's emotional well-being, in contrast to the burden of an
unclean, heavy conscience. Consequently, the clergy, as the gatekeepers of

absolution, have the ability to selectively reward or punish penitents based on the "correctness" of their conduct, but the imperative of absolution largely eclipses the perceived rights and wrongs ascribed to the actual behaviors. Examples abound of women confessing to using contraception, repenting, and receiving absolution only to do it again. Some women confess having had an abortion, expecting absolution, which they usually get. The clergy also strategically deploy stigma by forbidding the unrepentant to participate in church services or specifically disallow taking communion.[20] Maya's experience of being "cursed out of the church" until she "corrected" her behavior could be particularly detrimental to women living in smaller communities without the option of changing to another parish, although for Maya such an option existed. The visibility of being forbidden to return in one's church community stigmatizes the follower and serves as an additional coercion to "correct" one's behavior. This community enforcement of expected behaviors and the self-censorship experienced by the individual work here synergistically to produce a powerful form of moral governance through fear and coercion.

The personal encounter of confession (and the threat of withholding absolution) offers an important opportunity for the priest to redirect some penitents toward the "morally correct" behavior. Since the church finds only one fertility control method morally acceptable,[21] namely periodic abstinence known as kalendarzyk małżeński ("the little marriage calendar"), which is popularly understood as calculating fertile days and abstaining, priests are instructed that "it is then licit to take into account the natural rhythms immanent in the generative functions, for the use of marriage in the infecund periods only, and in this way to regulate birth without offending the moral principles."[22] Kalendarzyk can therefore be recommended by the priest during confession in those cases when a married penitent confesses to using contraceptives. According to the clergy in my study, some of the priests that teach premarital courses at their parishes have also been learning how to calculate a woman's fertile days based on the dates of her menstrual cycle. Women in the parish who need assistance in this matter have been encouraged to meet with these priests and allow them to create a calendar of their fertility.

Aneta's Story

But not all women follow the priest's directives like Maya. In some cases, women seek other, more progressive priests, or abandon the practice of confession altogether rather than comply. For example, Aneta, a twenty-four-year-old cook who worked in a downtown restaurant in Kraków and had a vocational degree in gastronomy, explained that "faith is more important for me than the practice: I need faith, but I don't always need the practice." After Aneta started a romantic relationship with Tadek when they were nineteen, a series of events led to her decision to no longer go to confession at the local church. Aneta stated, "When Tadek and I started dating, I wanted to have premarital sex because, as they say, it's good to try things out." Within a year Aneta and Tadek had wpadka, or "an accident"— she became unintentionally pregnant with twins, but after she told the good news to Tadek, he disappeared and would not answer his cell phone, so she decided to pay a visit to his parents' apartment, with her own parents in tow. "His parents were people who believed in God, but they felt no responsibility," she recalled. After a short and tense conversation, Tadek's parents offered Aneta money for an abortion, which she took but decided to keep the pregnancy. The doctor in the local clinic where Aneta belonged based on her residency decided that a twin pregnancy constituted what is known in Poland as "endangered pregnancy," requiring Aneta to be taken entirely off work during most of the pregnancy. Her employer was visibly displeased when Aneta presented her doctor's note, and within a week he hired a permanent, rather than temporary, replacement for her job, even though legally Aneta was entitled to return to her position following maternity leave. Once the twins were born, Aneta found herself in a very difficult financial situation mainly having to rely on social support benefits and part-time cooking jobs on those days when her mother, working full-time herself, was able to watch the twins. She explained, "I go to the church every Sunday but I didn't have a christening for my twins because I had no money. People would ask me: 'Aren't you afraid?' Apparently there was a possibility to have them christened at the hospital for a lesser fee than at the church but nobody told me that." Christening in Kraków can cost 200–500 złotych (approximately \$65–162),[23] depending on whether the organ player had to be paid separately—a sum Aneta could not afford. During the customary visit of the priest in Aneta's home in December (also know as the Kolęda ritual)[24] the twins became the subject of inquiry:

> During the Kolęda a few years back, the priest noted in my file that my twins had no christening, and they have been asking me ever since. The last time I went to confession, the old priest recognized me and said he can't give me ab-

solution because my children have not been christened. The priest was talking so loud that I'm sure that all [the people] waiting in line to the confessional heard him. It was a horrible situation at the confessional. That's why many people go to other parishes; they run away from priests that know them. . . . The priests now ask questions about contraception and sex life! When I was seventeen, my priest—an old man with grey hair and shaky hands—was asking me this! That's none of their business. They missed their calling, they should've become doctors. (Interview with Aneta, Kraków, 2002)

Most upsetting for Aneta was the realization that priests showed so little understanding of her predicaments. After the twins, Aneta went on the pill: "Of course, I didn't tell the priest, but later when he started to question me whether I was using contraceptives, I didn't want to go to confession anymore. It's been three years since I confessed." She explained that she never intended to resist the teachings of the church, but she found the church requirements impossible to satisfy given her personal and material situation.

What About Men?

The manual for confessors also instructs priests on how to manage the husbands of the women who use hormonal contraception, noting that it is un-Christian for husbands to cooperate with their wives' desires to use contraception. Although it is clear that the manual recognizes that the husbands could play a role in the use of contraception and that the church condemns cooperation as sin, the document ultimately depicts them as innocent bystanders perceived as victims of their wives' unilateral decisions to use birth control. The woman's use of contraceptives is viewed by the church as a form of "violence or unjust imposition on the part of one of the spouses, which the other spouse in fact cannot resist."[25] Further, the man "is sinned against rather than sinning";[26] thus, in the eyes of the church the man is largely free of responsibility and blame compared to the woman. The church takes a clearly gendered approach and makes a distinction between the type of regulation and disciplining that it applies to women as compared with men. Because women are constructed as the agents of the wrongdoing, the manual specifically instructs the clergy to remind women penitents that they are not sovereign individuals, and that "[in] the task of transmitting life . . . they are not free to proceed completely at will, as if they could determine in a wholly autonomous way the honest path to follow."[27] Therefore, from the perspective of the church, the only path they can follow is through the "formation of correct judgments through docile respect for God."[28] Punishing contraceptive practices that enhance women's reproductive and sexual autonomy while teaching women docility and acceptance of church surveillance constitute significant governance of women's conduct.

The Priest Also Makes House Calls: The Kolęda Ritual

One of more prominent rituals in the Polish Catholic tradition is the priest's yearly visit to people's homes between the end of December and the end of January, known as Kolęda. All parishes mobilize their priests to walk door-to-door, knocking on people's front doors to pay them a visit. The priest usually walks with one or two altar boys who often sing religious songs and ring bells while walking between the households. The group methodically combs the neighborhood knocking on every door with the assumption that all, or nearly all, households are Catholic and welcome the priest. While the priest is visiting a particular home or apartment, one of the altar boys typically scouts the next few households to establish whether or not all of them are planning to accept the priest. In the event that someone does not wish to host the priest, the altar boy finds out ahead of time, and this spares the priest the embarrassment of knocking on a door that never opens or the residents decline the visit. The priest will attempt to visit every resident in the parish area, not just those who attend the church or are Catholic, and households which declined to host the priest the previous year are not spared the knock on their doors the following year. The priests' visits are announced in advance during Sunday mass; however, given that only about half of Catholics regularly attend mass, the announcements are also distributed via posters taped inside apartment building staircases in each neighborhood, and by word of mouth to ensure that people will be home and properly prepared to host the priest on their designated day. Typically, the notices state that parishioners should prepare their homes, children in the house should prepare their religion notebooks, and every effort should be made to ensure that everyone in the household is present when the priest makes the house call. In recent years, parishes with websites began to also post their Kolęda schedules there, including detail listings of streets, buildings, and even identifying building entries or staircases that are scheduled for particular days and times.

The nature of Kolęda as a public spectacle and a tradition places significant pressure on people, especially in smaller communities, to accept the priest. The few families who reject him stand out as "nonbelievers," and so the social pressure to conform can be intense. The Polish anthropologist Janusz Mucha (1989, 216) observed that "under pressure from their family and social milieu they [the nonbelievers] marry and baptize their children," justifying the practice as "precaution against alienation" within the community and against "harassment on the part of priest-ridden public opinion." Mucha conducted his research during the peak of church attendance in Poland, amid the height of struggles against the state socialist regime in the late 1980s. He noted that "the vast majority of the whole category of unbelievers in Poland" (8 percent of the population) attended church services (Mucha 1989, 216). Not surprisingly, after the church peaked in public support in the 1980s, there was a gradual decline in religious practice. By 2009, only 2 percent of Poles who identified as nonbelievers attended services (Boguszewski 2009. 12). Nonetheless, the practice is unusual, indeed not found as such in other Catholic nations, and illustrates unique hegemonic pressures to publicly follow Catholic practices and display religiosity in Poland.

The Catholic Church dates the Kolęda ritual to the sixth century when it was carried out by the administrators of the king or the local bishop to collect money and goods from the peasants. Since then, the Canon Law established in the thirteenth century called for the head pastor of each parish to visit the houses of Catholics who were elderly, sick, poor, or living alone during the time of Kolęda around Christmas and the New Year.[29] Canonical Law no. 529 states that "in order to fulfill his office diligently, a pastor is to strive to know the faithful entrusted to his care" and specifically notes that a diligent pastor should be "strengthening them [families] in the Lord, and prudently correcting them if they are failing in certain areas."[30]

Over time, Kolęda expanded in Poland and currently includes visits to all households in priests' designated areas of the neighborhood. According to the clergy in my research, this ritual appears to have nearly disappeared in other Catholic locations around the world. In Poland, however, it continues to be administered by the church with great vigor. Each family is expected to prepare to host the priest by setting a table with a white tablecloth, a crucifix flanked by two candles, a plate with holy water retrieved from the local church during the previous few days, a special sprinkling brush, *kropidło*, used for sprinkling the holy water during the visit, the notebooks from the children's religious classes, and the envelope with money for the priest.

Kolęda includes three components: blessing the household, the collection of money from each household—the so-called *kopertówka* ("the envelope"), and updating the files the parish holds on each family. The priests I interviewed recalled that between approximately the fourteenth and sixteenth centuries the Catholic Church set a fixed amount of money that each family had to pay the priest; however, resistance on the part of the people as well as some priests resulted in allowing the amount to be determined at the discretion of the faithful. Only in the territory of Prussia was the Kolęda payment fixed. The priests have noted that in recent years some parishioners hand them empty envelopes, understood by the priest as a situation in which the poverty of the family is too great to spare any amount of money, but the shame of not handing an envelope is even greater.

It was quite common during my research to hear the sentiment that the Kolęda visit is mainly focused on the collection of money in expressions such as *przyszedł po kasę* or *chodzi po kasę,* which means "came to get cash" or "walks around to get cash."[31] The priests, rather familiar with this sentiment, protested, arguing that in fact, it is common for them not to take the envelope if it is apparent that the family is very poor or lacks employment. The priests I interviewed reported various uses for the money collected during Kolęda visits: they either combined and redistributed the collections evenly among the priests as a type of a salary supplement, or the funds were used in the parish for collective needs.

The central mechanism of surveillance that is inherent in the Kolęda ritual is the system of recording and monitoring individuals' behaviors through written records, which are permanently stored by the church. All parishes in Poland keep detailed files [*kartoteki*] on each family, which include information about every family member, as explained by the Archdiocese of Kraków: "Each parish maintains a file of its parishioners, where recorded are data, sacraments taken, information about the family situation, problems."[32] The degree of the observance of key Catholic rituals and notes related to conversations that the priests conducted with the parishioners during these visits are also recorded and followed up on during the next year's visit. Typically, the priest asks questions about children's attendance of religious classes, reviews their religion class notebooks, and gives them small colorful cards depicting religious themes. He also asks whether the family has been carrying out the proper rituals associated with births, deaths, marriages, and other life events requiring Catholic sacraments. One of the priests described such files as follows: "The files contain a variety of information. There's a list of people living in the household, dates of births, baptisms, and the sacraments of marriage. We note certain situations which are concerning or which would hinder the person from being able to fulfill the function of a godmother or a godfather. For example, people living without marriage, or in a demoralizing [*gorszący*] lifestyle, or lacking in the habit of monthly confessions."

The clergy in my study estimated that about 80 percent of households accept their visit.[33] Many of the priests notice that typically it is the women in the family who prepare the ritual table with the crucifix and who host the priest. Some of the husbands, the priests noted, leave the house right before the priest is due to visit. One of the priests related, "The wife tells me 'unfortunately, my husband is not at home,' but I know that he's hiding somewhere in the apartment." Consequently, at least some of the time, the priests speak with the women and children, rather than the men. It is during the Kolęda conversations that the priests question the adults about their marital and reproductive life, including inquiries about the number of children a couple is planning to have, and whether or not they have been married in the church. Given that the visits are short, the goal of the priests is to get the parishioners, particularly those who have committed transgressions, to agree to meet them in the parish at a later date for a longer discussion. Thus, Kolęda allows the clergy to go directly to peoples' homes and pursue those self-identified Catholics who fail to go to confession or mass, or who do so only sporadically.

During Kolęda, the clergy are sensitized to look for situations where, for example, a couple who has been married for a number of years has no more than one child. This indicates that the couple might be using contraception. Every attempt is made to establish whether the couple is using the calendar method or hormonal contraceptives. In the case of the latter, the priests' obligation is to strongly encourage the woman to meet with him for a discussion at the parish at a separate time to discuss alternatives that are acceptable to the church. When I asked the priests how they manage to talk about family planning in the presence of children, one of the priests explained, "If nothing else but for prosaic reasons, one cannot tackle such a topic in the front of the whole family." Another priest remarked. "If there appears to be a problem which requires serious discussion we recommend a meeting in the chancellery of the parish." However, the priests complained that appointments made for a later meeting "sometimes don't have the desired results because in some situations people claim they're too busy or they simply lack the courage to come to the parish."

Renata's Story

The increasingly common understanding that the Kolęda priest is likely to ask about sexual and reproductive practices, especially directed toward women, has led some members of the household to leave when the priest is about to visit or alternatively devise strategies to evade questions. For example, some of the younger, college-age women in my study described a strategy of texting or calling neighborhood friends who just hosted the priest earlier in the evening to find out whether the particular priest assigned to their block that year was asking "private" questions. I was told that the priest will typically repeat the same questions when talking to young, unmarried women in the house, and so the strategy allowed at least some of the women to prepare a ready answer or perhaps leave the apartment. But most women reported staying and experiencing the same questions year after year. Renata's story of her Kolęda experience is emblematic of the approach to childless marriages or those with too few children, in the eyes of the priest. Renata, at the time of my fieldwork, was a thirty-seven-year-old laboratory technician with a master's degree in chemistry and had been married since 1995. She and her husband, Peter, were voluntarily childless at the time of my fieldwork. Peter always stayed at home with Renata to host the priest during Kolęda even though he self-identified as a "nonbeliever." Renata related her story as follows:

> RENATA: Usually, I have this impression, the priests I've talked to
> during confessions, and they assume that I don't have any
> children due to a biological problem. But when the priest
> came with the Kolęda he started a conversation on the topic
> of why don't we have any children?
>
> AUTHOR: He started, without your initiative?

RENATA: Yes, he started; without any initiative. Because, I don't know, I don't at all take up this topic myself. So he started on this, and mentioning my career that, that's of course important (he was trying to be delicate about it), but nevertheless that here, in our nation, the population is generally falling and that I should try harder. . . . And in this moment you are supposed to explain yourself; and the situation is very awkward.

AUTHOR: So what did you tell him?

RENATA: I tried to change the subject, first of all. And second of all, I told him that such matters aren't always so simple and clear, that some [people] have children and others simply don't and that's it. . . . Every year a different priest comes here but from the same parish, and they all have my file so they all ask the same questions. (Interview with Renata, Kraków, 2002)

Renata became tearful when she told me that with every year the conversation with the priest is becoming more burdensome and uncomfortable, a notably different experience from the time of her childhood when she looked forward to the priest's visit and the small religious picture card he always gave her as reward for her nicely kept religion notebooks. She longed for the comfort of the faith, but not the pressure of being questioned about her private life: "I have always been a believer, but I never had much attachment to the directives [*zarządzeń*]." The priest rarely questioned Peter, as Renata explained, "probably because Peter was never christened, so they don't consider him a Catholic, and so it's easier for the church to accept him: it's like he never came to the church, and so he never left. It's worse when someone leaves—that's when they don't want to allow it." But Renata was never sure whether Peter's file noted him as unchristened; she reasoned so because the priests always focused on her behavior. But placing responsibility on Renata can also reflect the concept in the confessor's manual that Peter "is sinned against rather than sinning." Equally it can be attributed to the larger politico-religious discourse that blames women for a selfish and "irrational" refusal to reproduce the Polish nation amid a prolonged demographic decline marked by one of the lowest birthrates in the world.[34]

"Difficult" Households

Renata is what the clergy refer to as "difficult" because of her voluntary childlessness. From the perspective of the clergy, the overarching long-term goal of the Kolęda rituals is to "regulate" the situation of "conjugal life" according to Christian norms. The women in my study argued that the priests aim their "moralizing" or "criticizing" comments at the women in those situations in which there are too few children (usually referring to childless or one-child families), where there is a suspicion or confirmed knowledge that modern methods of fertility control are used, and where the children, based on their school notebooks, show frequent absences from religion classes. These are often labeled as "difficult" households in the parish files, requiring follow-up work.

Single motherhood is perhaps one of the greatest examples of "difficult" households, which is perceived by the church as a "moral problem" and discussed during the Kolęda visits. The single mothers I interviewed consistently reported that priests inquired about the whereabouts of the father of the children, explaining that it is their duty to encourage the family to get back together unless the couple has already divorced. The priests readily offer to be the mediators between spouses who have separated or are in conflict. They were also alert to any signs of what the church calls "de facto unions"—couples living together without a church marriage. Couples who have a civil marriage are also viewed as unmarried and in de facto unions, and, thus, living in sin. Paweł Kwiatkowski, one of the senior, more experienced priests in a parish in Kraków, explained his role during Kolęda visits as follows:

> As the shepherd of the souls, responsible for the common spiritual good, I have the right and the obligation to ask about religious practices, about life according to the sacraments, and to reprimand if I see that evidently the rules of Christian morality are being broken, such as concubinage [*konkubinat*]—the young living without marriage. . . . There should be no obstacles in completing the sacrament of marriage! (Interview with Kwiatkowski, Kraków, 2002)

Others among the clergy with whom I had discussions about Kolęda echoed Kwiatkowski, noting that this ritual served as their primary point of "defense" again "de facto unions." In other words, unlike during Sunday mass, going to people's homes allowed the priests to see firsthand who lived in the household and question them about their marital status. The trend of un-married live-in relationships, they noted, has been an emerging problem in Poland—an observation corroborated by demographers who find that co-habitation in Poland has been increasing and is often viewed as a potential stepping-stone for marriage (Mynarska and Bernardi 2007). This rather common trend across Europe is a practice that the church would like to curb, so much so that the Vatican was compelled to specifically address this issue in a document released by the Pontifical Council for the Family titled "Family, Marriage, and 'De Facto' Unions" (Trujillo and Hellín 2000). In it, the Holy See urges (2000, 5) the clergy to intensify their efforts in stemming this growing phenomenon, which is portrayed as a sexual lifestyle problem: "a certain way of living one's sexuality" that is characterized by "an under-lying mentality that gives little value to sexuality. This is influenced more or less by pragmatism and hedonism, as well as by a conception of love de-tached from any responsibility." Thus, "de facto unions" are perceived as threatening because they permit unregulated sexuality and what is seen as promiscuity; in contrast, fidelity is assumed in Catholic marriages.

Retrieving Catholics Gone Astray: The System of Cards and Stamps

The church has a wide-reaching net, a system of cards and stamps, which functions as a backstop to catch those Catholics who have gone astray. For example, Kolęda priests typically distribute confession cards to members of each household, except to children who have not yet completed their First Communion. Cardholders are expected to go to confession in the first few weeks of Lent, and at that time have the cards stamped and turned in to the parish. This way, the church keeps track of how many people who accepted the Kolęda visit also followed through with confession. The un-returned cards indicate individuals who accepted the Kolęda priest but ne-glect other, equally important rituals, which can be noted in their file for future follow-up purposes. Similarly, most parishes issue confession cards during the Easter holiday. Each card is numbered, and a record is kept of the numbers and names of those to whom the cards have been issued. The penitents later return these cards, and their names are checked off the list. Thus a record is kept of all those who have satisfied their obligation—a system that allows better monitoring and more concentrated effort with those who are falling behind.

The system of cards and stamps can serve to reach even those who have not been observing any church rituals whatsoever but who have been asked by a family member to become a godparent to a newborn child. Since over 90 percent of Polish children are christened, practically every adult at some point will be asked by a relative or a close friend to become a godparent. The godparent's role during christening is to hold the child for the duration of the ceremony. To become a godparent, however, the church requires a documented proof of recent confession. Thus, the future godparent is given the confession card, which must be stamped by the priest as proof of having confessed and received absolution before participating in the baptism. Culturally, it is very awkward to decline the role of a godparent in Poland, and a refusal might be taken as a grave insult. At the same time, new parents rarely select godparents based on religiosity. More commonly, financial means, personality, or familial reciprocity obligations are considered in the selection. Thus, religious and nonreligious relatives alike are targets for godparenthood. The required confession can pose a dilemma for nonreligious kin, but this condition can occasionally be circumvented with the help of a friendly priest.

Likewise, the system of cards and stamps also plays an important role in Catholic marriages. A couple planning a church wedding is required to complete a premarital course organized by one of the parishes in the area. The women I interviewed who completed such courses before the 1990s noted that the topic of contraception was rarely discussed in those courses, and if so, it was done superficially. Rather, the courses focused mainly on general aspects of upholding a Christian morality within the family, and the importance of completing Catholic sacraments of baptism, confirmation, confession and communion (also known as penance and Eucharist), marriage, and sacraments during burials. Greater attention to family planning in premarital classes began in the early 1990s. The standard approach has been two-pronged: to teach the calendar method as the only acceptable method of fertility control; and to discourage other methods by teaching that hormonal contraceptives have an abortifacient or early miscarriage (*wczesnoporonne*) function, and that condoms are largely ineffective and might actually have holes.[35] In cities with Catholic gynecological clinics that offer instruction on the use of the calendar method, the future brides might be referred there to complete that portion of the premarital course. Although the calendar or kalendarzyk is indeed the common term used by Poles for this method, in reality many of the parishes and clinics try to depart from using the term because of its association with religion. Moreover, the calendar method is perceived by many women and couples as a generally ineffective method, and is even the butt of popular jokes (What do you call a Catholic couple using the calendar? Parents). Nevertheless, a significant minority of women in my study use it as a default method (similar to withdrawal) particularly during times when they cannot afford other, more costly methods. As a way to augment the legitimacy of the church-sanctioned methods, Catholic clinics and premarital courses advertise Natural Family Planning (NPR, Naturalne Planowanie Rodziny) or the Billings Ovulation Method—approaches of fertility monitoring that try to establish the fertile and infertile days of the cycle through the observation of vaginal discharge and/or measuring of body temperature upon waking. This method is promoted as a scientific rather than religious approach. For example, the Catholic weekly *The Sunday Guest* heralds, "NPR—scientific and effective," and appeals to the reader with the following rhetorical question: "Why render yourself infertile during that time of the month when your body is already not fertile? After all, there are only a few fertile days during the month. The most important methods of recognizing fertility are currently being taught in Poland. All of them are based on the consideration of the natural cycles of fertile and infertile days in the life of a woman. . . . Fertility recognition methods have scientific basis and are effective in planning or postponing conception."[36]

Because of the church's effort to imbue kalendarzyk with scientific legitimacy, numerous Catholic organizations[37] with networks of instructors of natural family planning have emerged since the 1990s across Poland. In Kraków, the Małopolska Pro-Family Health Clinic and Dr. Malina discussed in chapter 2 offer one such center for natural family planning courses. The instructor employed by the clinic was an enthusiastic young university student, who quickly assured me that she was engaged and therefore qualified to teach about the Billings method to married couples. Although sexual experience was not a prerequisite for instructors (after all nuns and priests also teach and theoretically are inexperienced), she believed that couples are more receptive to natural family planning when taught by instructors who use the method themselves. She also insisted that her fiancé participate in our conversations (as we generally met in coffee shops rather than the clinic) in the spirit of maximizing his opportunities to learn about the method that they both were to use once married. Most parishes around the city also teach some form of natural family planning in their mandatory premarital courses. However, instructors can vary widely and can include nuns and priests tasked by the parish with teaching, as well as laity hired by the church. Premarital courses have a popular reputation of being the "necessary evil" that couples have to endure in order to hold a Catholic wedding, and some women in my study described elaborate evasion strategies to avoid attending the course while still getting the necessary stamp from the priest. These included attempts to obtain a personal abbreviated course from a befriended priest or traveling to an "easier" parish. The experience of Aleksa and her fiancé Tomasz, owners of a small neighborhood grocery store in one of the new subdivisions in Kraków, serves as one such example.

Aleksa and Tomasz decided on a Catholic wedding because "it was just easier" and "the normal" thing to do, even though neither of them was a regular churchgoer. But they enjoyed partaking in the major Catholic holidays along with the rest of the family, and a Catholic wedding was expected. Aleksa felt that forgoing a Catholic wedding, even if it would make for a less expensive event and more money could be stashed toward a flat of their own, would inevitably trigger questions from some of the elder relatives, so she preferred to avoid such frictions and focus on enjoying the wedding instead. Both, however, were dreading the premarital course but thought they could somehow maneuver through that obstacle as well:

> ALEKSA: We heard a lot of bad things about premarital courses, and so we didn't look forward to it. I heard that they really pressure women on the calendar [method] but the guys can just sit and listen.

> AUTHOR: Which church did you use for the premarital course?

> ALEKSA: The choice was either my parish or his, but I heard that Saint Anne's church was the best to use because they cater to university students and seem more modern and tolerant. We pleaded with my parish priest to allow us to transfer there by claiming that Saint Anne's was where we'd like to get married, so he should let us take the course there too. In reality, we just wanted to do the course there.

AUTHOR: How was the course? What did they go over? . . .

ALEKSA: The course turned out tragic! Most of the information was about procreation. The instructor said that some condoms are full of holes[38] and so that you never know if you have a good one or a bad one. He also said that when one couple he knew stopped using condoms the woman's skin cleared of acne because the sperm was good for that. . . . He said that "pulling out" was bad because it caused psychological problems for both people. Tomasz and I just looked at each other and laughed.

AUTHOR: Interesting. . . . Seems at least that they had a pretty even approach to men and women in the course . . .

ALEKSA: Well, actually no, because the woman instructor who came later, took the women separately into another room for more instruction, while Tomasz was finished. We had to go over the "mucus-rhythm" method with her, and at the end of this class she said that we have to use this method for one month and record everything in a little book she gave us. After a month we were supposed to come back and show her the results. Tomasz and I were using condoms at the time, and I was not interested in natural methods so I didn't do it. I borrowed the book from a friend of mine who did it, and I copied all her results. That's how I got checked off for it at the church. . . . They told Tomasz that he can take a separate class on the calendar method, but his was optional. At the end of the course they actually gave us an exam! I just laughed! (Interview with Aleksa, Kraków, 2002)

Aleksa and Tomasz received the needed stamp, but felt that Saint Anne's turned out to be no easier than what they heard about their own parish. Their friends' reports of gender bias proved to be true and was off-putting to Aleksa, but she believed that a Catholic wedding is still desirable enough to go through the required hoops. Thus, the system of cards and stamps constitutes an effective method of creating opportunities for surveillance and "corrective" teaching, even if these teachings do not always take. Catholic weddings and godparent privileges continue to form enticing inducements with which to pull some of the less religious Poles back to the confessional and face-to-face with church teachings.

Purifying Women, Purifying the Nation

As postsocialist gender politics demonstrated an ever-increasing regulation of bodily conduct after 1989, the justification for an increased surveillance of women's behavior was rooted in the religious and nationalist constructions of Polish women as the custodians of Catholic purity. This purity was predicated on the restraint and the self-control of women's sexuality as well as on the appropriateness of their reproductive practices within the context of heterosexual marriage. The purification of Polish women, and therefore the nation, of the alleged contamination wrought by the alleged licentiousness, permissive sexuality, and the corrupted, secularized mentality of the state socialist era emerges as the central goal of the church in the 1990s. Consequently, both the direct surveillance of women's conduct by the clergy demonstrated in this chapter and the indirect regulation of conduct via reproductive laws discussed earlier greatly intensified after the fall of the state socialist regime.

From the perspective of the Catholic Church—irrespective of how these regulatory mechanisms are circumvented or not—the intensified reproductive governance served to bolster the public consolidation of Polish Catholicism in the early postsocialist years. As Pope John Paul II envisioned in 1991, the larger goal of this consolidation was the reevangelization of secularized Europe with Polish leadership as the "Christ of nations," which has suffered for the sake of a future European Christendom (Byrnes 1997, 438). Although some might argue that this is an exaggerated understanding of Polish influence on Europe, the rhetoric of Poland's unique role in demonstrating how the moral purification is done persisted. In October of 2004, five months after Poland's entry into the EU, the pope continued to call on Poland to play an active role in bringing Christianity back to Europe. The moral governance of reproduction through sustained and wide efforts to monitor sexual and reproductive conduct in Poland has been vital in both rhetoric and practice toward fulfilling this vision.

The postsocialist state at different times since 1989 has been an active collaborator in this vision, as Solidarity policymakers and other conservative groups ushered in legislative changes that restricted reproductive rights and bolstered the public role of the church, all without holding any referenda. This was true when abortion was banned, when health care policy changes removed contraceptive coverage, when religion was introduced in schools, and when the Concordat with the Holy See was signed.

Aside from the particular moral agenda at play, policies and other disciplinary mechanisms directed at women that could potentially promise an increase in Polish birthrates have also been viewed as advantageous by a wide range of politicians, conservative and liberal alike. The low fertility rate in Poland has been used in the political discourse as an alarming trend that in the eyes of some politicians justifies restrictions on family planning. Likewise in Russia, a legislative proposal to restrict abortion care by requiring a married woman to get her husband's permission to access abortion has been depicted as a viable way to bolster Russian men's masculine identity, and therefore presumably prompt them to take charge of the low birthrates there (Rivkin-Fish 2010, 723). In Poland, calling for more births serves both the neoliberal market and nationalist agendas, and so regulation of women's reproductive and sexual conduct with the goal of stimulating population growth, be it of "good Catholics" or "good consumers," has become a shared political agenda of the church and the state.

Despite the restrictive reproductive policies and the myriad of mechanisms of direct surveillance of women's' conduct, Polish women cannot be understood as excessively passive or immobilized by the disciplining mechanisms to which they are subjected. I have shown here how some women simultaneously accept the Kolęda priest but defy what they church expects them to do when it come to their sexuality and reproduction. In other words, some women enact their own unofficial and unsanctioned agendas. Furthermore, the "docile body paradigm" (Deveaux 1996, 214) in which women lack the ability not to conform or to actively contest the disciplining mechanisms proves false when we consider the diverse ways in which the various restrictions, be they legal or informal, are selectively navigated or circumvented altogether. In particular, the women in my study turn out to be anything but docile when it comes of navigating legal restrictions on abortion.

5 ⫿ Abortion, Polish Style

WHEN THE 1993 ABORTION ban went into effect, some Polish gynecologists immediately began to perform abortions clandestinely, and patients migrated to this unregulated private sector. As shown in the preceding chapters, the Polish abortion ban is one of the harshest in Europe. In a nation where key mechanisms of unwanted pregnancy prevention are missing—namely, no sex education in schools and limited access to modern birth control methods due to a lack of health insurance coverage for contraceptives—the illegal provision of abortion has been flourishing. The severity of the current abortion ban in Poland allows for very limited exceptions. The law criminalizes abortion under all but three circumstances: (1) when the woman's life or health is in danger, (2) when a prenatal test shows a serious, incurable deformity of the fetus which is threatening to its life, and (3) when the pregnancy is the result of rape or incest which has been reported to the police. Abortions that qualify as lawful can be performed only in a public hospital. Even under one of these circumstances, the pregnancy must be less than twelve weeks to qualify. Since 1956 only 3 percent of all abortions had been performed for these three reasons, therefore, the 1993 law is de facto a near ban on abortion in Poland (Nowakowska and Korzeniowska 2000; Johannisson et al. 1997).

Where Did All the Abortions Go?

Until the 1993 ban, Poland has had a relatively high rate of abortion, similar to other Eastern European nations and Russia. Since the ban and the

emergence of the clandestine abortion sector, it has been difficult to estimate the number of illegal procedures that Polish women obtain annually
because the estimate would have to include not only the abortion underground but also abortion travel outside of Poland, and other less visible
methods such as purchases of remedies online as well as self-induced
abortions. But the Federation for Women and Family Planning has attempted the task and estimates that 80,000 to 200,000 clandestine abortions are performed annually in Poland (Nowicka 2001; Stefańczyk 2004,
2).[1] This estimate is consistent with how many women were getting abortions before the restrictions took place. For example, after abortion was
legalized in 1956, there were 150,418 abortions performed in 1960, and the
use of the procedure began to decline in the late 1960s. This drop in the
utilization of abortion coincided with a major increase in contraceptive
use: from 1969 to 1979 there was a sixfold rise in sales of birth control pills
in Poland (Okólski 1983, 269). Following this drop, the rate leveled off at
about 130,000 abortions per year (Mazur 1981, 197). Procedures performed in private offices were not included in state reports since doctors
were not obligated to report them; thus the state underestimated these
data significantly.[2]

The number of abortions performed legally began to drop in the late
1980s when gradual restrictions on access to the procedure were taking
place, significantly increasing cost and creating delays that pushed many
women outside of the legal time limit. These new obstacles included requirements that women seeking abortions obtain permission from three
doctors and a psychologist, rather than from just one physician, as was the
case until then (Nowakowska and Korzeniowska 2000, 220–25). After the
1993 ban, the numbers dropped well below 1,000 per year, reaching the all-
time low of only 123 abortions in 2001.[3] For a nation of 38 million people
with a historical record of high abortion utilization, such extremely low
numbers of abortions recorded by the state are clearly not reflective of the
actual number of abortions taking place. Furthermore, because access to
modern contraceptives in Poland is limited to those who can afford to pay
out of pocket,[4] and at other times it is limited by doctors who refuse to
prescribe contraceptives citing conscientious objection, it is reasonable to
expect a similar rate of unwanted pregnancy as had been the case before
1989. In fact, although the use of modern contraceptive methods has increased in Poland over the last two decades, still only 53 percent of the

sexually active population uses such methods (as compared to 60–80 percent in most other European nations) (Mishtal and Dannefer 2010, 235). That is despite the "fear of unwanted pregnancy" being most often cited as a concern in the sexual lives of young people (Izdebski 2006, 124). But this is not surprising, given that as of 2014 only one type of contraceptive pill has been subsidized (even if sold in four name brands), and it is of the "old generation" of pills containing high levels of hormones, and women generally avoid it because of the unpleasant side effects. The wide range of "new generation" low-hormone contraceptives made available to women elsewhere in the world, including the popular Nuva ring and IUDs, are not covered by health insurance.

The restrictions on family planning options and the lack of sex education in Poland might reasonably lead to the expectation that more births would take place as a result of women's inability to plan childbearings. Yet paradoxically fertility control in Poland is highly successful, as the Polish birthrate is one of the lowest in the world at just over one child per woman per lifetime (a topic I address in detail in the final chapter). Graph 5.1 illustrates this phenomenon and shows that births have fallen significantly since 1989.

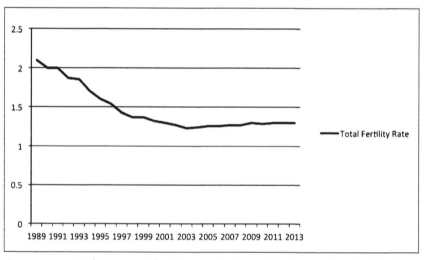

GRAPH 5.1. Birthrates: total fertility rate for Poland beginning after the fall of state socialism in 1989 and through 2013. Data source: *Statistical Yearbook of Poland*, 1989–2013 (Warsaw: Central Statistical Agency).

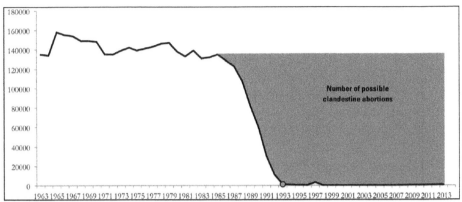

GRAPH 5.2. Number of legal abortions per year in Poland, 1963–2013. *Data sources:* COE—Council of Europe (2003) and GUS—Główny Urząd Statystyczny (2003–12).

What explains this apparent paradox, in addition to contraceptive use by women who can afford it, is the likelihood that a significant number of unwanted pregnancies that ended in legal abortions before 1989, are now terminated in the clandestine underground (indicated by the gray-shaded area in graph 5.2).

"White Coat" Abortion Underground

Following the 1993 ban, doctors who previously provided abortions in public hospitals, as was the practice for decades until then, began to offer them illegally in their private offices, creating a "white coat" abortion underground (*podziemie aborcyjne*), staffed mainly by experienced gynecologists. Thus, clandestine abortions have been widely available in doctor's private offices, albeit for a very high fee. Gynecologists and obstetricians who perform illegal abortions advertise their services in major Polish newspapers, including the largest Polish daily *Gazeta Wyborcza*, but also in major regional newspapers like *Dziennik Bałtycki*, published in the Gdańsk and the Tricity region (the contiguous cities of Gdańsk, Gdynia, and Sopot) on the Baltic coast. Advertisements for clandestine abortion can be found posted under the "Health" section, and the "Gynecologists" subsection in the advertisement area of the newspapers.[5]

Abortion ads are very short and simple and often contain only a mobile telephone number, and one of the following euphemisms signaling abortion services: "all services provided," "cheap," "vacuum method," "safe," "anesthesia," and "discreet," among others. The doctors who advertise illegal abortion services compete for clientele with phrases such as "A-Z gynecology" or the use of "AAAAaa" opening at the start of the ad to ensure that one's ad is listed first (see figures 5.1 and 5.2). Some doctors seem to place multiple ads in the same paper: tracking the number of original telephone numbers in these ads over a period of three months during my research in Gdańsk, I found that only eight original numbers were used to place an average of twelve ads per day in the *Dziennik Bałtycki* paper. Occasionally an advertisement is more explicit, such as "pharmaceutical recovery of menstrual cycle" or "No period? We will help." The phrase "new procedures" signals either medical abortion—a nonsurgical use of medications—or the offer of the vacuum method, which is a departure from the traditional dilation and curettage (D&C) surgeries widely employed in Poland. Newspapers containing offers for illegal abortion can be purchased across Poland in numerous kiosks, grocery stores, bookstores, and gas stations for an equivalent of a US dollar or less. Thus, clandestine abortion listings are generally widely available. Major Polish Internet discussion forums also contain information on accessing illegal abortion services in various question-and-answer conversations taking place online.[6]

A woman seeking an illegal abortion has to call the listed number to find out the price and the location, and abortions are typically scheduled either for the same or the next day. Physicians who are located centrally in large cities, for example Kraków, Warsaw, or Gdańsk, charge higher fees than those in nearby smaller cities to which the woman would have to travel on a train or bus. Part of the high cost, ranging from 1,000 to 4,000 złotych, is related to the fact that abortions in Poland, be it in the underground or in the lawful sphere, typically require the synchronization of two doctors: a gynecologist and an anesthesiologist. This is because in Poland abortion is still mainly performed using the older method of dilation and curettage, which must be performed under general anesthesia. It is from the D&C procedure that the popular synonym for abortion—skrobanka, or "little scraping"—comes. The use of D&C subjects women to an unnecessary risk of uterine perforation and scarring, and general anesthesia carries greater risks that local anesthetic or sedation, but as doctors explained to me, D&C is the method that Polish gynecologists who performed abortions before the ban are most familiar with, and moreover, they lack access to training

OGŁOSZENIA DROBNE | 23

FIGURE 5.1. *(left)* Examples of advertisements of illegal abortion services in Poland, Gdańsk, 2012. Key euphemisms depicted here include "safe, inexpensive," "bringing back the menstrual cycle pharmaceutically," "inexpensive," "safe," "discreet," and "full discreetness."

FIGURE 5.2. *(right)* Examples of advertisements of illegal abortion services in Poland, Warsaw, 2014. Key euphemisms depicted here include "all services," "bring back menstruation," "inducing of menstruation," "inexpensive," "full range [of services]," "pharmaceutical" (indicates medical abortion service), and "professional procedures."

and equipment to employ the newer vacuum aspiration method.[7] Doctors in this study reported hearing of colleagues who trained in vacuum procedures abroad, but this appears to be a small minority, judging by the ads that usually advertise "new procedures" or "vacuum" method as a draw to a particular clinic. The few abortions that are still performed lawfully in hospitals all involve the D&C method and general anesthesia. Some doctors theorized that maintaining older methods is "for their patients' benefit," assuming that their patients prefer to be asleep and unaware of the procedure, and wake up only when it is all over. The women in my research, however, had little awareness of the options of newer methods (although some had heard about the "abortion pill"), and generally assumed that abortions in Poland involve D&C and general anesthesia.

What is significant about illegal abortion in Poland is that it is a "white coat" underground, serviced by trained and licensed gynecologists; therefore, clandestine procedures in Poland are relatively safe and rarely take place in "back alleys." Poland belongs to a small number of nations where despite the restrictive abortion laws maternal mortality is low due to the relatively safe provision of illegal procedures. Nevertheless, some cases of deaths due to unsafe abortion in Poland have been exposed (Nowicka and Girard 2002).[8] Moreover, in a setting where doctors are criminalized for offering the service, dealing with complications and emergencies might be delayed as physicians and staff feel reluctant to seek external help. Likewise, women might delay securing an abortion because of money or wherewithal, and therefore present in a later gestational stage, which can increase the procedure's complexity and associated risks. But generally the police leave the clinics alone because they are significantly underresourced and catching the doctor in the act would require a tip-off.

The Story of Hania

Despite the accessibility of clandestine services and the clinical setting in which abortions are performed, the experience is harrowing. When I first met Hania she was twenty-two and had been getting ready for her summer job in Greece as a tour guide for Polish tourists traveling to Athens. She moved from the rural town of Wieliczka to Kraków in 2002 to pursue studies at the Academy of Physical Education, Department of Tourism and Recreation. She viewed tourism as a perfect career: a secure and lucrative job and a chance to travel outside Poland. Hania's mother, a nurse, partially supported Hania, but their finances were limited since Hania's father had died two years earlier and the family had incurred debts during his illness. Her summer job was a valuable opportunity to earn money and gain work experience, particularly since the main alternative among her peers was far less desirable fruit-picking seasonal work in Spain.

Hania dated Marek for only four months when she said they had a wpadka, an accident—she unintentionally became pregnant. She said they typically used condoms because the pill was too costly but occasionally relied on the less effective withdrawal method to prevent pregnancy. This practice was not unusual, as many couples resorted to less reliable methods, especially withdrawal but also the calendar method, at times of financial strain. I asked Hania how she reacted when she realized she was pregnant:

> I wanted to get an abortion *that* day. I knew they made it so we can't have them anymore, but I went to Dr. Jacob at the Academy who prescribed my [birth control] pills in the past hoping she'd give me a referral, but she told me to pick a doctor from the newspaper. So I got the paper and started calling. I called two ads that said: "vacuum method." One doctor was in Katowice and he wanted 1,200 [złotych], and the other was in Kraków and wanted 1,400, both could see me that day. I came up with a thousand but had to borrow the rest from two friends, as an emergency favor, and I chose the Kraków clinic since he let me bring a friend. The first friend I called couldn't come; the second met me right away. The clinic told me I was to meet their driver at a specific location, and to hold an empty *reklamówka* [plastic shopping bag] in my left hand. A man pulled up in an old car and told us to get in. We got in, frightened, but we got in. The situation felt anxious and secretive, I don't know, but basically he tried to be pleasant as he drove us outside the city to the doctor's private house. The sign at the gate said: "Doctor of Gynecology," which calmed me down a bit. The office was very elegant: it was tiled and the older woman anesthesiologist was quite friendly. She said the procedure is easy, like pulling a tooth. She came from her hospital just for this . . . . I never learned the doctors' names. When I woke up from the anesthesia, he wanted my phone number in case of complications and told me to return for a checkup, but later I decided I didn't need to come back. My friend and I were dropped off on the same street corner, and from there I took the bus home. I was glad to have it behind me. (Interview with Hania, Kraków, 2002)

Hania told me she never went back to the clinic because she was feeling well, and in any case she worried there might be an office visit fee—she could not remember if the doctor told her the follow-up was included in the abortion fee or not, and decided to err on the side of saving money. In retrospect, she had few complaints about the experience, despite enduring the fear and the financial burden, and would go to the same clinic again, if need be. Hania and her friend found getting in the car with a strange man behind the wheel more frightening than any other aspect of the ordeal, and once inside the clinic, which clearly appeared to be a functioning and well-equipped medical facility, she believed she was in the hands of professionals. Later that summer, Hania went on her first bus tour from Kraków to Athens, working as a guide.

Common Knowledge, but Exclusive Access

Hania benefited significantly from knowing from some of her close friends at the academy how the process of illegal abortion works, and therefore she had a sense of what to expect. Nearly all the women I spoke to during my research had extensive knowledge about how the abortion underground functions, including where to look for a provider, the cost and how it varies between different geographic locations, and the way clinics typically look.[9] Most personally knew of someone who had obtained an abortion clandestinely, and a few women also offered to discuss their own experiences.[10] Some indicated that referrals to abortion providers can be obtained from their own physicians. The following five excerpts from interviews show women's knowledge and the consistency of their understanding about the abortion underground:

> Sure, everybody knows about abortions. You can read about it in teen magazines like *Bravo*. There are also ads that you can see in the newspapers—they always advertise by saying "inexpensive" or "discreet" and such. Everyone knows about this, but that's not something people will talk about. The prices are going down, I hear: it used to be 1000 [złotych], but now you can get one for 500. If I had to recommend to someone where to go, I'd just say, "Check the paper," you can find all the ads there. (Grocery store inventory clerk, age 21, interview Gdańsk, 2007)

> All you need to do is just call one of the ads in the paper, like my friend did it. A car pulled up at a designated place and picked her up. They drove to a private

office in the suburbs, and when they got there, the driver pulled right into the garage at the doctor's villa. She got out and went straight upstairs to his office without having to go outside. The same driver took her back after it was over. She said she didn't have to travel far; it was fairly close to the center of Gdańsk. (Nurse, age 34, interview Gdańsk, 2007)

Five of my friends had abortions in recent years. They all had accidents [wpadki] with partners who were kind of occasional, not regular, you know. Abortions can be costly, but you can certainly find them all over newspapers; for example, *Dziennik Bałtycki* has a list of ads with words like "discreet," "inexpensive," "professional." Then you just pick one and call. (Clerk in human resources office, age 31, interview Gdańsk, 2007)

A number of my friends had abortions in private offices—the offices are usually quite beautiful, and it costs about 2000. You can find out which doctors perform them in many ways. One of my friends recommended a doctor to another friend, and two sisters I know used the same doctor for their abortions. If I needed a doctor I would go to my gynecologist and ask her first. She won't necessarily be the one who'll do it, but she can refer me since all abortions are done locally. (Store manager, age 32, interview Gdańsk, 2007)

Well, I used it myself. At the time when I got pregnant my relationship with my husband wasn't going well, so both of us were in favor of terminating. I decided I didn't trust the newspaper ads, so I went to my gynecologist and asked him. He told me he didn't do abortions, but that he knows another doctor who does and gave me his cell phone. This was a good method; I would highly recommend going through your own gynecologist, because they all know each other. My abortion was 1500 złotych, and was done in very good conditions; it was very professional. It was a nice private clinic, and everything went well. (Border and customs officer, age 36, interview Gdańsk, 2007)

Although women with sufficient financial means can circumvent abortion restrictions rather easily by paying for clandestine services, women who are poor, adolescents, the unemployed, and migrant women have a more difficult task. Clandestine abortion services are indeed expensive, as many women in my research pointed out. Prices in Warsaw, Kraków, and Gdańsk typically range between 1,000 and 4,000 złotych, $319–$1278, an equivalent of about two months' salary for a state-employed teacher. This is similar (if not higher) to the abortion cost in the United States, where women pay an average of $451 per procedure; however, at least 30 percent of US women deflect the cost by using health insurance (Jones, Finer, and Singh 2010; Jones and Kooistra 2011). In contrast, Polish women pay entirely out of pocket and have a much lower average income.[11] Moreover, women's disposable income is likely smaller yet, as the economic woes in Poland affect women disproportionately. Scholars have documented the "feminization of poverty" in Poland, where women are fast becoming the new economic "underclass": they are twice as likely to fall below the poverty line as men, and constitute the majority of the unemployed (Ciechocinska 1993; Domański 2002; Fodor 1997, 2002; Tarkowska 2002). While various types of economic gender inequities were present before 1989, women's poverty on a mass scale did not exist during state socialism the way it does now (Kocourkova 2002; Leven 1994; Molyneux 1995).

The combination of low income and the high cost of abortion allows mainly the better resourced women to access these services. Some women in this research explained they would "organize" (*zorganizowałabym*) the money if the need arose, which is typically a euphemism for borrowing from relatives or friends. For instance, Hania had to borrow 400 of the 1,400 złotych from two of her friends, while others try to arrange to pay doctors in installments, although it is normally expected that services in private clinics are payable in full at the time of service. Doctors in smaller cities charge less—Hania had the option of taking the train to Katowice, 67 km from Kraków, for a less expensive procedure—but such travel can be more burdensome physically, and might require lodging or extra time off work. Therefore, a woman's ability to circumvent the ban on abortion is closely related to her socioeconomic situation, as middle-class women and those who have the ability to "organize" the money can turn to the private sector for clandestine services. The rest are left with few alternatives.

Travel, Pills, and "Life Windows"

In parallel with the underground in Poland, abortion travel had developed to the neighboring nations of Slovakia, Czech Republic, Lithuania, Ukraine, and Belarus. More visible in the early 1990s, this practice has somewhat declined due to the wide availability and convenience of local abortions. Some of these options might be less expensive but require additional time and planning, and travel to an unfamiliar location. Foreign clinics appear to compete with the local providers by offering an environment free of the fear, indignity, and secretiveness inherent in Poland's illegal activity. For example, the Centrum Klinika—Private Clinic for Procedures (*Prywatna Klinika Zabiegowa*)—and Klinika-Ginekologiczna.com publicize abortion services in Slovakia and the Czech Republic in the Polish language and specifically target Polish women.[12] The website of the Centrum Klinika emphasizes the illegality of abortions performed in Poland and even states falsely that a woman who gets an illegal abortion in Poland can be punished with jail time (in reality, only those who perform or assist with abortion are criminalized, but not the woman). In contrast, the clinic advertises "Safety—Certainty—Comfort—Full Anonymity," and therefore the site encourages one to travel abroad instead. Třinec, where the clinic is located, is a medium-sized town in the Czech Republic only 5 km from the Polish border, and 21 km from the Slovak border. A significant minority of the population in Třinec is Polish, and therefore the Polish language can potentially be used during the travel. Since abortion is legal in both the Czech Republic and Slovakia, the website contains detailed information about the clinic, the procedures used (both surgical and pharmaceutical terminations are available), and photographs of its facility and staff. The proximity to the Polish border makes it accessible by train or bus from Kraków, Katowice, and other cities and towns in the southwest region of Poland, although the connection is often indirect since Třinec is not a major destination city otherwise. In the Czech Republic a procedure can cost around 1,000 złotych ($315 or €240), and in Slovakia 2,000 złotych (exactly €459 at the Klinika-Ginekologiczna)—these prices fall within the lower range of clandestine abortions in Poland, but would involve travel expenses and additional time.

Numerous other clinics abroad advertise to Polish women, including major clinics in Germany and the Netherlands, some of which run telephone hotlines in Polish.[13] In Germany, these clinics are also close, including in Schwedt (4 km from the border), and Prenzlau (45 km from the border), with Berlin and Frankfurt being further away but with more convenient train connections. Some clinics offer overnight accommodations in simple but comfortable rooms right at the clinic or assistance with nearby pensions and inexpensive hotels. Travel to the UK and Austria has also been recorded. In the UK, those women who can get a temporary work permit (understood as relatively simple to obtain) can access fully subsidized abortion care. In 1996, at least twenty Polish agencies offered abortion travel assistance by organizing bus trips to clinics in southern and eastern border nations (Nowicka 2001). The health care officials in some nations, especially in the UK, Germany, and the Netherlands, keep track of the number of Poles who pursue abortion annually there. A recent count indicates that approximately 30,000–40,000 procedures are performed abroad for Polish women (Bunda 2010). The cost in Western European clinics can vary from around €280 to €600 ($365–$785), but the availability of inexpensive travel on intra-European airlines such as Ryanair can make this option accessible, at least to some.

The question of abortion travel gained even more currency recently due to the implementation by the EU in October 2013 of the Cross-Border Health Directive, which gives EU citizens the right to seek health care in other states and have the costs reimbursed by their home nations (providing that a given service is legal in the home country). This would allow for the possibility that Polish women who qualify for an abortion procedure under the strict Polish law and travel to obtain the service across the border in Germany or the Czech Republic, for example, could seek reimbursement of costs upon their return to Poland. This avenue would potentially offer women a way to avoid conscience-based refusals of care in Poland and seek treatment in a more respectful and welcoming environment. The Polish state, however, promptly placed limits on the use of the Cross-Border Directive by requiring patients to first seek permission to travel for care outside Poland—a regulation in violation of the Cross-Border Directive. As of May 2015, this issue continued to be hotly debated, with feminist and patient rights groups voicing protest against the government's scheme to restrict the use of the directive.

A nonsurgical option for women is to purchase pills online for an abortion with self-administered misoprostol medication, which is commonly available as a treatment for ulcers, or with a mifepristone-misoprostol regimen, which is more effective.[14] As of May 2015, several Polish Internet forums offer information about where to buy the pills. But not all sources of these pills are legitimate. Recently, the Federation for Women and Family Planning has been reporting a new wave of newspaper advertisements for medical-pharmacological abortions, but sales of fake pills have been reported in Poland. During my fieldwork in Gdańsk in 2007, one woman related just such a story, describing a purchase of "expensive pills" at the central market square in Gdańsk. The purchase was arranged by phone from a newspaper advertisement, and she described the transaction scene as akin to the proverbial back alley purchase: "Literally here was the vegetable store, and here was the shoe store, and here was the person selling these pills." But "nothing happened for a week," so she decided to not wait any further and found a gynecologist to perform a surgical abortion. The pharmaceutical option is appealing because the pills, besides being less invasive, are also less expensive than a surgical procedure (200–400 złotych), and therefore might be more feasible for women who cannot afford other options. But in addition to the possibility of fake, expired, improperly stored, or substandard products, this method becomes far less effective after the ninth week. To address these concerns, some international reproductive rights NGOs took up the provision of the pills on the Internet. Internationally known is the Dutch organization Women on Waves (discussed in chapter 3), which reports being contacted primarily by Polish women; therefore, its website offers Polish language guidance, instructions about the purchase, and details about what to do and expect (Nowicka 2008a, 25–27). Some local Polish online discussion forums "virtually hold one's hand" through the process of a pharmaceutical abortion (Podgórska 2009). It appears as though the women who provide online advising to others have gone through the experience themselves and now help a newcomer who asks for help on the forum.

Self-administered medication abortion lacks direct medical supervision, and the issue of whether such supervision is necessary in these circumstances has been of concern, and at times a subject of vigorous debates in the reproductive health community in the United States and internationally. Recently, however, reproductive health providers and researchers have suggested that teaching women how to self-administer these medications in settings where abortion is illegal can actually be a form of harm reduction—a model of public health intervention to minimize harm due to human behaviors that have been driven underground as a result of policy or stigma—because this method has been associated with a decrease in complications and death from unsafe back alley abortion in Latin America and Africa (Hyman et al. 2013). However, in the Polish setting the situation is more nuanced in that illegal abortions are for the most part safe and performed by professionals. Nevertheless, the harm reduction rationale for self-administered misoprostol is relevant to concerns about those women who cannot afford the high cost of clandestine surgical procedures or travel abroad.

Some women who experience an unwanted pregnancy decide to give up the infant for adoption, and some cases result in abandonment. In the 2000s, stories of infants abandoned and found (some dead, some alive) near police and train stations or parks have appeared regularly in the Polish media. In 2006, the first so-called window of life (*okno życia*) (known outside of Poland as "baby boxes" or "baby hatches") was opened to provide a safe location where an infant could be abandoned, and currently there are approximately fifty such windows in Poland (Wiśniewska 2012). Forty-three of the fifty windows belong to the Catholic Church and are located in parishes, convents, the Caritas charity group, and the House of the Single Mother facilities. Only seven windows are state run or belong to a public hospital. The fact that most of the windows are typically constructed by the Catholic Church in buildings that belong to local parishes has been the subject of public debate about the relative benefit and harm of funneling these infants through the church system, and depriving the child of the chance of a so-called open adoption wherein the identity of the biological parents can be recorded in a formal legal process (Wiśniewska 2012). Indeed, the United Nations Committee on the Rights of the Child appealed for a ban on "baby boxes" on these grounds (UN 2012). It is questionable whether removing these windows in Poland would encourage more formal processes of relinquishing the infant for adoption. Given that infant abandonment is stigmatized and Polish women receive little support and respect from the state for their ability to make their own reproductive decisions, it is doubtful whether the closure of these windows would be enough to achieve the lofty goal of the UN. In the case of Poland, it could potentially increase abandonment in unsafe locations as was the case before the first window opened in 2006.

Illegal Is Easier Than Legal

Women I interviewed in my research commonly understood that when someone qualifies for a legal abortion because her situation falls within one of the three exceptions, it is easier and faster albeit a lot more expensive to get an illegal abortion compared to pursuing abortion legally.

Well-known cases of denial of lawful abortions by hospitals abound in the media, among them the cases of Alicja Tysiąc and Agata discussed earlier, which are just two of numerous examples. Lawful abortions can be difficult to obtain because it is not uncommon for conscientious objection to be declared by the directors of hospitals on behalf of the entire staff. My interviews with physicians and women patients revealed that doctors who performed abortions illegally in their private offices were also on staff in hospitals where they were known to refuse to perform the same procedure. Women who encountered a refusal of service at the hospital reported that the doctor would hand them a business card with contact information for his or her private clinic, accompanied with a discreet mention that "possibilities exist" outside of the hospital. When I discussed with one of the doctors what degree of freedom he felt he had in his private practice, he simply summed with: "Let's just say that *everything* is possible" (interview, Kraków, 2002).

The use of conscientious refusals to deny lawful abortions in public hospitals while performing services clandestinely and privately has several implications: doctors can earn far more in their private clinics, and they shield themselves from potential, or perceived, harassment by the church, leaving the women patients to endure the secrecy and stigma of a clandestine procedure for a large fee.

Despite the obvious existence of the underground since the early 1990s, authorities rarely policed clinics and almost never followed the trails of newspaper advertisements in the initial years following the ban. The approach to mainly ignore the underground in those years was consistent with the public denial of the underground's existence by the Catholic Church and the state, which claimed that the ban on abortion "works"— namely that the ban is in fact preventing abortions altogether and therefore constitutes a good policy. Owing to the efforts of the advocacy community to bring international attention to the widespread existence of illegal services, the church and the state eventually acknowledged the existence of the underground. But with it came policing and prosecutions of doctors. According to estimates reported in the Polish media, approximately three hundred cases of prosecution for illegal abortion are launched annually, typically as a result of a third party complaint, most commonly waged by a former boyfriend or fiancé of the woman who obtained an abortion (Bunda and Perzanowski 2010, 2–3). Normally, neither doctors nor patients expose any information. Whereas a woman who seeks or undergoes an illegal abortion cannot be prosecuted, a doctor who performs an illegal procedure or anyone who helps her in obtaining one can be punished with up to three years in prison (Zielińska, 2000).[15] For example, in 2009 the mother of a sixteen-year-old girl in Lublin received a sentence of two years in prison, suspended for three years, for accompanying her daughter to get an abortion (Bunda and Perzanowski 2010, 3). And in 2011, Dr. Jerzy Gawroński (who, unusually, allowed the media to reveal his name) received a sentence of one year in prison, suspended for two years, plus a fine of 4,000 złotych for performing two illegal abortions, while the assisting midwife was given seven months in prison, suspended for two years and a 1,000 złotych fine.[16] Many of these cases are dismissed because the evidence needed is difficult to produce since the police must catch the doctor "in the act" of performing the procedure to count as a crime. Therefore, occasionally a raid on a clinic takes place if the police are tipped off ahead of time, or the clinic might be placed under police surveillance, but solid evidence is elusive. Therefore, most cases that result in arrests and trials often end in suspended sentences, fines, and temporary suspension of medical licenses (Nowicka 2008a, 29–30). None of this appears to be deterring the doctors, perhaps because they support reproductive rights and/or perhaps because illegal abortion is a lucrative business.

Acting on their own by pursuing illegal abortion and helping each other, Polish women beat the system using strategies that not only defy the abortion law but also stand in defiance of the state and the church, both of which urgently call for more births. But to what extent can these individualized and privatized strategies be considered a form of protest or resistance vis-à-vis the reproductive governance launched by the religious and nationalist politics of the postsocialist era? Surely, obtaining an illegal abortion or using contraceptives against the church's prohibitions accomplishes precisely what the women want—shaping their lives according to their wishes, plans, and possibilities. But I would also suggest that this can be understood as a form of resistance—a form of civic and religious disobedience—however limited politically, and a stopgap strategy for dealing with larger social and collective concerns about reproductive rights and health as well as gender inequality that should be addressed with collective and policy solutions.

Anthropologists who have theorized resistance argue that intention is significant in interpreting whether a practice amounts to resistance, and that some scholars perhaps see resistance where none is present (Abu-Lughod 1990). Others, however, argue that resistance among the "weak" and marginalized populations can manifest in limited and subtle ways (Scott 1985), like attacks of spirit possessions among Malaysian women working in oppressive factories (Ong 1987), or the practices of gossip or pilfering to resist oppression (Scheper-Hughes 1992), or even black humor as a way to cope with injustice and trauma (Goldstein 2013). The spectrum of what constitutes resistance has been extended to include deliberate inaction as an informed, strategic response to power (Halliburton 2011). Contestation can therefore assume a number of forms that are subtle and perhaps based on pragmatic sense, but which undoubtedly form resistance-like practices and express dissent (Lock and Kaufert 1998, 13). The most overt forms of resistance in Poland have been waged by feminist reproductive rights groups, but these efforts have been without a major effect on legislation, mainly because of the widespread political passivity of the society at large, but also because there is a political climate hostile to any contestations of the church.[17] And significantly, the medical community and the public have generally abstained from joining the struggle.

The "Tension Diffuser"

The Polish abortion law, despite its obvious detachment from reality or perhaps because of it, acts as a kind of "tension diffuser" by allowing a degree of political passivity on almost all sides. The fact that some doctors invoke "conscientious objection" as professional protection against scrutiny in public work settings reflects the avoidance of engagement with abortion politics.[18] Despite the daring provision of clandestine care under legal circumstances that threaten them with imprisonment, Polish doctors chose political nonengagement regarding abortion for several reasons. The postsocialist cuts in health care froze doctors' wage increases, which were already relatively low during the state socialist era; thus, physicians vigorously promote private practice as a way to boost dismal salaries (Tymowska 2001). One clandestine abortion in large cities like Kraków and Warsaw can equal more than a physician's monthly wage in a public health facility. The anthropologist Agata Chełstowska argues (2011, 98) that Polish doctors are "turning sin into gold" and estimates that illegal abortions in Poland generate around $95 million annually for doctors, tax and record free.[19] Numerous women interviewed in my research pointed out (from both experience and hearsay) that doctors who perform illegal abortions have tiled floors, rather than linoleum, in their clinics, and drive "Western" cars, which are understood as typical signs of personal wealth.

The lucrative nature of clandestine abortion and the notable lack of an alliance between providers and advocacy organizations creates a challenging political climate in which to advocate for reproductive rights. When the newly powerful church launched its antiabortion rhetoric in the early 1990s and the feminist groups opposed the church's discourse, doctors stayed conspicuously out of the struggle. Physicians' organizations were banned under communism across the Soviet region, so the historical lack of unity in medicine may contribute to doctors' political passivity at the critical time of political transition. This disparity between the active national and international advocacy of reproductive rights NGOs and the political nonengagement of the local medical community means that political campaigns to decriminalize abortion in Poland have had to turn to the supranational governance of the European Union. The EU provides some legal venues in which to advocate for legal changes, in particular the European Court of Human Rights, as was the case with Alicja Tysiąc and Agata. But these verdicts have had a minimal impact on the status quo in Poland since according to its Accession Treaty, Poland is entitled to sovereign decisions regarding issues of "morality." Likewise, the lack of support for abortion rights and the efforts of the Catholic right to discredit feminist advocacy by linking reproductive rights to communism make an association with advocacy organizations unattractive to many physicians.

The reproductive rights NGO, the Federation for Women and Family Planning, conducted a study in 1999 with Warsaw-based obstetricians and gynecologists and found that both conservative and liberal doctors see the current abortion law and the clandestine provision of services as a "tension diffuser": the ban is needed for the Catholic right's ideological expression, and the underground functions to provide services (Nowicka and Zielińska 2000). Since the medical community as a whole has been reluctant to advocate for liberalization of the law, advocacy is left entirely to local and international NGOs. As long as the two sides leave each other alone, the situation generates little debate among doctors. Instead, gynecologists focus on private practice and rarely speak publicly against the law, thereby not exposing themselves to attacks from the conservative right or their local parish.

Meanwhile, the Polish state has demonstrated a very low interest in investigating illegal abortions and their health consequences, and gathers no data regarding the prevalence or the complications resulting from these procedures. Thus, health consequences are also unclear, and the rates of maternal mortality specifically due to abortions performed illegally are not known. (The ratio of maternal mortality actually declined since the 1993 abortion ban from 17 in 1990 to 5 in 2010 [WHO 2012b, 43]). Even so, it is unknown whether or not the Polish maternal mortality ratio includes deaths due to illegal abortions. Lack of such data also acts as a kind of "tension diffuser": this status quo benefits the Catholic Church, and also reduces the ability of reproductive rights groups to advocate for legalization of abortion for safety, in particular since maternal mortality due to unsafe abortion has long been a powerful statistic in favor of political reforms in other geopolitical settings (Haddad and Nour 2009; Hodorogea and Comendant 2010).

As for ordinary women, their responses to the continued status quo have been to develop their own *unofficial biopolitics*—distinctly different from what the church prescribes—by coping with the risks of unintended pregnancy, on the one hand, and by rejecting the church's strictures, on the other hand. Their own biopolitics include circumventing the legislation by pursuing illegal abortions, seeking guidance and sharing knowledge about ways of preventing pregnancy on the Internet, and by searching for doctors willing to provide desired services. These are what the anthropologist Rivkin-Fish (2005) identified as individualized and privatized strategies for dealing with social and collective concerns about reproductive rights and health as well as gender equality—issues that ought to be addressed with collective and policy solutions. Using these strategies women not only defy the abortion law, but also stand in defiance of the state and the church, both of which urgently call for greater fertility, a topic I turn to next.

6 ⫼ The "Dying Nation" and the Postsocialist Logics of Declining Motherhood

POLISH WOMEN NOT ONLY manage to find ways to circumvent laws that limit their family planning options but control their fertility in a remarkably effective way. Almost simultaneously with the reproductive rights restrictions that took effect in the early 1990s, women in Poland began to limit their childbearing to a single child or occasionally two, on average. This continued "refusal" to bear children has been the source of intense anxiety for the state and the church (especially the nationalistic elements) and enthusiastically highlighted in the media.

In November 2002, when Poland hit the bottom of its fertility drop with 1.22 children per woman, the major political analysis weekly, *Polityka*, announced, "There are too few of us" (*"Mało nas"*), warning that the Polish family is dying out due to a shift of young women's priorities—a shift that goes "against the natural characteristics of the female psyche and degenerates the economic prospects of the nation."[1] That same year, the First Polish Demographic conference held in Warsaw for the purpose of assessing the results of the recent population data, dramatically declared: "This year we'll need more coffins than baby cribs," leading the press to this rhetorical question: "Shouldn't Polish women be thinking more about their first child, instead of their first job?" (Henzler 2002). As the demographic "crisis" continued in subsequent years with negligible signs of improvement, *Gazeta Wyborcza*, the largest Polish daily newspaper, suggested that we look to women and their inability or lack of desire to birth, and proposed that for

"Europe: looking to regain its lost sense" it must take on "the battle in the bedroom," i.e., "If women in the EU don't start birthing more, we won't be able to reverse the escalating trend of aging in Europe" (Pawlicki 2005). Common imagery in the media and political discourses depicts Poland as "depopulated"—indeed, the nation has experienced negative population growth for the twenty years since state socialism collapsed. For a nation with 86.7 percent affiliation with Roman Catholicism and restricted family planning options, including a ban on abortion, a major fertility decline might seem surprising.

Fertility decline is not new. In the preceding few decades a decline had been observed in nearly all locations around the world, with the exception of sub-Saharan Africa. However, the situation in Eastern Europe is particularly dramatic because fertility essentially plummeted across this region at a rapid rate only after the fall of the Soviet Union. During the years preceding the present slump, Poland's total fertility rate (TFR) had been at or above replacement since World War II. During the latter thirty years of state socialism TFR fell gradually from 2.98 in 1960 to 2.1 (replacement level) in 1989. However, after the regime's collapse in 1989, Poland's TFR plummeted to 1.22 by 2002 (*Abridged Statistical Yearbook* 2008, 124). Since then it has increased only marginally to 1.3 in 2012, and dropped again in 2013 to 1.26 (*Abridged Statistical Yearbook* 2014, 127). In the EU, Poland has the third-lowest TFR, surpassed only by Romania and Hungary, both of which dip below 1.3.[2] In urban areas the TFR is only 1.21, whereas in rural Poland it is a bit higher at 1.43, commonly explained by stronger Catholic traditions; however, the higher births in rural regions can also be due to lesser access to illegal abortion (women would have to travel to cities) and fewer options to choose doctors who are not conscientious objectors to family planning. In addition to the pill, IUDs, condoms, and illegal abortion, fertility is also controlled in Poland by the withdrawal method, which has been popular in Europe for well over a century (Izdebski 2006; Schneider and Schneider 1996). Poland's population decline is compounded by significant emigration, especially to Ireland and the UK, after Poland's entry into the EU in 2004.

Demographers, having for some decades studied declining fertility around the world, have taken a keen interest in the Eastern European phenomenon after the fall of the Soviet Union. Scholars rapidly began to describe demographic trends in Poland that have been seen elsewhere:

specifically, women have been postponing having their first child from age twenty-three in 1989 to age twenty-seven in 2010;[3] the number of marriages has systematically dropped since 1989; the number of children born outside of marriage has risen; divorces have increased in frequency; and cohabiting relationships without marriage have also increased (Caldwell and Schindlmayr 2003; Dey 2006; Frątczak 2004; Sobotka 2004).

In addition to these demographic trends, Poland also reflects the recent demographic observation that unemployed or underemployed women tend to curb their fertility. In the past the reverse was true: high female unemployment and employment structures that deterred women from working had been associated with higher fertility. However, recent cross-national findings show a reversal of this pattern: a postsocialist labor market in Eastern Europe that is unfriendly to female labor participation is now associated with lower fertility (Castles 2003). To explain this phenomenon, some scholars have proposed the "tempo effect," arguing optimistically that the very low fertility in Eastern Europe is driven by the postponement of childbearing, and that the system will eventually "catch up" (since it is assumed that women cannot postpone having children indefinitely due to age-related biological barriers), following which fertility will at least partially recover, making the current situation just a temporary adjustment to new economic circumstances (Bongaarts 2002; Caldwell and Schindlmayr 2003; Sobotka 2004).

As fertility in Eastern Europe, including Poland, showed no signs of recovery during the last twenty years, demographers began to look to social and cultural reasons, not only macro-economic ones. A convincing argument put forth by Reher (2007) and McDonald (2006) presents an opposing view to the "tempo effect." They assert that while the postponement of childbearing is an important factor in European fertility decline, "extremely low fertility has been around for too long for it to portend anything other than major long-term social change" (Reher 2007, 194). Although a degree of recovery (perhaps reflecting a tempo effect or improved social policies) did materialize in the Nordic nations, states in Southern and Eastern Europe show no signs of improvement and in some locations fertility has continued to fall. Indeed, "waiting for tempo is beginning to look like waiting for Godot" (McDonald 2006, 487).

Significantly, new demographic theories propose that *gender inequities* experienced by women are decisive in discouraging motherhood because the burden of care work combined with desired, or necessary, employment proves too overwhelming for many women to manage (McDonald 2000). Yet the persistent myth of a temporary phenomenon and the concomitant disregard for the gender inequities theory in fertility decline have prevented many European states from taking relevant policy action to make motherhood more feasible through subsidies for child care, paid parental leave, and so on. Poland is a stark example of this problem. The Polish state responded in 1999 with the Profamily Program, based on the Vatican's Family Rights Charter (Profamily Politics of the State Program 1999). The program consists mainly of political rhetoric that calls on women to have more children and stresses the importance of the nuclear family, but it is void of any meaningful policies to help women combine work and motherhood (as has been done with success in Scandinavia and France). The program succeeded in making expressions such as "demographic low" (*niż demograficzny*), pronatalist politics (*polityka pronatalistyczna*), and profamily politics (*polityka prorodzinna*) a quotidian part of the Polish vernacular. But the program has utterly failed in its mission as birthrates have fallen even further since the launch of the program in 1999.[4]

Without work-family reconciliation policies on the horizon, the experience of very low fertility in Poland has now become a structural problem with virtually certain long-term consequences. Seriously altered age structures and a falling number of women of reproductive age will make the future labor market dependent on the postponement of retirement by the older generation. The complexities of the Eastern European demographic situation and the culturally specific differences between the nations in this region call for caution in applying unidirectional demographic transition theories that imply a predictable evolutionary process of social or economic change (Bernardi 2007; Dey 2006; McDonald 2000; Rivkin-Fish 2003). In fact, the concept of "demographic transition," which focuses on the macro-economic picture, is inadequate as an explanation for why Polish women have postponed and significantly limited childbearing for well over two decades. Indeed, there is nothing transitional about this situation. Similarly to abortion politics, understanding Poland's drop in fertility requires attention to the institutional context—in particular the role of the Catholic Church, the conservative state administrations, and the nationalist discourses—within which women negotiate their new circumstances, and it is necessary to explore women's experiences and perspectives on motherhood before the observed macro population trends can be theorized and understood.

In theorizing fertility decline and how states try to "engineer" reproductive outcomes, Foucault's ideas once again prove useful to think with. His historical analysis traces states' management of individuals to beginning in the eighteenth century, through a variety of surveilling mechanisms, in particular a systematic census-like accounting of behaviors. In the context of population decline, demographic knowledge and pronatalist policies constitute the expression of what Foucault refers to as biopower—a set of state techniques that "brought life and its mechanisms into the realm of explicit calculations and made knowledge-power an agent of transformation of human life" (Foucault 1980, 143). He observes a consolidation of state power via new administrative attention to the health of populations, but reconfigured in the service of the state. In Poland, the notion of population health is recast as numerical population growth, and women are simultaneously recast as "biological citizens" expected to live responsibly and rationally in order to maximize their contribution to the growth of the population (Rose and Novas 2005). But whereas Foucauldian biopolitics is a secular rationality promoted in the name of optimizing the well-being of the citizen and the society, the nature of Polish biopolitics lies in its religious and moral governance promoted in the name of Catholic-nationalist state-building. The statistical surveillance of women's reproductive behaviors that generate annual total fertility rates and birthrates and the accompanying demographic knowledge serve at the state's disposal to substantiate the implementation of state policies aiming to reverse negative population trends. In recent years, the Polish Central Statistical Office has been generating briefings prepared specifically for press conferences at the start of the new year in January that report estimates of the previous year's reproductive performance of Poles. The opening statement of the 2013 press release announced in bold yet another year of "negative population growth," and a loss of 37,000 people as compared to 2012.[5] Biopower is simultaneously the production of knowledge or "truth discourses" about, in this case, reproductive behaviors, and the response to these changes with particular policies aiming to "improve" the life or health of the population (Rabinow and Rose 2006, 197).

In the Polish case, the Catholic-nationalist rhetoric has long been that childbearing is a reflection of patriotism. Emblematic of this is the argument in "Truth, Children, and Money," an article in the Catholic publication

Fronda that urges universal "rational thinking" (*racjonalności świata*) that rejects "moral relativism" and dictates higher birthrates to build "a strong state and a strong nation" (Piłka 2013, 6, 1). From this imperative to reproduce the nation came restrictions on access to family planning and sex education that are being justified by the "demographic crisis."

Given the aggressive political and media rhetoric in Poland warning about a demographic crisis and women's presumably confused priorities, in this final chapter I consider several questions: How do Polish women explain their reproductive decisions in light of the state and church's critique of their reproductive decision making? What concerns do they consider central to their reproductive strategies? If the majority is Catholic, how can women justify going against the Catholic principles that disallow deliberate fertility control?

The Makings of a Demographic Crisis

Polish women's ability to reconcile work and family looked very different during the state socialist period and after its collapse. Before 1989, the state implemented a number of new policies that expanded access to education, health care, and employment, especially for women, thereby creating substantial improvements in the living standards of the population. As the anthropologist Katherine Verdery describes it (1996, 24), the socialist state established itself as the "benevolent father" providing for the basic welfare of all. Women, however, were the major beneficiaries. Social services grew; new benefits relieved women of many of the burdens of caretaking; and women were encouraged to enter paid employment. The state provided many households with basic appliances and opened a network of public child care centers—from infant care facilities to library-like places for teens. Welfare benefits were expanded to include cash provisions to supplement families' and single mothers' wages, purchase school books and supplies, and support the care of disabled children. Food was relatively inexpensive, and health care was state-subsidized, though not always adequate. As a result of these policies, Polish women's full-time employment rose to 78 percent during state socialism (Fodor et al. 2002, 371–72).

Women, not unlike other workers, experienced unprecedented job security in the new structure. As a capital-poor system, state socialism relied heavily on labor and created an inflexible employment structure that provided a great deal of work security with virtually no threat of unemployment. This was especially significant for women who were now able to easily enter the job market, interrupt their work for childbearing, and return to the safety of their jobs with minimal or no loss of wages. Simultaneously, and consistent with the socialist gender equity rhetoric, the state greatly expanded women's access to education—during the socialist period women exceeded men at every educational level, except vocational training.[6]

The expansion of reproductive rights that gave women greater freedom in family planning decisions during state socialism was also highly significant for women's ability to balance work and family. Of course, the Catholic Church strongly opposed such legislation, but its power to influence policy was tenuous at best, given the strongly secular nature of the state socialist regime. This separation of church and state indeed benefited women. One of the important feminist critiques of state socialism, however, is that despite the progressive policies that helped women in education and employment, the state failed to reduce gender inequalities within the family—women were still expected to manage the household and care for children, husbands, and elderly or sick relatives—as well as in the workplace where the gender wage gap persisted. Yet gender relations were certainly reconfigured as women pursued careers, financial independence, and greater reproductive and sexual autonomy.

The Neoliberal Turn

In the last two and a half decades since the fall of state socialism, Eastern European nations underwent profound economic transformations, shifting from the security provided by generous welfare states with guaranteed education and employment to the instability of free market economies marked by large-scale deregulation. The policies that had been critical in helping women reconcile work and family began to be rapidly dismantled. The situation in Poland was particularly ironic since the fall of the regime resulted from a decade of mounting opposition waged by the Solidarity labor union, coupled with a failing economy. As the upper echelons of the labor union took power after 1989 for the ensuing five years, headed by Lech Wałęsa, the new government wholeheartedly embraced neoliberal economic principles that give market forces primacy in solving both economic and social problems to the detriment of workers and organized labor. The political scientist David Ost (2005) describes this betrayal of the working class as the "defeat of Solidarity" by its own embrace of the global capitalist agenda.[7] President Wałęsa, himself a former electrician in the Gdańsk shipyard (which, as such, is now mostly shuttered thanks to neoliberal policies), rapidly proceeded with antiworker policy changes that targeted women especially, including major cuts in maternity leave, subsidies for child care, and other critical social services.[8]

Comparative studies of welfare provisions in Eastern European nations show that Poland has had one of the harshest reductions in family and maternity benefits (Fodor at al. 2002, 477–83). The postsocialist state closed or privatized most of the child care facilities and reduced family cash benefits. The state rhetoric now emphasized the primacy of motherhood and naturalized gender roles in which women stay at home to take care of their children; therefore, they should not need child care facilities or benefits. Such rights were routinely portrayed as discouraging motherhood, harming the well-being of the family, and contrary to "normal" biologically destined gender roles (Siemińska 1994). Wałęsa also launched privatization of health care. Many health care subsidies were eliminated; for example, subsidies of medicines dwindled from 100 percent before 1989 to 35 percent in 2004, the lowest in the European Union, and many basic services were removed from universal coverage (*Economist* 2004). According to the 2006 World Health Report, Polish government expenditure on health care was 9.8 percent of total government expenditure, the second lowest in the EU after Latvia (WHO 2006). In terms of perinatal health care, the former minister of health, Ewa Kopacz, approved the continued exclusion from state coverage of anesthesia during childbirth. Epidurals are thus placed alongside aromatherapy as extras during deliveries. In fact, some hospitals decline to provide epidurals altogether, claiming that they lack full-time anesthesiologists, but media reports that it is more likely a matter of savings, as the national insurance pays hospitals the same flat fee for a delivery, whether with or without anesthesia (Klinger 2013).

Wanda Nowicka and the Federation for Women and Family Planning argued in an open letter, to no avail, that this excludes many women from otherwise available advances in health care and constitutes a violation of patient's rights and human rights (Nowicka 2010). In 2012, the new minister of health, Bartosz Arłukowicz, began discussions to subsidize anesthesia during childbirth, but as of 2015 nothing had come of the idea; therefore, women who give birth in Poland continue to have to pay out of pocket for care that is considered basic in other European nations (Mishtal 2010). In general, women's health as compared to men's in Poland has been declining as a result of the transformation to the market economy (Niemiec 1997; Wróblewska 2002; Szaflarski 2001).

In the area of employment, job security was no longer guaranteed, unemployment soared, especially among women, and preferential hiring practices began to favor applicants with inside connections. Job opportunities became elusive and required greater dedication of time, making planning one's future more difficult. According to the World Bank's Development Research Group's assessment of Eastern Europe, the transition from state socialism to market economy has been accompanied by one of the largest and fastest increases in inequality on record (Milanovic 1999). Indeed, economic changes are driving a new socioeconomic class stratification in Poland—the Polish Gini coefficient (a measure of the inequality of wealth distribution; a value of 1 indicates perfect inequality, while a value of 0 indicates perfect equality) went from 0.26 in the 1980s to 0.33 in 2011, and is the second highest after Russia in the post-Soviet region.[9] Polish women are bearing the brunt of this stratification as many fall below the poverty line, and women constitute the majority of the unemployed due to acute gendered discrimination in the workplace (Domanski 2002; Zajicek and Calasanti 1995). In rural areas women are turning to kin networks for resources and support, and to traditional strategies of home production of clothing and food (Pine 2002). Polish feminist groups have been highlighting the detrimental effects of neoliberal economics but with little effect. It is in response to this historical, politico-economic, and ideological shift observed and experienced in the political, legislative, and public realm that Polish women began to postpone motherhood.

The Postsocialist Logics of Declining Motherhood

"So I'm happy we're having a demographic crisis; it's what the government deserves!" exclaimed Alina, a forty-year-old information technician who at the time of this research in 2007 had an eighteen-year-old son. She explained that the core of the issue lies in the dwindling social support that she and her mother had been able to enjoy before 1989. She went on: "I'm so mad at the government. I think it's great that we're having a demographic crisis because the state doesn't give us any support—no support for women who are pregnant or women with kids. I had my son just before 1989 and it was no problem to have kids back then, even though I was a single mother" (interview with Alina, Gdańsk, 2007). Sentiments like these, expressing both anger squarely directed at the postsocialist policies and almost nostalgia for the communist era when women were more easily able to reconcile work and family, dominated many of the conversations with women during this fieldwork.

Confirming what has been shown in the anthropological scholarship on Eastern Europe, the women I interviewed who grew up during state socialism perceived motherhood and work as simultaneous endeavors, an aspiration that is proving far more difficult to attain after the fall of the regime (Dölling et al. 2000; Erikson 2005; Stoilkova 2005). Combining work and family is implied in the pragmatic sense of "self-realization" (*samo-realizacja*) that is part of Polish women's vernacular, at least among the middle classes, and the imagined sequence of life events reflects this thinking, as Mariola, a twenty-one-year-old student at the Jagiellonian University in Kraków, explained:

> Really, women don't think anymore that they should give birth *first*, and then, later, they'll get everything else figured out. Now we think, "Finish the degree, find some kind of work, in the meantime it might be good to find a husband," and then at that point, after some time, think of having a child. Among my friends the dominant opinion is that a child is a luxury. If the material situation is normalized enough, then that couple, or that woman, can decide to have a child. Still, the majority of women want at least that *one* child. (Interview with Mariola, Gdańsk, 2007)

Yet postponement of pregnancy in favor of securing jobs has been depicted by the Catholic Church and the right-leaning media as a rejection of motherhood. Nearly all of the women in my research, regardless of education or employment, explained that far from rejecting motherhood, they desire to have at least one but preferably two children, in an ideal situation. A common expression heard in the interviews was "the first child is for oneself, the second child is for the first," which was explained to mean that parents need a child to take care of them in their old age, while the second child is important to prevent the first one from becoming selfish or spoiled. In reality, however, women felt that a second child is rapidly becoming an economic luxury from several perspectives, in particular because of the lack of child care, which makes it difficult for them to reconcile work and family. The state eliminated subsidized child care, and babysitters are still rarely used since the idea is quite new, the service is very expensive, and "you simply can't trust strangers with your kids," as one woman summed up.

For many the only way to hold down a job is to get help from one's *Babcia*—literally, a grandmother—referring to the tradition of having a mother or mother-in-law who is available and willing to provide child care for the grandchild. However, with the increased geographic mobility in Poland after 1989, and the greater push to look for jobs in other cities, fewer relatives are on hand to provide child care. Women who had babcias considered themselves lucky. The issue of child care was closely intertwined with the way that employers viewed women job applicants. The experiences and perspectives of Celina and Ewa that follow are emblematic of those of nearly all other women in my study, whether these experiences were their own or the experiences of their relatives, friends, or coworkers. When I interviewed Celina, a thirty-four-year-old border customs officer without children, she expressed some sense of job security in her current position because she works for the government but related the following experiences from recent years:

> Of course, I went through my share of problems before I got this position; I had three unpleasant situations. When I was looking for a job one of the employers asked me if I'm planning to get pregnant, and if so, whether I had a babcia at home on hand to do my child care; I said I didn't. Another employer told me that he requires a current pregnancy test as a condition for the employment. I totally disagreed with this practice and just left. And another employer told me he'd give me the position if I declared I wouldn't get pregnant for two to three years. I left there too. The main reason [that I don't have kids]: no child care! I have no kids, but ideally I would like two. I've been married for nine years. (Interview with Celina, Gdańsk, 2007)

Since Celina has no children but has been in a long-term relationship, I was interested in her thoughts about the government's calls for women to have more children and whether this rhetoric mattered to her. When asked, Are you concerned about the demographic crisis we are hearing about or not? She immediately replied:

Absolutely not. I'm very opposed to the current government, especially to its right-wing policies. My views are really opposite; so naturally the government has no influence on my thinking or my life. If a new leftist government called for higher fertility *and* provided protection for women who are interested in having kids, then I might consider [having a child]. My mother is a good example of what happened here: she was a single mother with two kids ages nineteen and seven right during the '89 transition and she lost her job as soon as Solidarity came to power. They fired a single mother! What we need is legal protection for single mothers and women against being fired. It was also easier in the old system to get a place for your child in the infant care center or in a preschool. Now there's no space, and you have to pay. (Interview with Celina, Gdańsk, 2007)

Ewa, who is a thirty-three-year-old physician in general practice with two children and has been working for a number of years in a stable position at a major health clinic, was one of a few women I interviewed who were able to afford a babysitter: "I would like a third child, but we would need child care, first and foremost, and second, we'd need a larger apartment. We badly need a babcia! We had a couple of nannies, babysitters, but that didn't go well—one of them burned my child with coffee! My husband helped with the child care a little bit too. But all in all, it's very draining financially to pay for child care" (interview with Ewa, Gdańsk, 2007). When our discussion turned to the state's alarmist calls to women to have more children and its ubiquitous rhetoric of profamily politics, I asked Ewa whether the state's concern about the demographic situation in Poland mattered to her. She replied: "I can't say that the state matters for me that way. That's because the state first and foremost needs to change its politics toward women, to offer child care and protection at work for women. Currently, the state's political position is *anti*family, not profamily." Despite her relatively comfortable economic position, Ewa echoed many other women's understanding of the problem, arguing that what is needed are "major changes in policies that would guarantee greater social services, child care, health care, and the protection of women in the workplace."

Deeper conversations about work experiences revealed that widespread fear of discrimination by employers against pregnant women, new mothers, and women with small children drives women's decisions to postpone or refuse having a child (Mishtal 2009a). The majority of women in my research either directly experienced gendered discrimination in employment or knew of women who had. These narratives recounted problematic employer practices that had an adverse influence on women's fertility decisions, such as firing women who returned to work following maternity leave or child-rearing leave, and encouraging or requiring women to sign a contract pledging not to get pregnant for two to three years as a contingency for their hire. Women also complained about illegal practices such as asking female job applicants if they have small children and hiring permanent employees to replace women on maternity leave. Hanna, a thirty-four-year-old sales clerk in a long-term relationship and with one child but with a desire to have two related the following experience with her employer, which echoes the concerns of other women, who like Hanna are likely going to forgo the second pregnancy in favor of employment:

> We don't want any more kids under the current circumstances. One is enough. Thankfully, I was able to return to my job after our son was born but I had only three months off. I made an agreement with my boss that I would take only three months. It was also better for me since I needed the money; I couldn't really afford to go on the child-rearing leave. But besides, I had a babcia at home to do the child care, so I was able to work again. I was certainly concerned about my work because some of my friends were fired once they became pregnant, so it was on my mind. About a year ago my boss fired an acquaintance of mine when she got pregnant. After a few months I decided to ask him very casually about that. He said he had the *right* to fire her. I didn't want to pursue it any further so I dropped it. (Interview with Hanna, Gdańsk, 2007)

In reality it is against Polish labor law to fire a pregnant employee. Hanna told me she was aware that the boss had no right but was afraid to challenge him or appear confrontational, in case she "catches his eye in a negative way" (*podpadnie*). However, many employees are often unfamiliar with their rights, and likewise, bosses are unfamiliar or unwilling to follow the law. Katarzyna Kurkiewicz, a labor lawyer who specializes in gender discrimination and works closely with a feminist organization, the Network of East-West Women in Gdańsk, corroborated the experiences of the women in this research, saying that "these practices are increasingly common in Poland." Kurkiewicz explained that even though it is unlawful for the employers to ask women about their pregnancy status, whether they have children, or to request that they sign an agreement pledging not to get pregnant for a period of time, these practices have become customary, leaving women with little choice but to answer the questions or sign the agreements. The employer cannot fire a woman who states that she is pregnant; hence harassment techniques are used to drive women out "voluntarily" (interview with Kurkiewicz, Gdańsk, 2007). Legal recourse for victims has been practically nonexistent due to the extraordinary delays and expenses that accompany legal procedures in Poland.

Many women told me that employers discriminated against applicants with small children, using the interview process to identify women who might miss work because of child care. Yet after experiencing work discrimination and limited maternity leave with the first child, women became discouraged about having another. As Zofia, a twenty-seven-year-old sales clerk, who was in the eighth month of her first pregnancy at the time of the interview and in a long-term relationship explained:

> We are in a bad financial situation, so after this pregnancy we'll just have to wait and see. I would really like two kids because a single child *needs* a sibling, otherwise it'll turn out selfish. . . . I'm not sure if I'll even have my job when I go back, because when I got pregnant my boss started to make things difficult for me, all of a sudden he made everything an uphill battle for me—every time I needed to go to the doctor he would make a fuss or any other requests he always made it look like I'm asking for too much; he wanted me out. It just wasn't convenient for him to have any of the employees pregnant. My doctor took me off work when I was in my fourth month because it was time for me to get more rest. . . . I'm still theoretically employed, but I have a feeling that my job will be gone by the time I return. . . . I've seen it in my own job: my boss never hires women with small children. He always says it's better if the kids are preschool age, like at least six or so. (Interview with Zofia, Gdańsk, 2007)

Rather than making "irrational"—as in misguided or unreasonable—decisions to delay motherhood and drive the aging Polish nation deeper into a demographic hole with confused priorities favoring careers over motherhood, the women I interviewed consistently expressed a strong sense of responsibility toward their families and their children. As Renata, a twenty-nine-year-old environmental engineer poignantly observed, "It's easy to birth ten kids, but then they are reared in poverty. Everyone is responsible for their own kids and their own decisions of what they can manage and what is in their best interest, the family and their children" (interview with Renata, Gdańsk, 2007).

Women also consistently would prefer more children if state policies supported their efforts to reconcile work and family. Paid employment was both necessary to support the family and assumed as a fulfilling part of a woman's life—a perspective that might have been somewhat more prevalent in my research because of the predominantly middle-class sample owing to the higher educational and social standing of many of the women I interviewed. Women wanted to "self-realize," to be treated fairly and decently, and feel materially stable to ensure their and their families' well-being. Women used these expressions to convey this point: "give women security that they can return to their jobs," "protection of women at work," "guarantees that women won't be fired," "stop the practice of firing women from their jobs," "legal protection of women in employment," and so on.

The current labor and health policies of the state continue to offer no tangible protection for women in the job market. The main "Profamily Program" response from the Polish state came in 2005 when it introduced a one-time baby bonus known as *becikowe*—literally, money for a baby blanket—of 1,000 złotych (approximately $325) per newborn. Becikowe was restricted in 2009 to only those women who began monitoring their pregnancy under the care of a gynecologist not later than the tenth week of the pregnancy, thereby drastically narrowing the eligibility for the benefit.[10] Women in my research deemed the payment "absurd" and "laughable" given the magnitude of financial and employment difficulties they deal with. Since the baby bonus has failed to change the demographic situation, the Polish minister of finance and other policymakers from time to time debate eliminating it altogether.[11]

Russia offers an interesting comparison here. In 2007, President Vladimir Putin offered a payment akin to becikowe to women who gave birth to or adopted a second child; however, his was much more substantial— the "maternity capital," as it is know, was equivalent to $10,000 and has since been increased. In the larger scheme of postsocialist hardships, even this is a meager amount, but what was significant about Putin's announcement, as Rivkin-Fish argues (2010, 702), was that he acknowledged "that bearing and raising children have negative consequences for woman's power; he further assumed state responsibility for addressing this inequality." Despite reinforcing the "woman-mother" discourse with assumptions that women care for children and men's role in care work is optional, Putin nevertheless offered a counterpoint to the dominant neoliberal "responsibility" model embraced in Russia (and elsewhere) by recognizing the role of the collective in women's and families well-being (Rivkin-Fish

2010, 716). In contrast, the Polish becikowe, which in 2015 remains at the original 2005 year level of 1,000 złotych, and has in fact been recently limited to low-income parents only, is essentially negligible in a financial sense and no more than a symbolic offer. Similarly, in 2014 the Polish state also extended maternity leave to a generous fifty-two weeks; however, only a small proportion of women who hold a "work contract" (*umowa na pracę*) are eligible. In reality, the vast majority is hired on what are known as "trash contracts" (*umowy śmieciowe*), which include schemes used by employers to hire women on a part-time, temporary, or "per assignment" basis in order to avoid payments to their social security pension fund.[12] Not surprisingly, Polish birthrates have remained consistently low, despite becikowe, and the new maternity leave is unlikely to motivate any changes in childbearing decisions.

In the end, women in my research were highly aware of the "demographic crisis" and many worried about the future of their retirement pensions and the aging of the society, but almost none of them felt compelled by the state's calls for increased fertility because of the ubiquitous perception that the state is not doing anything to facilitate motherhood and employment, and the widespread awareness that the government had dismantled the many social service programs that had been in place under state socialism.

But perhaps even more significantly, women are discouraged by their experiences of postsocialist gender inequalities.[13] Demographic debates in Poland clearly reflect the naturalized and instrumental gendered logic of "woman-mother" in assumptions that women will leave employment to provide care work, and that the state can try to dictate and shape birthrates (Rivkin-Fish 2010, 717). Although the notion of state support of parenthood with specific policies resonates with women who are struggling economically after the massive cutbacks in public services since the fall of state socialism, the obvious lack of attention to gender equality has a significant and discouraging effect on women's desire to have children. Rather than promoting gender equality through, for example, parental leave policies that require the fathers to take time off work (as is the case in some Scandinavian nations with "use it or lose it" leave earmarked for fathers), and specific and enforceable employment laws that protect women in the labor market, the Polish state mainly keeps silent about the negative social and economic consequences of childbearing for women.

Between a Rock and a Hard Place

To balance personal desires, cultural expectations, and economic constraints, women in Poland walk a fine line between the expectation and desire to have one child and the increasing difficulty to have another—a bind that is underpinning the persistent fertility rate of 1.3 children per woman. The powerful cultural and Catholic stigma against voluntary childlessness makes childbearing less a free choice than a highly constrained one; still, Polish demographers are observing a slow increase in voluntary childlessness, though no data are yet available on the extent of this phenomenon (Frątczak 2004). But what is most striking in Poland, given its enduring demographic crisis, is the existence of an equally powerful stigma against "multi-child families," which are commonly referred to in the Polish vernacular as *patologia socjalna*—literally a "social pathology," a behavior outside the norm. The expression is used rather liberally and unselfconsciously in the political discourse, the media, and the professional world of social work (where much of my early research in Poland took place). It commonly conjures up "reckless" reproduction in the context of a rural and old-fashioned lifestyle, poverty, and perhaps alcoholism and domestic violence. How many children are deemed too many and therefore pathological? This can vary depending on the context.

The lower-income Polish and immigrant women, especially the Roma, are typically the target of the pathology label, but the phenomenon is not unique to Poland.[14] According to the anthropologist Jane Schneider and the sociologist Peter Schneider (1996, 8–13), who studied population decline in Europe, Italy in particular, the politics of reproductive stigma originated in the late twentieth century. As the gap between the number of children for the well-off and the poor families widened after World War II, the practice of limiting births began to be considered normative for the Western middle classes, thus distinguishing so-called respectable and disreputable families based on their childbearing patterns. Soon social pressures emerged to avoid the reproductive stigma of having "too many" children. My participant observation work at the welfare offices of the City Center for Social Assistance (Miejski Ośrodek Pomocy Społecznej, MOPS) in Kraków revealed that multichild low-income families were often judged as exercising poor sexual control and showing lack of responsibility and sensibility. Even in the eyes of some of the most dedicated social workers who tried to blame the Catholic Church for blocking access to sex education and therefore setting off "reckless" reproduction, high fertility among the poor was still seen as draining limited welfare resources. The church opposes the general negative stereotype of a multi-child family as irresponsible, poor, and uneducated.[15] Schneider and Schneider (1996, 12) have shown that reproductive stigma vis-à-vis the poor and the immigrants became normative when Europe began its demographic transition. As a result, they argued, the "historical experience of limiting family size through sexual discipline—and in a context of social hierarchy—left behind a cultural residue that makes it easy to attribute any number of social ills such as backwardness, underdevelopment, and poverty to reproductive practices that elude consciousness or 'rational control'" (Schneider and Schneider 1996, 13).

But in the context of postsocialist Poland, the stigma of having "too many" children appears to stretch across classes: although the "pathology" label is liberally applied to the poor, the label of "Matka Polka"—literally, the Polish Mother—is used for middle-class women. Both are stigmatizing and socially punishing in their implication that the woman has too many children, thus a poor sense of judgment. Matka Polka is also used as a nationalist symbol of a self-sacrificing mother and a protector of the Polish nation derived from the Catholic cult of Mary. The story of Krystyna, a social worker at a welfare office in Kraków, when she decided to have a second child is emblematic of this discourse. Krystyna and her husband, also a social worker, struggled financially on their state salaries but decided nonetheless that it was psychologically beneficial for their first child to have a sibling. Krystyna explained that when she was pregnant for the first time, her coworkers were approving and supportive, but when she got pregnant the second time, she became the target of jokes. Her supervisor (herself married with one child) gave her the nickname "Matka Polka." In the postsocialist era of the desirability of "modern" lifestyles Matka Polka is perceived in the popular discourse as an antiquated ideal of a religious woman. Krystyna recounted the story to me several years later in 2002 with a great deal of resentment and said that she tried not to get angry but nevertheless felt compelled to justify her decision to her boss by saying that "a child must have a sibling for proper socialization." Krystyna's reasoning was promptly mocked by the supervisor who dismissed it as simply "a typical way of thinking for a Matka Polka."

It became clear in the course of my research that some women who work in the middle and upper socioeconomic class settings have experienced both types of pressures from their coworkers: to have a child, but to not have more than one child. Thus, having only one child appears to be not only a necessity for many women, but also a middle-class marker and a "rationality" that separates the middle classes from the lower socioeconomic stratum, and alleviates some of the anxieties produced by the profound politico-economic instabilities that threaten many women's and couples' class standing. The association between a modernizing postsocialist lifestyle and low fertility is increasingly more common in the popular discourse and in the media, despite the demographic alarm. In the case of Krystyna and her middle-class family, the stigma lay in Krystyna's embrace of an "old-fashioned" religious female identity, namely that of a sacrificing Polish mother. She was the only one in a department of six women with more than a single child.

"The Feminine Genius"

In the context of Poland, and other predominantly Catholic nations, the religious pressures for unimpeded or "natural" fertility can be substantial. This distinct religious rationality also underpins the policies and discourses around reproductive conduct. In response to declining fertility the Vatican has been outspoken, as have Catholic churches at local levels, with warnings of irrational "self-destructive tendencies" of individuals (read: women) who postpone marriage and childbearing for the benefit of careers. Other threats responsible for the "demographic winter" are homosexuality and "so-called new rights" for same-sex couples, single parenthood, cohabitation, "prodivorce mentality," "antibirth mentality," and religious relativism which makes people think that "one religion is as good as another" (Trujillo 2003a). In an effort to revitalize reproduction as constitutive of womanhood, Pope John Paul II in his 1995 "Letter to Women" introduced the expression "the feminine genius," arguing that women "fulfill their deepest vocation" through motherhood, hence their reproductive capacity is their "genius":

> It is thus my hope, dear sisters, that you will reflect carefully on what it means to speak of the *"genius of women,"* not only in order to be able to see in this phrase a specific part of God's plan which needs to be accepted and appreciated, but also in order to let this genius be more fully expressed in the life of society as a whole. . . . *The Church sees in Mary the highest expression of the 'feminine*

genius," and she finds in her a source of constant inspiration. Mary called herself the "handmaid of the Lord" (Lk 1:38). Through obedience to the Word of God she accepted her lofty yet not easy vocation as wife and mother in the family of Nazareth. (John Paul II 1995b)

The Polish church also condemned the "evils of liberal pedagogy" and feminism as ideologies that promote individualism and egotism, thereby driving women to reject the self-sacrificing Matka Polka identity in favor of careers (Bartnik 2010). Warnings about the spread of a "contraceptive mentality" are aired pervasively, as the Polish church owns a number of television and radio channels, especially the ultra-conservative Radio Maryja (Kubik 2001). The church forbids all forms of contraception, including condoms and the withdrawal method, allowing only for periodic abstinence (kalendarzyk, discussed earlier). Yet the demographic situation is making it obvious that Catholic women in nations like Poland, Italy, Ireland, and Spain manage and limit their fertility. How do Catholic women justify this practice?

It was clear throughout my research that using contraceptives to manage fertility was of high priority for Polish women, despite the ban on abortion and having to resort to clandestine procedures, loss of subsidies for contraceptives, and the religious condemnation of contraception (Mishtal and Dannefer 2010). In fact, an observation made during an interview in 2014 by one of Warsaw's veteran gynecologists, who has been in practice since the 1960s, that even women on a very low income "organize" enough money to get an abortion, if necessary, reflects the importance of controlling childbearing. The women did not characterize their decisions as driven by selfishness or irrationality; instead they offered pragmatic rationales, in particular their sense of responsibility to their families over any other considerations. The focus of women's narratives on "rationality" and "responsibility to their families" is symbolically highly significant, as women feel the need to defend their integrity as both mothers and rational actors in the face of religious and political discourses that denounce low fertility. However, in doing so, they are defining "rationality" narrowly and potentially further stigmatizing women with more than a single child, who then appear to lack this particular kind of "rationality," as was the perception of Krystyna.

Some women turned the tables on the church, as was the case with Ewa, who has two children and argued that it is the church that lacks rationality:

I attend mass every Sunday, and I completed a premarital course, which I thought was quite good. But the Catholic Church is *irresponsible* when it calls for higher fertility when there are no social provisions for women to be able to do this. Most of all, I feel responsible for my kids: I feel responsible for the well-being of the kids I have; therefore, my decisions regarding childbearing and the kinds of contraceptive methods I use are all my decisions, because I'm responsible for what happens to my children. Since the church takes no responsibility for child care or the upbringing of my kids, their opinions on this don't much matter to me. (Interview with Ewa, Gdańsk, 2007)

Urszula, a nineteen-year-old university student, who is moderately religious, justifies contraception in a way that exemplifies how women have reinterpreted what is and is not sin, and what aspects of life fall outside of the church's purview: "Most of all I want to be able to control my own fertility; therefore, I must protect myself against accidentally becoming pregnant. I'd never use the little calendar because it's simply not effective. The church says that everything is a sin but the calendar, but I disagree. To me it's not a sin to use whatever method gives the needed protection. That's most important. . . . If my financial situation is suffering, then that's all that matters, and the church has no impact in such situations; these are unrelated topics" (interview with Urszula, Gdańsk, 2007). Some women confessed to priests the use of contraceptives in order to symbolically cleanse, although they continued to use them, as Ela, a thirty-one-year-old sales clerk with one child, explains: "Right now I'm not interested in having more kids, so I definitely plan to use condoms. The calendar just doesn't work. I think it's a lesser evil to use contraceptives than to abandon kids. It's not a sin to use condoms, but I feel compelled to confess them anyway. When I confess I get mixed reactions from the priests—some get angry, some are more tolerant—but I always get my absolution in the end. It's my own initiative to confess" (interview with Ela, Gdańsk, 2007).

In a direct address on fertility decline titled *Declaration on the Decrease of Fertility in the World* the Vatican again argued for the protection of the heterosexual family against the dangers of the "so-called new rights." As is the case elsewhere in Europe where geographic or religious minorities are cast as politically threatening (Krause 2005a, 2005b; Schneider and Schneider 1996), the Vatican's pronatalist discourse is also about race and class and the dangers that immigrant populations, especially Muslim populations, represent to the "religious balance" in Europe.[16] Locally in Poland, the

Rzeczpospolita daily's headline in January 2010 asked, "Is Christian Europe Threatened by Islamization?"—the article, accompanied by a photo of a woman wearing a niqab, related the statement of Cardinal Miroslaw Vlk of Prague, in which he warned of an imminent "Islamization" of Europe due to the demographic crisis among Catholics (Szymaniak 2010).[17]

The Logics behind the Crisis

Far from irrationally rejecting motherhood, Polish women are highly pragmatic when delaying parenthood in order to navigate the new dilemmas marked by profound job insecurity, widespread gendered discrimination in employment, limited child care, and cultural pressures for having children but not "too many." Against the background of major cutbacks in the social services of the pre-1989 era, women I interviewed speak of new sources of economic instability and concern. Employer practices that are especially threatening to pregnant women and mothers highlighted in this research included questioning women during job interviews about their pregnancy plans, whether they have small children, and their child care arrangements—all illegal labor practices used by businesses to identify and exclude undesirable employees. The state has not been able or willing to protect women against discrimination.

The class character of the fertility decline in Poland is highly significant as well. The emergence of a single child as the middle-class norm based on "responsibility to the family" reflects not only a necessity for many women but also a class marker that separates middle-class "rationality" from the "pathological" reproduction of the lower stratum. This emergent middle-class identity in turn functions to lessen some of the postsocialist class anxieties produced by the instabilities of the neoliberal market that increasingly endanger women's economic footing. However, the narrowly defined "rationality" of having only one child also serves to further stigmatize women who lack the educational or employment resources or otherwise make choices that do not adhere to this form of rationality, and are punished with "pathology" or "Matka Polka" labels.

The role of the Catholic Church cannot be underestimated in maintaining the current situation. When the administration of the Kaczyński twins in 2007 debated improvements in child care services to help women stay at work, the church shut down the idea as antifamily, arguing that the only

profamily approach is for women to be full-time mothers and give up employment (Jackowski 2007). Given that work-family reconciliation policies
have increased birthrates elsewhere in Europe (France, for example), the
church's position clearly demonstrates that what is of greater importance for
the church is not to stimulate fertility but to dictate the *way* women should
reproduce. The church is using the demographic decline as an opportunity
to enforce a particular Catholic morality centered on the "proper" reproductive and sexual conduct of women, and the revival of a patriarchal family
structure, without regard to the realities of women's desires, expectations, or
the economic circumstances of their lives. Indeed, in the context of postsocialist democratization the church has been able to act as "a superb instrument of power for itself" (Foucault 1991b, 107), acting via legislative
mechanisms to insist on a distinct form of religiously sanctioned reproductive conduct and morality. Therefore, unlike the Foucauldian version of state
management of reproduction in liberal democracies as a way to improve the
health and welfare of the population, the Polish profamily program seeks to
intervene in reproduction with aims that are fundamentally different as they
focus on moral disciplining through a "proper" sort of reproduction.

The ineffectual response from the Polish state to women's predicaments
shows a fundamental lack of interest and political will to protect women's
rights, and to make work and family reconciliation possible. Rather than
implementing motherhood-friendly policies such as prosecuting gendered
discrimination in employment or reinstating subsidized child care, the state
has instead taken up the religious rhetoric of the primacy of motherhood
and the nuclear family in their failed Profamily Program.

The influence of religious rationalities and the Catholic Church as a
political institution in nation-building has long been recognized in population scholarship as a factor in reproductive politics and patterns. Although
the demographers who favor the theory of the tempo effect to explain declining fertility have relied on the notion of economic rationality, demographers have also criticized their own focus on economics, noting other
rationalities that shape different fertility contexts, in particular those that
are influenced by religious or cultural pressures (Caldwell 1976, 355). The
narratives of women in my research demonstrate that economic rationality
theories are also limited by their partial understanding of the Polish case
where the material and economic realities that circumscribe women's reproductive choices are in fact underwritten by *gendered* inequities. In this

sense, Foucault's gender-blind conceptualization of biopower fails to account for the pronatalist techniques' and discourses' gender-specific target and effect (Soper 1993, 29–30).

The biopolitical approach to understanding fertility decline also encounters another limitation in the context of Poland: it underestimates the complex responses of individuals to biopower (Lock and Kaufert 1998, 8–9). Although the state socialist biopolitics aimed at enabling women to obtain education and enter the labor market (succeeding on both accounts), the postsocialist biopolitics that restrict reproductive rights and ignore the need for policies to facilitate women's desire to balance work and family as well as fail to promote basic gender equality, are also failing to motivate women to reproduce. At the center of the postsocialist case are pragmatic women—for whom "demographic crisis" and religious discourses ring hollow—dealing with the real dilemmas experienced in the new politico-economic climate, in particular gendered forms of inequality in employment and health care. These dilemmas are often eclipsed by the rhetoric produced by the state, the church, and the media that blames women for low births. The focus on women as the locus of the problem therefore obscures the gendered inequalities inherent in the new power relations of the neoliberal state and labor market. In 2005, a group of Polish experts was asked in the weekly *Przegląd,* What should rational profamily politics look like? Answers ranged from recommendations of greater state support for job security and social services offered by Wanda Nowicka (then at the Federation for Women and Family Planning), to recommendations that economic rationality dictates that the state should stay out of the way offered by the economist Aldona Andrzejczak (Tumiłowicz 2005).

It is clear that the Catholic Church rationality and the historical context of regime change in 1989 have been decisive in the making and the persistence of the Polish demographic crisis. Even though religious calls for unimpeded fertility are falling on deaf ears, the religious discourses on the responsibility of women to reproduce, and by implication, the irresponsibility of nonreproduction, are ubiquitous and take attention away from the true dilemmas facing Polish women. In the end, the case of Poland raises questions about the place of women's rights in postsocialism and also highlights the limits of liberal democracy in which conflicts between religious agendas and women's rights challenge the liberal states' commitment to social and gender justice.

CONCLUSION ꘈ
The Future of Women's Rights in Poland

IN THIS BOOK, I have tried to apply empirical, theoretical, and humanistic approaches in examining the effects of postsocialist changes on reproductive rights and policies. I have shown how after the fall of the state socialist regime in 1989, the Catholic Church was able to implement a politics of morality based on individual surveillance and political intimidation to maintain legislative control over reproduction, despite declining numbers of practicing Catholics in Poland. Significantly, the church was able to consolidate its political power—the culmination of a long-term effort to establish close church-state relations—not just in relation to the state, but within the state structure itself. The singular political influence of the church in Poland thus ushered in an era of *moral governance* that infused the political, economic, social, and private spheres of life in Poland after 1989. It was implemented and enforced through myriad mechanisms targeting reproduction and sexuality, from health policy restricting reproductive health care, to educational policy implementing religion in schools, to individual controls through specific forms of surveillance directed toward women and embedded in religious rituals. The right of the Polish church to hold a powerful political role and maintain as well as bolster these mechanisms of moral governance has been further enshrined in the Concordat of Poland with the Vatican, virtually foreclosing the possibility of a separation of church and state in the near future.

Yet as I have argued, numerous social actors, from doctors to women patients to feminist activists, resist the church's strictures and, acting with their bodies, live very differently than Catholic morality prescribes. Women use coping strategies that circumvent the restrictive policies on abortion by pursuing services illegally, defying religious prohibitions on contraception, organizing themselves into advocacy groups, and helping each other in the process. By successfully limiting their fertility amid the demographic "crisis," Polish women have established a contentious relationship with the church and the state. They do so in a geopolitical setting where liberal bio-politics—the kind that aim to improve the health and well-being of the in-dividual in the name of societal good—are yet to fully develop. Instead, the pronatalist project is clearly identified by women as an expression of a po-litical agenda that pays little attention to the myriad gender inequalities with which women in Poland grapple. Thus, the pronatalist project has not succeeded thus far. Nor has religious governance through the church's pol-itics of morality succeeded in colonizing people's consciousness. Obtaining an illegal abortion or using contraceptives against the church's prohibitions accomplishes precisely what the women want—shaping their lives accord-ing to their wishes, plans, and possibilities. The resistances, contestations, and unofficial practices that Poles routinely engage in to control their fertil-ity reveal the sharp limits of religious governance and a different form of *unofficial biopolitics* in Poland.

Paradoxes as the New Status Quo

Over two decades after the escalation of morality politics and the ban on abortion in Poland, new contradictions emerge. The Catholic Church in Poland has suffered a progressive decline in popularity and respect, owing mainly to its involvement in politics and the ostentatious flaunting of wealth (Korbonski 2000). Yet as opinion polls and a low level of political engage-ment would suggest, the society at large seems to have settled into accepting restrictive reproductive rights policies ushered in by the church through backdoor legislative maneuvers. Simultaneously, the flourishing illegal abortion underground is popularly understood as the backdoor solution to the abortion ban, a resource available only to the well-off. The implication of this kind of "politics of duplicity" (Kligman 1998) is a sustained status quo, in which the population at large mainly prefers to avoid the controver-sial topic. The current state of affairs is a reflection of a telling expression I heard early in my research, that in Poland "the red rule" was replaced by "the black rule," referring to the black priestly cassocks, and the dominance of the church in what can and cannot be discussed.

There is also a prevailing sense of fatigue with the abortion issue, despite the fact, or perhaps because of it, that new abortion bills (mainly proposing a total ban) regularly show up for parliamentary votes. The unfortunate outcome is that many Poles see the abortion issue as a battle between two "extremes"—the Catholic right and the feminists—and too often the acceptance of the status quo is perceived as a compromise, a moderate approach, whereas in reality Poland's abortion law is one of the harshest in Europe. The discourse of "compromise" serves as a convenient rhetorical tool to silence or at least to shelve this difficult issue, rather than confronting the pretense inherent in the coexistence of the abortion underground and a Catholic abortion law implemented presumably for a Catholic nation. In their day-to-day lives, Polish women have settled into effectively circumventing the current abortion ban using individualized and privatized strategies rather than searching for collective solutions (Rivkin-Fish 2005). This situation harkens back to the state socialist era when nonpolitical, non-state methods were the best ways of getting things done. Currently perhaps the popular perception of the state as ossified in a symbiotic relationship with the church indicates that political avenues for reforms opposed by the church are limited. The church's constant political and media presence also reminds the society that this institution is ready and primed to fight against any attempt to liberalize reproductive laws. Meanwhile, women's subterfuges and resistances to the constraints imposed by the church and the state, however effective on the individual level, are limited politically, and a stopgap strategy for dealing with larger social and collective concerns about reproductive rights and health as well as gender inequality that should be addressed with collective and policy solutions.

The Struggle Goes On

It has been more than twenty years since Poland instituted the ban on abortion, yet the struggle around reproductive rights continues to occupy a central place in Polish politics. Catholic politicians and groups periodically introduce parliamentary bills for an absolute abortion ban.[1] For example, in March 2007, the Catholic League of Polish Families party (at the time, a member of the ruling coalition) proposed a constitutional amendment banning all abortions, that is, doing away with the few remaining exceptions that include saving the woman's life or health and in the cases of rape and severe fetal abnormalities. The proposal was rejected. But later that year a more severe measure was proposed. The minister of health, Ewa Kopacz, proposed legislation to register women who have a positive pregnancy test in order to track registered pregnancies and thus prevent abortions. In a response, Nowicka (at the time the head of the Federation for Women and Family Planning) fired back, highlighting that "under the pretext of caring about women and their health, the Minister wants to tighten the system of control over women, over their reproductive functions and decisions," and pointed out that such authoritarian control measure is "an idea from the times of Ceaușescu" when the Romanian dictator forced pregnant women to be monitored (Nowicka 2008d). Soon after, Minister Kopacz withdrew her proposal. In 2013, a bill seeking to ban abortion in cases of fetal abnormalities was considered, but failed again, and in April 2015, ahead of the parliamentary and presidential elections in Poland, the church announced a new campaign to collect signatures for yet another antiabortion bill to eliminate the current therapeutic abortion allowances. Still, activists at the Federation for Women and Family Planning as well as the Eastern European groups ASTRA are well aware and ready for such bills to be proposed in the future.

Even Prime Minister Donald Tusk, perceived as moderate in the West as compared to the previous administration's staunchly conservative Kaczyński brothers, allowed the consideration of a further criminalization of abortion. Ultimately, he too called for maintaining "the compromise," paradoxically referring to the current abortion law, and warned that "anyone who interferes with this compromise puts Poles in danger of an abortion war" (*Gazeta Wyborcza*, October 11, 2011). With the final vote in July 2011 of 261 against to 155 in favor of further criminalization, the proposal got a surprisingly large minority to give the bill a thumbs up. In fact, according to Karolina Więckiewicz, the attorney at the Federation in charge of legal counseling, and who assessed the situation in 2014, the proposed bill should have failed more decisively in the Parliament based on the parliamentarians' declared positions (interview with Więckiewicz,

Warsaw, 2014). However, voting is often maneuvered by the supporters of such bills to take place on a Friday, when attendance of the MPs is generally lower, but proponents of the bill make sure to show up, creating a skewed vote in which the rejected bill appears to have had more weight than it would have, had all the MPs been present to vote. Więckiewicz observes that MPs who clearly oppose such bills are not always sufficiently concerned about the efforts of the antiabortion movement or the issue "isn't that important to them."

In the realm of health care provision, a group of over 2,600 Polish Catholic doctors signed between March and June 2014 what is known as the "Declaration of Faith," pledging to refuse medical services according to the Catholic Church's guidelines. The affair triggered a wave of debates in the Polish media about the role of religion in access to reproductive health care, in particular whether objecting doctors ought to hold positions of power in public hospitals funded by taxpayers' money and potentially impose their particular position on subordinate health care providers. Despite heavy criticism from left-leaning politicians and women's rights groups, the declaration has made a strong symbolic statement of the church's continued effort to restrict access to family planning.

Because of these attempts to do away with even the most minimal protections of reproductive rights and health, paradoxically, women's organizations find themselves having to defend the current highly restrictive abortion law in an effort to prevent total criminalization. When I spoke to the reproductive rights activist Wanda Nowicka in 2007, she explained that she no longer believed that a national referendum would succeed today, the way such referendum might have stopped a ban on abortion back in 1993. She summed up the situation this way:

> A pervasive double discourse[2] dominates: it's politically correct to accept the ban, on the one hand, but this position doesn't reflect the reality that abortion and contraception are widely used, on the other hand. It's a double standard. Substantial damage was done to our cause three months ago [in 2007] when a total abortion ban was debated in the Parliament because the discussion clearly showed that greater value was assigned to the protection of fetal life than to the protection of a woman's life, which tells us that women's rights are becoming less and less important in Poland. Additionally, Polish youth that grew up in the last fourteen to fifteen years did not experience having abortion legal and accessible or having sex education in schools, so they have no understanding of

the difference, and cannot be counted on to vote for a change in the current restrictive law.

Seven years later in 2014, Więckiewicz offered the same outlook: advocacy efforts have to focus on not letting the situation get any worse. Despite important verdicts from the European Court of Human Rights in support of Polish women's reproductive health and rights, there is "too much to battle locally," she noted, to be able to take full advantage of the European Union tools and institutions. But in any case, the EU has no mandate to substantively influence the Polish abortion law, and their verdicts and recommendations operate mainly as "soft" authority, rather than "hard directives" that must be implemented. She ultimately observed that the reproductive rights situation in Poland is "commerce" [*handel*] and hoped that "women will realize, with our help, that their rights have been sold in a trade with the church, and become more engaged politically as well as work up the courage to start demanding their rights."

In June 2014, the Warsaw doctor Bogdan Chazan was fired from a hospital for refusing to provide a lawful abortion to a woman for a severe fetal abnormality—one of only three circumstances under which Polish women can still seek legal abortion care. The popular protest by women's groups, progressive politicians, and much of the Polish public against Chazan's use of conscientious objection to deny the procedure forced Warsaw's mayor, Hanna Gronkiewicz-Waltz, to dismiss him from his post as the hospital director. However, the headline in *Gazeta Wyborcza*, the largest Polish daily newspaper, astutely observed, "Chazan fired— problem remains," highlighting the fact that the dismissal of one doctor still does not guarantee access to the limited abortion services remaining in Poland (Siedlecka 2014).

Ultimately, laws banning abortion do not eliminate the pursuit and use of abortion services by women, and do not increase the birthrate, as numerous historical examples show, including the case of Poland. Furthermore, for anyone but the most superficial observer, such a law in Poland does not signify Catholic devoutness in the population. Since 1989, the Catholic affiliation in Poland has been dropping, and the church's influence in shaping moral norms and worldviews has also declined (Boguszewski 2010). The abortion ban as a way to institute Catholic values is a failed and unenforceable policy that disproportionately hurts poor women.

The "In Vitro" Struggle

The latest wrinkle in Poland's reproductive rights struggles stemming from the abortion ban comes from in vitro infertility services, which are strongly opposed by the Catholic Church. Assisted Reproductive Technologies (ARTs)—commonly known in the Polish vernacular as "in vitro"—have been provided in Poland for more than twenty years, and approximately forty clinics operate currently without any state regulation (Radkowska-Walkowicz 2012).[3] Lack of regulation means that standards of care and safety in these clinics are defined only by clinicians' goodwill and ethics, with no assurance that protocols for treatment are evidence-based (Dembinska 2012). Since only private clinics offer ARTs, these reproductive health services, once again, are accessible only to the well-off in Poland. Serious opposition to ARTs' regulation and health insurance coverage has come from the Catholic Church and affiliated policymakers (Kulawik 2009).

The church, in the name of "embryonic rights," prohibits the use of infertility treatments on the grounds that destruction or freezing of excess embryos produced during the process is equivalent to abortion; thereby these procedures violate the 1993 abortion ban. Moreover, the Catholic media in Poland stigmatize children born with in vitro assistance as physically unhealthy, socially alienated, and emotionally scarred (Radkowska-Walkowicz 2012). In response, a grassroots NGO called Our Stork [Nasz Bocian], in tandem with other reproductive rights groups, especially the Federation for Women and Family Planning, has been working against the stigmatization of children and for regulations of ARTs. They also prepared a bill debated in the Polish Parliament to establish a policy to regulate infertility care, but with little success thus far.[4]

The current political climate around this issue is highly polarized, and the policymaking efforts are stalled, although national opinion surveys show that the Polish public overwhelmingly favors regulation and access to infertility care: in 2012, 79 percent was in favor, while only 16 percent was against ARTs (Rogulska 2012, 3). Several ARTs bills from both sides have been proposed for a parliamentary vote, including proposals to create regulation, subsidies, and access, on the one hand, to proposals to revise the criminal code in order to jail doctors who provide infertility care, on the other hand. Any regulation of ARTs in Poland would de facto signal the validation and legitimation of such procedures by the state—an unfavorable outcome for the church. Therefore, despite some willingness from the state to consider regulation, such policy is unlikely to be adopted in the near future. Importantly, limited subsidies for 15,000 couples to undergo a maximum of three cycles (European standards allow up to nine) of in vitro care was approved by Prime Minister Donald Tusk in 2013, against strong opposition from the church; however, this is a temporary provision implemented by the Ministry of Health for the 2013–16 period. According to the Our Stork organization advocates, the provision has little stability and can be retracted with new elections or a change at the Ministry of Health. (In fact, conservative politicians are already going on record that they will seek to eliminate this provision.) Nevertheless, they perceive the program as a "slap in the face" to the Catholic Church, and therefore a promising move by politicians who traditionally defer to the church's agenda (interview with Anna Krawczak, Warsaw, 2014). Since 2012, some city governments also began to offer limited in vitro treatment subsidies for local residents. Ironically, the first and most substantial program of this kind is being offered, against the wishes of the church, by the city government of Częstochowa, the Catholic center of Poland and the home of the famous Black Madonna monastery. This program resulted mainly from the initiative taken at the local government level—a significant phenomenon in that local politicians took a position that stood in defiance of the policymakers in Warsaw as well as the Catholic Church.

Nearly all European nations where infertility treatment is available have policies that set standards of care and protect the citizens from the improper use of ARTs because there are serious public health concerns. Specifically, a high number of embryo transfers is associated with serious health problems due to low birth weight and congenital abnormalities, thus some Scandinavian nations, for example, permit only a single embryo transfer (van Heesch et al. 2010). In Poland, however, multiple embryo transfers are routine—a practice that is also hailed as in line with the church's prohibition on discarding or freezing of embryos. Moreover, in 2013, Novum, a major Polish IVF clinic, advertised "A chance for free treatment" if the woman qualified for the clinic's pharmaceutical trials of a new hormonal infertility medication. In an unregulated clinical setting, pharmaceutical testing on patients raises serious questions about the safety and ethics of such practices.[5] According to the activists at Our Stork NGO, it appears that ARTs clinics do not necessarily welcome state subsidies for treatment, given the fact that such coverage typically carries clinical guidelines of care, which in turn is perceived as undermining the "golden freedom" that Polish doctors currently enjoy (interview with Marta, Warsaw, 2014).

IVF treatments in Poland also attract a growing wave of "reproductive tourism," especially from the UK, Germany, and Italy, as Polish clinics are typically less expensive. Italian couples also travel to Poland because IVF has been severely restricted in Italy. Polish clinics cater to foreigners by advertising in multiple languages on their websites and offering assistance in finding hotel accommodations for traveling patients. However, unregulated care also means that couples from elsewhere in Europe, where clinical safety guidelines would limit the length or extent of treatment, can access unlimited procedures in Poland where such guidelines are not enforced.

In 2004, the EU released Directive 2004/23/EC requiring nations to control harvesting and storage of human tissues, and deemed ART regulation as necessary to protect public health. Poland was to establish such regulation by 2006, but failed to do so. In January 2013, the European Commission reprimanded Poland for lack of legislation regulating ARTs. In June 2013, Polish government launched a partial subsidy for IVF treatment for 2,000 qualified couples (a drop in the bucket as compared to needs), but no regulation has been advanced. In September 2013, Prime Minister Tusk justified "delaying on purpose" by saying he lacked a parliamentary majority to pass the IVF regulation bill (Siedlecka 2013).

The current in vitro stalemate functions as yet another compromise between acquiescing politicians and the church. Meanwhile, the private clinics that offer ARTs and those that provide illegal abortions make enormous profits from the legislative status quo at the expense of women who cannot afford their services. Clearly, "public morality" as the defining element of postsocialist democratization continues to be central to Polish national politics even as it is challenged internally by women's organizations and the everyday practices of women that defy the directives of the church and the state. These changes are also extremely relevant to present-day European Union concerns as Polish reproductive politics increasingly spill into the international political arena.

The EU and the Human Rights Approach

Throughout the course of this research that began in 2000, reproductive politics have become increasingly at the center of policy debates in Europe.

Access to abortion, contraception, and sterilization, and recently also to ARTs, has long been contentious as predominantly Catholic nations have historically argued for special sovereignty on "public morality" when these nations joined the EU. Ireland and Malta both enjoy such clauses, formally making them immune to the EU's incursion in their policies banning abortion and sterilization. Following on the Irish and Maltese precedents, Poland negotiated sovereignty on "moral issues" when it joined the EU in 2004, thereby protecting its own abortion and sterilization bans. More recently debates about the use of conscientious objection in reproductive health care have been escalating. This growing practice of refusals of lawful reproductive health services, especially abortion and emergency contraception, is fueling discussions about state sovereignty vis-à-vis the EU, and religious freedom of doctors versus women's right to health care. Growing demographic anxieties across Europe form an important backdrop for these debates. The primary line of tension is at the intersection of the secular agenda of the EU and the religious agenda of the Vatican.

Formally, the EU lacks a mandate to dictate any particular reproductive health policy to a member nation, yet the EU has taken explicit positions on abortion, contraception, and sex education. In 2002, the European Parliament adopted the UN Resolution on Sexual and Reproductive Health Needs and Rights, and urged nations to enact policies to ensure access to these services (Nowicka 2002). The EU's reliance on individual rights, explicitly utilized in these recommendations, is rooted in the European Convention on Human Rights (ECHR) established in 1950—the same year the European Court of Human Rights was developed to arbitrate human rights violations. All forty-seven nations in the Council of Europe, including Poland, are signatories to this convention. As described in earlier chapters, the ECHR recently judged against Poland in instances of refusals of lawful abortions in cases of rape and endangerment of health (the cases of Alicja Tysiąc and Agata, among others).

The ECHR has also ruled in cases of denial of abortion in Ireland. In 2007, the UN Committee on Human Rights criticized Ireland for the ambiguity of its abortion law, which was unclear about whether an abortion to save the woman's life is criminalized or not—an issue highlighted by the death of Savita Halappanavar who in 2012 was denied a life-saving abortion while in an Irish hospital in Galway (O'Toole 2012). This tragic case (ruled in Ireland as "medical misadventure") together with another ECHR ruling against Ireland in 2010 which called on Ireland to make the life-saving exception explicit in the law, triggered a vigorous political debate and resulted, in 2014, in a clarification that allows abortion when the life of the woman is at risk, including the risk of a suicide. It remains to be seen how this clarification will be tested in future cases.

But reproductive rights are not just a matter of access to health care. The court declared access to abortion in these cases to be within the scope of human rights on the grounds of the rights to privacy, liberty, and security. Earlier landmark conferences in Vienna, Cairo, and Beijing also defined human rights to encompass women's right to equality and self-determination. Reproductive rights advocates in Poland firmly believe that pursuing reproductive rights as human rights is the most promising avenue (Nowicka 2011). The large regional ASTRA network, consisting of thirty-four reproductive and sexual rights organizations from twenty Eastern European and former Soviet bloc nations is also taking the avenue of "reclaiming and redefining rights" in central and Eastern Europe along the UN's human rights pledges.[6] Likewise, reproductive rights advocates working with international NGOs and medical communities see human rights as the best strategy amid challenges posed by powerful religious influences within policymaking (Chavkin and Chesler 2005). The Federation for Women and Family Planning when working on behalf of the plaintiffs in the successful cases at the European Court of Human Rights specifically relied on the human rights framework, where advocating for women's autonomy and ability to make decisions about their own bodies and lives (rather than just health) was of paramount importance.

However, even though the human rights language in the various international agreements generated by the UN is strongly and unambiguously worded, activists are disappointed with the meager follow-up to ensure that conservative governments abide by the human rights convention and court recommendations. In 2011 Wanda Nowicka asserted that Polish reproductive rights activists are specifically concerned about the opposition to human rights on the ground of cultural and religious relativism, noting that the universality of human rights has "been questioned by a number of governments and scholars ever since the adoption of the Universal Declaration, primarily from a conservative standpoint," and that "assertion of culture and protection of religion can serve as vehicles to conserve a patriarchal model of inequality and discrimination against women" (Nowicka 2011, 126).

Anthropologists and other scholars have also identified the limits of moral relativism in the present times marked by pervasive injustices along gender, class, and ethnic lines, and growing inequalities both within and between nations (see, e.g., Levitt and Merry 2009; Scheper-Hughes 1995), but others note that the use of rights discourse can be a risky practice because rights-bearing groups can be pitted against one another (Morgan and Roberts 2012). This specter of a stalemate is already manifesting in Europe, as Poland, Ireland, and Malta—the three EU nations where the Catholic Church has a powerful grip on policymaking decisions and the only nations in Europe with abortion bans—working in tandem at the EU level have effectively paralyzed many nascent discussions about reproductive and sexual rights and health in Europe. Malta, with a population of less than half a million, has single-handedly put an end to such discussions at the Council of the European Union where unanimous voting is required to move certain topics forward. Paradoxically, while the EU is paralyzed about its own reproductive rights policies, it is simultaneously funneling significant amount of "development aid" to other nations for the same purpose.

What is emerging from this highly contested terrain is what Nowicka (2011, 121) refers to as the "terror of 'agreed language'"—yet another status quo between the conservative religious groups and the UN or the EU—which paralyzes any movement forward from the original Cairo and Beijing commitments. Worse, at times the achieved reproductive rights language is actually retracted. For example, during the 2012 Rio+20 United Nations Conference in Rio de Janeiro, the term "reproductive rights" was stricken altogether from the summit's final text as the Vatican delegation prevailed in its opposition to the wording (Ford 2012, 1). The concern voiced in Rio de Janeiro by Gro Harlem Brundtland, the former Norwegian prime minister, that removing specific references to reproductive rights is "a step backwards from previous agreements" (Ford 2012, 1) is precisely reflected by Nowicka's point that in the current political climate, rather than making progress on human rights and pressing the implementation forward, "women's movements have been pushed into a corner and have had to pull all our efforts into holding the line" (2011, 120). Nevertheless, international human rights obligations have been used successfully to liberalize abortion laws in a number of nations in the recent past, including Nepal, Mexico City, South Africa, Ethiopia, Colombia, Portugal, and Spain, although the Spanish law is again experiencing threats from the conservative government of Mariano

Rajoy Brey. This threat has been met with tremendous opposition with major protests held in Spain, Brussels, London, Paris, and Rome.[7]

As these struggles continue, the reproductive rights debates raise important questions about the meanings of EU citizenship for Polish women as well as other women in Europe, the scope of member states' sovereignty in the domain of reproductive rights, and the nature of democratization in the East European region.

The Limits of Polish Democracy

The political realignment during the 1989 transition period has given a distinct shape to Polish democratization in which the appearance of "formal democracy" gives the impression that Poland has transitioned successfully away from the repressive rule of the past. This "formal democracy"— mainly defined in political discourses as the dominant neoliberal rhetoric of free market openness—tends to conceal the gender inequalities and injustices that have emerged since the 1989 collapse of the state socialist regime in Poland. Likewise, class-based anger and struggles have also been suppressed by the neoliberal and globalization rhetoric (Ost 2005, 187–90; Rivkin-Fish 2004). Other forms of discrimination based on sexual orientation and immigrant and minority status have likewise intensified. The nationalist political spin of the low birthrate pitching the nation as "dying out" is fueling patriarchal reactions against reproductive rights and women's rights in general, with fewer people supporting the liberalization of abortion now than two decades ago when the abortion ban was first imposed. At the same time the state fails to offer tangible improvements to protect women's jobs or to ease their burden of care work. The phrase *harówka*—meaning grind or toil—was a quotidian expression that women in my research used to refer to their day-to-day lived experience. While Poland established a free market state, the quality of Polish democracy raises concerns, and it is crucial for anthropological and feminist observers to critically assess the role of new or newly powerful institutions advocating or legitimizing restrictions on women's rights.

The role of the state is highly significant in that it holds the power to directly shape gendered life experiences through specific laws related to reproduction, sexuality, health care, employment, and education (Connell

1990). Conversely, the state is also a reflection of the significance of gender, since historically the reconfiguring of gender relations around moral norms and "civilized" behavior has been crucial to the formation of power structures (Elias 1978; Kligman 1996, 1998; Mosse 1988). Poland is emblematic of the pivotal role of gender in nation-making.

This research also questions the role of women's rights in an ostensibly liberal democratic state. The hallmark of Polish postsocialist politics has been the disregard for women's concerns, including the rejection of the Solidarity Women's Section's protests about restrictions on abortion in 1990, the rejection of the petition with 1.3 million signatures calling for a national referendum on abortion in 1993, the implementation of an abortion ban that, according to surveys at the time, was clearly in conflict with the will of the population at large, and the subsequent denial or downplaying of the illegal abortion underground, as well as cuts in social services and diminished employment security, especially for women.

Some feminist scholars who have examined the marginalization of women's rights in the East European region after 1989 have argued that in the realm of social policy, issues that concern women are fundamentally the same in the East and West, and revolve around reproductive rights and health, equity in everyday gender relations, and political representation (Gal and Kligman 2000a, 2000b). But others have noted that the inferior role of women's rights is a reflection of the way that liberalism was historically understood here, even if common interests of women exist in both the East and the West. Nanette Funk, in her historical analysis of political thought in East Europe, proposes that it is the lack of political individualism in Poland that translates into the lack of support for women's rights, as even some of the most prominent Polish liberal thinkers "recognized collective goods and rights and emphasized individual duties, obligations of sacrifice and responsibility to others, the nation, family, God, and the state; these goods could override individual rights" (2004, 700). Thus Funk contends that the secondary status of individual rights ingrained in Polish political culture prevents the legitimation of women's rights in postsocialism.

Although lack of political culture or political individualism is important to consider, this research demonstrates that the special status of the church is decisive in that it undermines the liberal tenets of egalitarianism inherent in a liberal democracy. Gila Stopler argues that "the relationship between patriarchal religion and the state in liberal democracies adversely affects the rights of all women, and the liberal states cannot live up to their commitment to women's equality without significantly changing their relations with patriarchal religions" (2005, 191). A mere legalistic separation of church and state, as in Ireland or the United States, for example, does not predict the degree of political influence of religious institutions. In Poland, at any rate, a formal separation of church and state was criticized by Cardinal Glemp as a "communist-inspired" concept (*Economist* 1991, 51), and after 1989 the church successfully prevented the inclusion of such separation in the new Polish Constitution. More significant to consider is the degree to which religious actors enjoy access to politics, and therefore exercise power in the area of policymaking. The "liberal bind"—the conflict between a liberal state's protection of religious institutions and the protection of women's rights—cannot be simply resolved by a legalistic separation of church and state (Stopler 2005). As the case of Poland makes clear, the special status and recognition afforded to the Catholic Church, and enshrined in the Concordat, is highly significant for women's rights, because the church traditionally intervenes in those policies that particularly affect women, including reproductive rights and family policy. To deal with this contradiction the postsocialist liberal state must consider disestablishing religion from state matters both symbolically and financially or risk undermining the political legitimacy of its democracy.

Finally, the case of Poland also demonstrates that there are no straightforward relationships between formal democracy and the advancement or security of women's rights. Examining women's rights under a range of political regimes from democratically elected to authoritarian, Mala Htun (2003) observes that in some contexts women's rights (but not necessarily women's movements) fare better under less democratic states, where political elites play a greater role than grassroots social movements. For instance, advancement of women's causes has been more successful in Brazil and Argentina, where feminist elites have been decisive in the struggle for women's rights. In Poland, the few prominent feminists could potentially have a "multiplier effect" by sparking activist interest in the population at large or in the younger generation, most of whom have grown up knowing only restrictive reproductive policies and how to get around them. Although feminist role models are few and the antifeminist political climate difficult, the feminist elite has the potential of bringing women's concerns to the forefront of the political discourse long dominated by the right-leaning rhetoric, and perhaps encouraging greater involvement of women in politics. Among these leaders Wanda Nowicka stands out. Her reproductive rights activism progressed in visibility and influence from cofounding, with a small group of friends, the NGO Neutrum in 1990, which opposed the rapid church-state merging in the early days of transition, to becoming the first member of the parliament in 2011 with an explicit agenda of advocating for abortion rights and reproductive health. Nowicka appears to be the feminist elite activist that Htun (2003) envisions as capable of advancing a women's rights agenda. But when an American feminist scholar in New York, Ann Snitow, who has supported the Polish women's movement, asked me, Can Poland allow for an individual radical feminist to become a political star like Adam Michnik?, Can Poland have a feminist star?, the questions were mostly rhetorical. This is because of the deep entrenchment of religion in politics, the fear of the church in affecting elections, and the general antifeminist hostilities that tend to label frontline advocacy as extreme. Gail Kligman's observation from Ceaușescu's Romania bears repeating as it mirrors postsocialist Poland: "As long as women lack the freedom to control their reproductive lives fully, they will be unable to participate in the public sphere as full and equal citizens, and in their private lives as full and equal partners" (1998, 250). Ultimately, the Polish predicaments demonstrate a clear need for multiple locations of women's rights activism from articulations of radical independent thought challenging the policies and discourses of church and state powers to reproductive health services and feminist awareness-building on the grassroots level. Until then, women in Poland will continue to find themselves on the losing end of the postsocialist democratization process.

Notes

Introduction

1. Despite Pope Francis's media rhetoric that might suggest a less conservative turn, he has held firm to the established doctrines on abortion, contraception, sex education, assisted reproductive technologies, homosexuality, and other issues related to what the church understands as questions of "morality."

2. Earlier that year I was contacted by one of the older tennis players from another city whom I knew superficially but who asked if I would put her up overnight in my Warsaw studio where I lived in the state-subsidized housing for tennis players the last couple of years before my arrival in the United States. I learned that night that she was an activist in the Solidarity movement and was distributing clandestine literature. I was too young and naïve as well as uninformed politically to understand her efforts or to appreciate the gravity of the situation.

3. For example, in 1980 the Hyde Amendment, which prohibited the use of federal funds for abortions, was upheld by the US Supreme Court in the *Harris v. McRae* case, therefore continuing to limit access to reproductive health care for women who are poor and on Medicaid. In 1989, in the case of *Webster v. Reproductive Health Services*, the court upheld a law implemented in Missouri that prohibited the use of public facilities or employees to perform abortions that were deemed medically unnecessary, i.e., those requested for social or economic reasons. Numerous other challenges have followed since the 1990s. See http://now.org/about /history/highlights/, accessed March 26, 2015.

4. Scholars generally understand the 1989 transition as a set of "transformations" rather than as a simple and predetermined "transition" from state socialism to capitalism, with a spectrum of different and distinct outcomes, which may or may not appear like Western-style capitalism (Burawoy and Verdery 1999; Hann 1994; Verdery 1996).

5. I use the term "gender regime" following the feminist scholar R. W. Connell, and the theorist of transnational feminism Chandra Mohanty. According to Connell: "The state is a bearer of gender and each state has a definable 'gender regime'

that is the precipitate of social struggles and is linked to (though not simply a reflection of) the wider gender relations in the society" (1990, 523). Mohanty later clarified the term, noting that "the state delimits the boundaries of personal/domestic violence, protects property, criminalizes 'deviant' and 'stigmatized' sexuality, embodies masculinized hierarchies . . . , structures collective violence in the police force, prisons, and wars, and sometimes allows or even invites the countermobilization of power" (2003, 64). My own usage of the term in the context of Poland broadens its meaning to encompass both the state and the Catholic Church.

6. A notable exception is Romania, where abortion was banned under the dictatorship of Nicolae Ceauşescu, and therefore access to abortion and contraception was expanded after the fall of Ceauşescu's regime and his execution in 1989 (Baban 2000; Kligman 1998).

Chapter 1: "The Church Was Helping Us Win Freedom"

1. Paul Mojzes, a religious studies scholar, argues (1999) that it is more accurate to say that Roman Catholicism became the national religion rather than the state religion in Poland because the church at various historical times was able to oppose, or detach from, the state while maintaining national political authority among Poles. During the interwar years of 1918–39 and, during the postsocialist period, as I argue in this chapter, the phenomena of state religion and national religion have been conflated.

2. In contrast, Katherine Verdery argues (1991) that in the context of Ceauşescu's Romania, nationalism intensified under the state socialist rule, as Ceauşescu's regime appropriated national identity discourse to establish its own legitimacy and generate popular consent during the communist period.

3. The most repeated narrative of the heroism of the church in defending Poland is the story of the massive Swedish invasion in the 1640s commonly known as "the deluge." As Poland was near capitulation to the Swedish invaders, the monastery of Częstochowa, the home of the Black Madonna portrait that was believed to perform miracles, successfully resisted the Swedish assault, which was said to have mobilized Poles across the country to drive out the Swedes. The event has been depicted as a miracle of the Black Madonna and the Catholic Church in protecting the sovereignty of the Polish nation. This famous story of Catholic nationalism is taught in history and literature classes, since Henryk Sienkiewicz, one of Poland's prominent writers, had written a novel based on the story of "the deluge." The story was also made into a television series and later into a film. The monastery has recently been renamed the National Shrine Of Our Lady of Częstochowa ("National" was added).

4. Most of the state socialist systems repressed the churches as communist ideology associated religion with individuality, nationalism, and indolence but the degree of repression varied. The Eastern Orthodox churches were most vulnerable because they were structurally autonomous and materially dependent on the state, whereas the Roman Catholic Church was protected by the Vatican and was financially independent of the state. Generally socialist regimes attempted to isolate local Catholic churches from the Vatican but were only successful in Albania (Gautier 1997; Radic 1999; Trojan 1994).

5. *Tygodnik Powszechny* has been the main Catholic weekly newspaper in Poland since 1945. It was temporarily shut down by socialist authorities from 1953 to 1956 for the refusal to publish Josef Stalin's obituary (*Tygodnik Powszechny*, September 22, 1946, 1).

6. The small Catholic Left was accused by the church of acting as state spies in order to break up the church from within (Michnik 1993, 175; Monticone 1986, 15–16).

7. Not all leftists in the Soviet bloc region were hopeful—a small group believed that Soviet-style communism would never embody what Marx envisioned (Volkogonov 1996).

8. The church was also allowed to keep all property under 50 hectares (125 acres) throughout Poland and a substantial number of properties that were over 100 hectares in the areas of the city of Poznań, and in the regions of Silesia and Pomerania (Monticone 1986, 17). In contrast, the state socialist regime confiscated nearly all of the property of the Polish gentry; however, the nobility proved resilient—they were able to maintain their social capital and became once again an influential political group after 1989 (Jakubowska 2001, 2012).

9. As a result of these revelations the New Left formed in Europe and the United States, a movement that distanced itself from the authoritarian Soviet system and aimed for a more participatory and democratic style of socialism.

10. This play was written by the renowned Polish writer Adam Mickiewicz between 1823 and 1832.

11. The majority of the remaining Jewish population in Poland left the country following the riots of 1968. In 1968 there were simultaneous riots in many other locations around the world, especially in the United States, where protests were held against poor living conditions, unemployment, and various forms of discrimination.

12. Soviet bloc regimes also legalized abortion in Czechoslovakia (1958), Romania (1957), Soviet Union (1955), Hungary (1953), Bulgaria (1956), and Yugoslavia (1969). Romania is a notable exception, as mentioned earlier, where Ceauşescu's policies banning abortion in 1967 resulted in a surge in maternal mortality due to illicit abortions, as well as in infant abandonment, and infant HIV infections (Kligman 1998).

13. Pseudonym.

14. Poland's total fertility rate (the number of children per woman per lifetime) dropped from 2.98 in 1960 to 2.1 in 1989 (Frątczak 2004).

15. This distinction is known in Poland as Solidarity I and II—terms that highlight the ideological difference between the early and later phases of the Solidarity movement.

16. Scholars have proposed various points of origin for the Solidarity movement. The sociologist Maryjane Osa (1997) argues that Solidarity emerged as a religious movement rather than as a worker-based or worker-intelligentsia-based movement. David Ost (1990) argues that Solidarity originally formed out of a desire to create "subjectivity" and that the union initially rejected direct involvement in politics. Jadwiga Staniszkis (1984) sees the movement more broadly as a social force that transcended the free trade union formula and sparked a self-limiting revolution, while others see it as a democratic social movement of the working class that responded to the political opportunities of the time (Bernhard 1993; Laba 1991).

17. See Sunday practices table (referred to as "Dominicantes i communicantes"), table for 2012 on the Institute of Statistics of the Catholic Church (*Instytut Statystyki Kościoła Katolickiego*), http://www.iskk.pl/kosciolnaswiecie/179-dominicantes-i-communicantes-2012.html, accessed March 26, 2015.

18. Even though ideologically the Catholic Church is a monolithic institution, not all clergy were unified behind the cardinal's attacks on pluralism. For example, the priest Ludwik Wiśniewski of Wrocław wanted to hold political debates that aimed for constructive solutions and steered clear of inciting conflict among groups of different political or religious beliefs (Kenney 2002, 38–40). Nevertheless, dissent within the church is uncommon, and if present it typically meets with swift reprimand from the Vatican.

19. The role of Pope John Paul II was significant in weakening Soviet rule by advancing Catholic nationalism in Poland (Weigel 1992, 16). Jan Kubik (1994) further argues that the Catholic imagery and symbolism used by the Solidarity movement had the effect of publicly chipping away at the legitimacy of the regime. Ultimately, the collapse of the regime in Poland was the result of a combination of internal and external factors (Lee 2001).

20. The theme of Poland as the "Christ of nations" is evident in much of the Polish nationalist literature. The Polish poet Adam Mickiewicz uses the story of Christ's suffering, death, and resurrection as a metaphor for Polish national history in his famous book *Dziady* (*Forefathers' Eve*) published in 1832. Various adaptations of *Dziady* are ubiquitous in Polish theaters, and the book is also required reading in all public schools.

21. The pen is now on display at the Solidarity museum in Gdańsk.

22. The Vatican signed concordats with the following European nations: Austria, Croatia, Italy, Latvia, Lithuania, Luxemburg, Malta, Portugal, Slovak

Republic, Slovenia, and Spain. France and Czech Republic declined signing a concordat (EU Network of Independent Experts on Fundamental Rights December 14, 2005).

Chapter 2: Restricting Access to Reproductive Services

1. The anthropologist Lynn M. Morgan in her ethnography *Icons of Life: A Cultural History of Human Embryos* (2008) demonstrates through a meticulous historical analysis of science how women have been written out of the language of pregnancy: initially the scholarship in the area of embryology and new imagining techniques discussed embryos as "science," but eventually, as Morgan shows, embryos became "persons" used for political agendas.

2. Jane Bayes and Nayereh Tohidi, scholars of political science and women's studies, observe a "fundamentalist turn" in John Paul II's philosophy brought on by the belief that "radical capitalism" in the form of globalization, feminization of the labor market, and sexual "permissiveness" led to the acceptance of contraception and abortion (2001, 23, 67).

3. For further discussions of reciprocity networks of exchange during the state socialist era in Poland see, for example, Nagengast (1991).

4. For example, Reporters Without Borders described in their annual report for Poland in 2003 an account in which a Polish journalist, Zbigniew Wiśniewski, writing for the daily paper *Trybuna*, was fined $6,421.00 for insulting Pope John Paul II by calling him "an unsophisticated country vicar" (Reporters Without Borders 2003, 1).

5. During the state socialist period, women in the Soviet region, including Poland, spent nearly double the hours per week on domestic labor as did men (Corrin 1992).

6. Familism rhetoric together with "remasculinization" promoted by the state emerged across the postsocialist region (Gal and Kligman 2000; Haney 1996; Haney 2003; Rivkin-Fish 2005, 12–13).

7. A few examples of Catholic clergy on state or state-sponsored bioethics committees include the priest Wojciech Bołoz—the Ministry of Health (see http://www2.mz.gov.pl/wwwmz/slajd?mr=m4&ms=1&ml=pl&mi=5&mx=0&mt&my=5&ma=00311, accessed March 26, 2015); the priest Stefan Gralak—Ministry of Health representative at the Council of the Healthcare Worker in Warsaw—a nationwide organization of health professionals (see http://www2.mz.gov.pl/wwwmz/index?mr=mo&ms=&ml=pl&mi=904&mx=0&mt=&my=9&ma=02752, accessed March 26, 2015); the priest Arkadiusz Nowak—who advised the minister of health on issues pertaining to HIV/AIDS (see http://aids.nazwa.pl/www/ekontra/?act=2006&id=35, accessed March 26, 2015).

8. Conscience-based refusals of reproductive health services are being observed in many parts of the world, despite the fact that the major international professional associations, including the World Medical Association and the International Federation of Gynecology and Obstetrics, FIGO, hold the position that the provider's right to "conscientiously refuse to provide certain services must be secondary to his or her first duty, which is to the patient" (Chavkin, Leitman, and Polin 2013, S45). In the context of the United States, conscience-based refusals are also at the center of public health controversy about mergers between Catholic and nonsectarian hospitals. These mergers result in the adoption of religious ethics guidelines that prohibit emergency contraception and sterilization in the merged facility. Merger Watch, a patients' rights advocacy nongovernmental organization, has been at the forefront of tracking the effects of such mergers on access to reproductive health services in the United States. See http://www.mergerwatch.org/, accessed May 26, 2014.

9. Kulczycki (1995, 475) cites abortion data provided by the Polish Ministry of Health for 1988 to be 105,333 and reports a major drop to under 31,000 in 1991. Rich (1994) reports that by 1993 lawful abortions fell to 777.

10. In Poland, Bayer Schering primarily promoted birth control pills initially. Since 1994, the company registered with the state the first intrauterine device and two medications used in hormone replacement therapy. See http://www.bayer.com .pl/#, accessed May 26, 2014.

11. Most abortions are still done using dilation and curettage; therefore, the popular synonym for abortion is *skrobanka*, or "little scraping," and a doctor who performs abortions can be referred to as *skrabacz*, or "scraper."

12. According to the postsocialist concordat, the church reserves the right to reject burials for a variety of reasons, even in areas of Poland where no other cemeteries are available. The refusal of burial as punishment has also been observed in Malta where Catholicism is the de facto state religion; for example, people who voted in favor of anticlerical politicians have been refused burials in church cemeteries (Koster 1991, 113)

13. See http://www.iskk.pl/kosciolnaswiecie/179-dominicantes-i-communicantes -2012.html, accessed March 26, 2015.

14. In practice, the calendar method is typically understood in Poland as periodic abstinence on the woman's fertile days, calculated based on the dates of her menstrual cycle, but theoretically this method might also include basal body temperature measurement or the observation of the viscosity of vaginal discharge.

15. The issue of the unregulated use of conscientious objection is a growing phenomenon in Europe and the United States, and has been the subject of recent debates at the Council of Europe (Mishtal 2014). In the United Kingdom in April 2014, the Royal College of Obstetricians and Gynaecologists considered barring

doctors who object to prescribing contraceptives from receiving diplomas in sexual and reproductive health. But the issue of regulation remains a challenge for policy-makers due to its highly politicized and complex nature.

16. In 2012, a group of Catholic pharmacists submitted a legislative proposal that would allow pharmacists to not sell contraceptives and claim conscientious objection on behalf of the entire pharmacy. However, after an intervention from the Federation for Women and Family Planning, their proposal was rejected by the main pharmaceutical inspector, Zofia Ulz, who stated that a pharmacy has no right to decline to fill a doctor's prescription and that pharmacies that do will have their licenses revoked. See "Aptekarze muszą sprzedać środki antykoncepcyjne," http://kobieta.wp.pl/kat,26355,title,Aptekarze-musza-sprzedac-srodki-antykoncepcyjne,wid,14566983,wiadomosc.html?ticaid=112218, accessed March 26, 2015.

17. Some scholars momentarily believed that this was a promising shift toward left-leaning politics in Poland and toward greater political attention to growing socioeconomic class concerns (Szelenyi, Fodor, and Hanley 1997).

18. The EU is primarily a system of political and economic integration based on international treaties between member states. It also refers to the expanding system of governance, even though much of the EU's involvement occurs via the individual state's administrative institutions (Bellier and Wilson 2000). In recent decades the EU has been widening its governance to include social issues of gender equity (Beveridge, Nott, and Stephen 2000). The EU integration has been a difficult process because the diverse cultural politics, including differences related to views of gender equality, at times challenge the EU's aims to develop unifying economic, social or health policies (Rossilli 1999; Shore 2000; Vogel-Polsky 2000).

Chapter 3: Women Respond

1. Poland has thousands of NGOs registered with the state, but the number of active feminist or explicitly women's rights groups that have a national scope is less than twenty. Some active NGOs, such as the Center for Women's Rights, have multiple branches. Most concentrate in large cities, especially Warsaw. See http://historia_kobiet.w.interia.pl/p-or-ko.htm, accessed March 26, 2015.

2. Rural NGOs in Poland face even greater challenges with funding as well as opportunities to access professional expertise and information (Regulska 1999).

3. NGOs focusing on gendered issues have proliferated across the post-Soviet region, occupying the so-called Third Sector, but many have struggled to obtain sufficient funding to develop projects that are useful and appropriate locally against the new economic dilemmas due to neoliberal market reforms (Hemment 2007; Regulska 1999).

4. I also conducted research with members of the OŚKA Foundation, which is an informational center for women and a support organization for other women's rights NGOs in Poland, as well as Labrys and Campaign Against Homophobia—both groups conduct LGBT advocacy; however, the latter is particularly visible and often collaborates with the Federation for Women and Family Planning.

5. While "shock therapy" style reforms were instituted in Poland, Western financial aid also arrived in this region but not always with positive effects. Scholars have argued (Creed and Wedel 1997; Wedel 1998) that some Western aid to Poland was inappropriate, and it served the political agendas of the donors rather than the local needs.

6. Real names are used with permission (or by informant's request) for Kinga Dunin, Małgorzata Fuszara, Anna Giza-Poleszczuk, Anna Krawczak, Katarzyna Kurkiewicz, Hanka Lipowska-Teutsch, Wanda Nowicka, Kazia Szczuka, and Karolina Więckiewicz. All other names are pseudonyms.

7. Rivkin-Fish (2005) examines the disenfranchisement of doctors in Russia and some of the consequences of this disempowerment for the provision of maternity health care.

8. Hungary offers an interesting parallel here: although abortion remains legal in Hungary, state subsidies for abortion were withdrawn in 1992 as a result of pressure from the Catholic Church. Similar to Fuszara's observation about Poland, the debate about restricting reproductive rights in Hungary in the early 1990s galvanized feminist groups there as well (Petö 2002, 368; McMahon 2002). Elsewhere in the region the number of women's rights NGOs also increased but not always for the same reasons; in Bulgaria, for example, the main concerns were the trafficking of women and gendered discrimination in employment (the latter is a pressing issue in Poland, as I will show later in the book), whereas reproductive rights were not in jeopardy owing to the relatively weak political authority of the Orthodox Church (Chimiak 2003, 19).

9. It has been related to me during research that some tensions between gay, lesbian, and feminist groups have surfaced in the past over concerns about stereotypical approaches to women on the part of some gay activists, as well as incomplete inclusion of lesbians into the feminist groups. These tensions led at times to the weakening of cooperation between these groups or to the retreat of some individuals from participation in advocacy. Still, in September 2010, four diverse groups—KPH, the Federation for Women and Family Planning, the Feminoteka Foundation, and the Polish Society of Anti-Discrimination Law—collaborated to sign a joint letter to the Members of the European Parliament requesting the dismissal of Elżbieta Radziszewska, a conservative politician who publicly expressed homophobic views while, ironically, holding the office of the Plenipotentiary on Equal Status. (She was dismissed, but not until a year later.)

10. Any kind of political organizing is difficult, and political involvement of Poles has been observed to be "marginal": a national opinion poll found that 52 percent believed that involvement in any social movement has no effect on what is happening in the nation (Wciórka 2000, 3–4). More recently, a survey about the attitude of Poles toward different forms of protest indicates that 47 percent, a signficant portion, believe that protest "doesn't do anything" (*nic nie daje*) (Pankowski 2013, 6). A shift toward the political right since 1989 might also be discouraging citizens from political and civic participation (Regulska 2009, 551). These findings are peculiar for a nation where the Solidarity oppositional movement has been the first political movement in the region and instrumental in toppling the communist regime.

11. Nationalist-Catholic discourses that included the "noble knighthood" gender model dominated while Poland was occupied by Russia, Prussia, and Austria from 1795 to 1918, and although Poland was absent geopolitically, the nation was held together significantly by the efforts of the church. See Hetnal 1998.

12. See the following case studies from Brazil, Sweden, Denmark, and Norway: Alvarez 1990; Curtin and Higgins 1998; Dahlerup 2002; Halsaa 2002.

13. After the end of the military dictatorship strong alliances between the Brazilian feminist movement and medical institutions (including the Ministry of Health and the Brazilian Federation of Gynecology and Obstetrics) have resulted in the establishment of and improvements in reproductive health services in Brazil, including abortion care (De Zordo and Mishtal 2011, 34–35). This shift took place despite the significant influence of the Catholic Church in Brazil.

14. Women constituted less than 8 percent of the Solidarity Congress, whereas they formed about 50 percent of the union's membership (Hauser, Heyns, and Mansbridge 1993, 262; Kenney 2002, 67; Ost 2005, 139).

15. Yet an analysis of opposition during the state socialist era, and before the consolidation of Solidarity, shows that resistance was gendered in that the state showed greater willingness to accommodate the demands of women (grounded in household concerns with family budget, food availability and prices, and care work) than those of men before 1989 (Kenney 1999).

16. In the discourse of Solidarity that divided workers into "skilled" and "unskilled," the male management of the union automatically categorized women and peasant-workers as "unskilled" and therefore expendable, despite the fact that women were paid far less than men and also maintained equipment and inventories (Ost 2005, 139, 145).

17. See voter turnout statistics compiled by the International Institute for Democracy and Electoral Assistance: http://www.idea.int/vt/countryview.cfm?id=179, accessed March 26, 2015.

18. TRR (Towarzystwo Rozwoju Rodziny), briefly discussed in chapter 2, refers to the Society for Family Development. It is the oldest state-funded health

education organization, active since the 1970s. Since the fall of state socialism, the organization has struggled due to lack of funding, but the group is surviving in a scaled-down form, in part with the help of the International Planned Parenthood Federation.

19. During my fieldwork between 2001 and 2014, it was not uncommon to see a clergyman or a politician representing the extreme right Catholic party, the League of Polish Families (somewhat marginal in terms of the electorate but a vocal organization), invited to offer the opposing view for television debates about reproductive politics.

20. Women's Foundation eFKa was formed in 1991 and, unlike other NGOs, receives much of its funding from the German Heinrich Böll Foundation, in addition to the European Commission and a few other funders. Eliza related that when eFKa struggled financially and there was no money to publish another issue, she approached the Heinrich Böll Foundation for funding by pitching *Zadra* as a piece of popular press that would be interesting and accessible to a large cross-age, cross-gender population. The donor agreed, and *Zadra* has been funded since then, but the distribution never grew beyond its rather small number of issues (less than 2,000), and the magazine is mainly enjoyed in academic circles. In some measure probably owing to the national antifeminist rhetoric, *Zadra* might not reach a much larger population; however, it constitutes an important activist and intellectual anchor for the established community of feminists.

21. Miłosz refers to *ukąszenie heglowskie* in his *The Captive Mind (Zniewolony umysł)* (1953); this expression gained popularity in everyday speech among the educated in Poland.

22. For discussions of the influence of Western feminism on feminist consciousness-raising in this geopolitical region see, for example, Funk (2004), Fuszara (2000a, 2000b), Gal and Kligman (2000), Ghodsee (2004), Goven (2000), Maleck-Lewy and Ferree (2000), Marody and Giza-Poleszczuk (2000), and Matynia (1995).

23. Although the political capital of Western feminism has been highly significant in validating the local struggle in Poland, relatively few scholars, mainly those working in this region, explicitly acknowledge the grassroots feminist heritage in Poland (Einhorn and Sever 2005, 23–53; Petö 2002, 361–71; Šribar 2002, 372–77). This heritage is sometimes poorly understood in Western scholarship, which tends to overestimate the role of the West. For example, the work of Maria Nemenyi, a Hungarian sociologist, and Susan Gal's ethnographic work in Hungary show that women are not politically apathetic or lacking in social consciousness, as some Western scholars have argued (Gal 1994, 1996; Nemenyi 1996). In relation to Poland, arguments that Western NGOs had to teach Polish activists how to talk about women's rights, claiming they lack this language (McMahon 2002), or that feminist thought was exported to Eastern Europe only after 1989 (Ghodsee 2004), or that

Polish women's groups lacked knowledge of teamwork and had to be taught how to arrive at agreements (Coyle 2003)—all these ideas have been contested by the participants in this research as misconceptions of activists' background and skills. Additionally, the perception of the postsocialist civil society as a sort of blank slate without relativizing the concept to consider local history has been criticized in anthropology scholarship as a simplistic Western application of this concept (Buchowski 1996; Gal 1996; Hann 1996; Phillips 2002).

24. This effort to dichotomize feminism and motherhood has been criticized by scholars of, and in, Eastern Europe; some have noted that feminism understood as a forced choice between a woman's interests and her family would find little popularity in a setting where the family was historically seen as a haven vis-à-vis the socialist regime (Goldfarb 1997; Marody 1993). Others have pointed out the ways in which this false understanding of feminism has been used as a political tool to hinder consciousness-raising, as exemplified by the Jesuits' textbook (Fuszara 2000a, 2000b; Watson 1993).

25. Several scholars observed the phenomenon of the professionalization of a nascent women's movement during times of political transition because of foreign funding and funder-preferred, intervention-oriented effort, rather than grassroots consciousness-raising; see Sabine Lang's (1997) analysis of the "NGOization" of the East and West German women's movements in the 1980s and 1990s, Sonia Alvarez's (1998) examination of Latin American women's movements, and Veronica Schild's (1998) observation of the same trend in Chile.

26. Projects sponsored by Western funders uninformed about local historical experiences and cultural logics might backfire. This has been demonstrated by Rivkin-Fish (2004, 2005), who describes a WHO project focused on women's empowerment in the context of maternity health care, but which was rebuffed by local doctors as misguided in the context of post-Soviet shortages and physicians' experiences of marginalization.

27. The strategy of working from within the government was conducive to women's rights advocacy in Slovenia. When abortion rights were threatened there in the early 1990s due to pressure from the Catholic Church, women responded with a massive protest, which resulted in the dropping of such consideration from the parliamentary debate. The protest was successful because "the renamed Communist Party" (the equivalent of the Polish SLD party) provided the management and the political structure through which the protest could exert pressure on the Slovenian Parliament to keep abortion legal (Šribar 2002, 373–74).

28. The British Broadcasting Corporation, for example, reported on the mock tribunals as highlighting the larger "chilling effect" of the already restrictive 1993 abortion law and noted that doctors and hospitals are fearful of being prosecuted if provide abortion care under the current exceptions to the abortion ban, thereby

resulting in denials of abortion "under any circumstances." "Poland's tough abortion law comes under fire at the women's rights tribunal in July 2001." See http://www.bbc.co.uk/worldservice/sci_tech/features/health/sexwise/sw-news/views7.shtml, accessed March 26, 2015.

29. According to the data reported by the Polish Ministry of Health, adolescent girls ages twelve to nineteen have a high rate of unwanted pregnancies in Poland and constitute 7 percent of all women having children.

30. The Polish expression for a "single mother" is *samotna matka*, which literally translates as a "lonely mother." Likewise, other expressions of singleness (*samotna osoba, on/ona jest samotny/a*) traditionally use the word "lonely." In recent years, the word "lonely" has been at times replaced with "free" (*osoba wolna*), and most recently, the English "single," as in *singielka*, has been adopted in the Polish language as an effort to do away with the term "lonely," especially in the left-leaning media and in the feminist communities.

31. In Portugal in 2004, *Langenort* sailed to the town of Figueira da Foz but was blocked before reaching the harbor by a Portuguese Navy warship, ironically named *F486*; but despite not setting foot on land, the campaign triggered enormous media reverberations. (Abortion was legalized in Portugal in 2007.) WoW has also launched safe abortion hotlines in several nations in South America and Asia. See the section titled "Campaigns": http://www.womenonwaves.org/set-450-en.html, accessed March 26, 2015.

32. The event became the subject of hundreds of news stories in Poland and international media outlets. See http://www.womenonwaves.org/article-232-nl.html, accessed May 27, 2014.

33. The ASTRA network, consisting of twenty-eight organizations, tracks all news and developments in reproductive and sexual health policies and rights in the region, including in Russia, and dispatches electronic bulletins globally to the interested academic, health care, and advocacy communities; it also facilitates collaborations between groups on a variety of projects, both national and international. ASTRA has been advocating for a wide variety of causes that relate to women's rights, including the separation of church and state at local and EU levels, and gender equality broadly defined, and the case of Alicja Tysiąc at the ECHR. See http://www.astra.org.pl/, accessed March 26, 2015.

34. Other similar cases have been filed by the Federation, working on behalf of the plaintiffs, against Poland at the ECHR in recent years. This includes, for example, the case of Z. *v. Poland*; a pregnant woman died as a result of being denied access to comprehensive medical care for ulcerative colitis because her doctors were afraid of harming the fetus (Z *v. Poland*, App. No. 46123/08, Eur. Ct. H.R. (2008). This also includes the 2002 case of RR, whose prenatal tests showed that the fetus suffered from a genetic abnormality, but these results were withheld from her; later she was

repeatedly put off after requesting an abortion until the twenty-four-week time limit had passed. After her infant was diagnosed with Turner's Syndrome (following which her husband left her), RR worked closely with the Federation, which took the case to Polish courts but received little justice. The lower court outright dismissed her case, saying that no crime was committed because doctors are not "public servants," and higher courts offered insufficient compensation. In 2004 she took the case to the ECHR. The court's verdict, announced in May 2011, declared that RR's human rights had been violated and that withholding lawful medical care or information about her state of health amounted to inhuman and degrading treatment (ECHR 2011).

35. "Rząd odwoła się od wyroku w sprawie Alicji Tysiąc." See http://www .wprost.pl/ar/108621/Rzad-odwola-sie-od-wyroku-w-sprawie-Alicji-Tysiac/, accessed March 26, 2015.

36. Notably, the Catholic weekly *The Sunday Guest* (*Gość Niedzielny*) compared Tysiąc's pursuit of abortion to the practices of "Nazi murderers"; Tysiąc sued, won (the judge declared the paper's comparison as the "language of hatred"), and received an apology and damages from the Katowice Archdiocese, which publishes the paper (*Gazeta Wyborcza,* March 5, 2010).

37. This case was filed at the ECHR as the *Case of P. and S. v. Poland.* The complete judgment can be found at http://hudoc.echr.coe.int/sites/eng/pages /search.aspx?i=001-114098#{%22itemid%22:[%22001-114098%22], accessed March 27, 2015.

38. Committee on Economic, Social and Cultural Rights, *Concluding Observations: Poland,* paragraph 28, UN Doc. E/C.12/POL/CO/5 (2009).

39. Before 2009, medical grievances could be reported directly to the Ministry of Health, but the appointment of the ombudsman dedicated to this issue has resulted in a far greater number of cases submitted for review (*Rynek Zdrowia* 2010).

40. "Rząd się nie odwoła. Agata wygrała walkę o swoje prawa." (The government will not appeal. Agata won the struggle for her rights.) *Gazeta Wyborcza* portal. See http://wyborcza.pl/1,75248,13337640,Rzad_sie_nie_odwola__Agata _wygrala_walke_o_swoje_prawa.html, accessed March 27, 2015.

Chapter 4: Confessions, *Kolęda* Rituals, and Other Surveillance

1. See Sunday practices table (referred to as "Dominicantes i communicantes"), table for 2012 on the Institute of Statistics of the Catholic Church (*Instytut Statystyki Kościoła Katolickiego*), http://www.iskk.pl/kosciolnaswiecie/179-dominicantes-i -communicantes-2012.html, accessed March 27, 2015.

2. A decline in the strength of the Catholic Church resulting from revelations of sexual abuse scandals and cover-ups has been observed in a number of nations.

For example, evidence exposed in the Ryan Report in May 2009 in Ireland, containing nine years of investigation of physical and sexual abuses of over 1,500 children housed in Irish Catholic residential "reformatory and industrial" schools, and compiled by the state-funded Commission to Inquire into Child Abuse, has had a detrimental effect on the image of the Catholic Church in Ireland (Commission to Inquire into Child Abuse 2009). In Poland, abuse scandals have also chipped away at the authority of the church. A 2013 national opinion poll titled "The Problems of the Catholic Church in Poland" showed that "pedophilia among priests" is listed as the worst problem, followed by "homosexuality among priests" and "involvement of the Church in politics" (Pankowski 2013, 2).

3. Statistical data related to the Polish Catholic Church are maintained since 1972 by the Institute of Statistics of the Catholic Church (*Instytut Statystyki Kościoła Katolickiego*), Societas Apostolatus Catholici *(*SAC), 1998. See http://www.iskk.ecclesia.org.pl/index.htm, accessed March 27, 2015.

4. The three most important of these documents initiated or promulgated by Pope John Paul II to address the Catholic world on the topic of Christian family values and reproduction are the Apostolic Exhortation *Familiaris Consortio* (John Paul II 1981), the *Catechism of the Catholic Church* (Catechism 1993), and the Encyclical *Evangelium Vitae* (John Paul II 1995a).

5. See the section titled "Documents of the Holy See" on the website of the US Conference of Catholic Bishops: http://www.usccb.org/issues-and-action/marriage-and-family/natural-family-planning/catholic-teaching/, accessed March 27, 2015.

6. For example, the Catholic weekly *Tygodnik Powszechny* in an article titled "Contraception in the Confessional" published an extensive interview with the priest Ksawery Knotz, a professor of the theology of marriage and family in Kraków who teaches natural family planning and authored a book about sexual life in a marriage. The point of the article was that contraception is a legitimate topic to pursue during confession, and that the *Vademecum for Confessors* underscores the importance of doing so as well as gives this practice the authority and legitimacy needed to pursue a sensitive topic (Sporniak 2003).

7. All quotations on this and the following pages regarding the manual refer to the *Vademecum for Confessors concerning Some Aspects of the Morality of Conjugal Life* (Trujillo and Hellín 1997).

8. Ibid., 3.

9. Because contraception and abortion are recognized as politically controversial by the Vatican, the position of the church on these issues is theoretically subject to change, according to the doctrine of "papal infallibility," which states that politically divisive issues are deemed not infallible (Noonan 1986).

10. Trujillo and Hellín 1997, 4.

11. Ibid., 3.

12. Ibid., 5.

13. IUDs, in addition to preventing fertilization, alter the lining of the uterus. In theory, this may prevent pregnancy by preventing the implantation of a fertilized egg, should fertilization occur, but this possibility has not been shown empirically. See http://www.who.int/reproductivehealth/publications/family_planning /9789241500999/en/, accessed March 27, 2015.

14. To substantiate this claim, Vatican documents cite the following statement by Pope John Paul II: "It is being demonstrated in an alarming way by the development of chemical products, intrauterine devices and vaccines which, distributed with the same ease as contraceptives, really act as abortifacients in the very early stages of the development of the life of the new human being" (John Paul II 1995a, 10).

15. Trujillo and Hellín 1997, 6.

16. Ibid., 7.

17. Ibid., 9.

18. Ibid., 7.

19. Ibid.

20. This form of disciplining, discussed in the Polish media, is also used or threatened in situations in which a parishioner is known to have voted for policies or politicians that the church disapproves of as well as against those who have used in vitro fertilization.

21. The Vatican released a number of documents directed to Catholic parishes around the world specifying acceptable and unacceptable methods of birth control. The latest of these documents is titled, "Family Values Versus Safe Sex: A Reflection by His Eminence, Alfonso Cardinal López Trujillo," authored by the president of the Pontificate Council for the Family and released on December 1, 2003 (Trujillo 2003b).

22. Trujillo and Hellín 1997, 15.

23. Traditionally, it is understood that church sacraments were to be offered without a specific expectation of a payment, but on a so-called "*co łaska*" donation basis—which literally means "whatever grace" or "whatever mercy"—thus, whatever the individual is able to donate the priest will be appreciated. Nowadays, payments for christenings, weddings, burials, and other church services are expected, but churches do not openly disclose their prices; therefore, individuals exchange information in discussion forums or comments sections online or through word of mouth about the price lists of particular parishes.

24. The ritual of Kolęda is discussed in detail later in this chapter.

25. Trujillo and Hellín 1997, 8.

26. Ibid., 18.

27. Ibid., 14.

28. Ibid., 13.

29. The Kolęda ritual is sometimes traced as far back as the third century when St. Atanas called for priests to visit the homes of the faithful for the purpose of blessing the household and the family. The canon law that establishes the requirement of Kolęda is number 529, paragraph #1 (Kodeks Prawa Kanonicznego). See http://www.newadvent.org/cathen/09056a.htm#IV and http://www.vatican.va/archive/ENG1104/_P1U.HTM, accessed March 27, 2015.

30. Ibid., Can. 529, §1.

31. This sentiment can also be seen in Polish online discussion forums in relation to the question of how much money is appropriate to put in the envelope for the priest, and whether or not it is necessary to pay the priest to begin with. This topic was taken up by the television channel TVN on January 9, 2012, 10:48 a.m., in a program titled "*Ile dać księdzu po kolędzie?*"—"How much to give the *Kolęda* priest?," and in the discussion forum that followed (Chrzanowska-Kozioł 2012). See http://dziendobry.tvn.pl/video/ile-dac-ksiedzu-po-koledzie,1,newest,18109.html, accessed March 27, 2015.

32. See http://www.diecezja.pl/archidiecezja/aktualnosci/wizyta-duszpasterska-koleda/, accessed March 27, 2015.

33. In recent years, some priests have been cited in the Polish press as observing a trend of a decreasing number of households accepting the Kolęda priest. In 2012, the church distributed a letter titled, "Why Kolęda?" to parishes across Poland, which was posted on numerous church websites. The letter is directed to the faithful and urges their participation in the Kolęda ritual. It also voices a concern about those who identify as "believing-not practicing" (*wierzący-niepraktykujący*). The Kolęda visit is considered an important direct opportunity to retrieve and bring this group back to the church. See Archdiocese of Kraków website: http://www.diecezja.pl/archidiecezja/aktualnosci/wizyta-duszpasterska-koleda/, accessed March 27, 2015.

34. I address the topic of "irrational reproduction" and the birthrate decline in Poland in chapter 6.

35. The Vatican forbids the use of condoms as part of a general opposition to all methods of family planning except for periodic abstinence (Trujillo 2003b). This document takes the additional position that condoms are ineffective in comparison to chastity in terms of prevention of pregnancy (2003b, 12) and sexually transmitted infections alike, and that latex material is porous to infectious agents (2003b, 13). Because of this position (see the section "HIV/AIDS Increase and Decrease with Condoms and Chastity, Respectively" [2003b, 17–19]), the church has been accused of contributing to the AIDS epidemic in Africa (Simpson 2009). In May 2006, Pope Benedict XVI began the first stage of deliberation on the possibility of allowing the use of condoms within a heterosexual marriage in which one of the spouses is infected with HIV, and in 2010 he allowed that the use of condoms by male prostitutes with HIV could be acceptable (Donadio and Goodstein 2010). These deliberations

suggest that the upper echelons of the church consider condoms to be effective; however, the official position is unchanged as the church continues to teach about the ineffectiveness of condoms to its faithful worldwide.

36. This article, titled "The Pill Is against Nature" byTomasz Gołąb, is representative of texts in the Catholic press dealing with family planning in that the typical approach is to juxtapose criticism of hormonal contraceptives with praise for natural family planning (Gołąb 2006). See http://gosc.pl/doc/761443.Pigulka-przeciw -naturze/2, accessed March 27, 2015.

37. A few prominent examples include the Polish Association of Natural Family Planning Teachers (*Polskie Stowarzyszenie Nauczycieli Naturalnego Planowania Rodziny*), http://www.npr.csc.pl/; the Society for Responsible Parenthood (*Towarzystwo Odpowiedzialnego Rodzicielstwa*), http://www.tor.org.pl/; and the John Paul II Institute for the Treatment of Marital Infertility (*Instytut Leczenia Niepłodności Małżeńskiej*). See http://www.leczenie-nieplodnosci.pl/pl/, accessed March 27, 2015.

38. The opinion that condoms have holes was an idea repeatedly encountered by those women in my research who completed premarital courses. This idea can be traced to the Vatican's seminal position paper on contraceptives titled "Family Values versus Safe Sex", which states that latex material is porous, and therefore condoms can fail as a barrier method (see the sections titled "Condom Failure and Pregnancy" and "Condom Failure and Its Latex Material" in Trujillo 2003b, 12–13).

Chapter 5: Abortion, Polish Style

1. The Federation for Women and Family Planning conducted estimates of the number of illegal abortions in 1993 and 1996; the survey was repeated in 1999 and 2000 with similar results. The wide range of the estimate (80,000 to 200,000) is not unlike the ranges of estimates that were made in the United States before *Roe v. Wade* legalized abortion in 1973. According to Allan Rosenfield, the late dean of the Mailman School of Public Health at Columbia University, and one of the most prominent women's health activists before and after legalization of abortion in the United States, estimates of illegal abortion in the United States before *Roe* also had a wide range because of the difficulty in accounting for all the different ways in which women pursued clandestine abortion (personal communication November 14, 2006). In general, maternal mortality can offer some indication of the prevalence of clandestine abortion, but in the case of Poland maternal mortality is not a useful measure because Polish illegal abortions are for the most part performed safely by experienced doctors who performed them before the 1993 ban went into effect.

2. In addition to the state data, up to 85,000 unreported abortions per year maybe have been performed in private clinics in Poland before 1989 (Okólski 1983, 265).

3. There was a small temporary increase in 1997 when abortion was briefly legalized. In 1996 the Polish Parliament, temporarily holding a left-leaning majority supported by President Kwaśniewski, passed the Family Planning Act, which liberalized the 1993 law by including socioeconomic reasons. But the following year the parliamentary power shifted once again in favor of the Catholic Solidarity Election Action (AWS), which promptly took the liberalized abortion law to the Constitutional Tribunal, where the law was changed back to its 1993 form, claiming socioeconomic reasons for abortion to be unconstitutional (Zielińska 2000, 34).

4. In addition to growing out-of-pocket costs, the Polish health care system, as has been described in post-Soviet Russia, requires that patients offer providers informal payments to ensure quality of care (Czupryniak and Loba 2004; McMenamin and Timonen 2002; Rivkin-Fish 2005).

5. The online versions of these newspapers do not contain health advertisements.

6. For example, the forum "zapytal.onet.pl" contains a discussion stream, prompted by the question, "How much is an abortion procedure and where can it be done?" The discussion that follows offers rather accurate advice from multiple respondents about the cost and even provides recommendations for clinics abroad. See http://zapytaj.onet.pl/Category/004,007/2,14508821,Ile_kosztuje_zabieg_aborcji _i_gdzie_go_mozna_wykonac.html, accessed March 27, 2015. Also see the forum "wizaz.pl" with a similar discussion vignette: http://wizaz.pl/forum/showthread .php?t=328206, accessed March 27, 2015.

7. In 2009, the International Planned Parenthood Federation compiled information about abortion methods and laws in thirty-six European nations, including Russia and the former Soviet republics located in Eurasia. According to this report, Poland and Lithuania are the only nations where the D&C procedure is officially the sole available method used in abortions. The vacuum aspiration method and medical abortion are available in all other nations (IPPFEN 2009). In Romania, where curettage has been traditionally used, newer methods such as vacuum aspiration might be sometimes "finished" with a "little curettage, just to be sure" (Lorena Anton 2013, personal communication). In 2012, the World Health Organization in its technical and policy guidance for health care systems states that "vacuum aspiration is the recommended technique of surgical abortion for pregnancies of up to 12 to 14 weeks of gestation. The procedure should not be routinely completed by sharp curettage. Dilatation and sharp curettage (D&C), if still practised, should be replaced by vacuum aspiration" (WHO 2012a, 2).

8. A review of unsafe abortions in Central Eastern Europe and Central Asia indicates that the overall quality of abortion care remains poor in this region mainly

because of the use of older and less safe techniques discussed earlier, namely routine D&C and general anesthesia (Hodorogea and Comendant 2010).

9. During my later research in Gdańsk, I pursued the topic of knowledge about illegal abortion further and found that forty-seven of the fifty-five women I interviewed that year (i.e., 85 percent) had extensive knowledge of the underground.

10. Research on threatening or illegal practices such as clandestine abortion has successfully employed the "three-closest-friends" methodology (Sudman et al. 1977), in which proxy questions pertaining to the informants' friends are used to explore the topic in depth, but allowing research participants to not disclose whether or not they have personally participated in illegal activities (Gipson et al. 2011, 61).

11. Poland's average household income of $14,508 a year ranks near the bottom—thirty-third out of thirty-six countries—among OECD nations, which include European and other more economically developed nations around the world (OECD 2011).

12. See the clinic's website: http://aborcja.cz/, accessed March 27, 2015. For Klinika-Ginekologiczna.com see http://www.klinika-ginekologiczna.com/, accessed March 27, 2015.

13. See, for example, the Polish language website with information for clinics in the Czech Republic, Germany, and the Netherlands: http://www.aborcja-polska .org/adresy-klinik#c, accessed May 27, 2014. Abortion is also legal in Ukraine and the Polish-Ukrainian feminist organization Gender Lviv offers basic information about abortion travel from Poland to Ukraine, emphasizing that the cost is lower than traveling to other nations, although no specific clinics are mentioned. See http://genderlviv.u-f-a.pl/node/184, accessed March 27, 2015.

14. According to the International Women's Health Coalition, a network of reproductive rights and health NGOs, in contrast to misoprostol (the anti-ulcer drug), mifepristone, also known as RU-486, is a registered abortion medication and therefore unavailable in Poland and other settings where abortion is illegal. In these settings misoprostol is instead used for clandestine abortions because of its common availability. Most effective is a mifepristone-misoprostol regimen which is used in legal settings as the standard method for medical abortion. See International Women's Health Coalition: "Abortion with Self-Administered Misoprostol: A Guide For Women," pp. 1–4. http://gynuity.org/resources/info/abortion-with-self -administered-misoprostol-a-guide-for-women/, accessed March 27, 2015.

15. In addition, if an abortion is performed and the fetus is deemed to have been able to live independently, the prison sentence may be increased by an additional eight years.

16. "Lubuskie: ginekolog skazany za nielegalne aborcje," *Rynek Zdrowia,* January 26, 2011, 1. See http://www.rynekzdrowia.pl/Prawo/Lubuskie-ginekolog -skazany-za-nielegalne-aborcje,105785,2.html, accessed March 27, 2015.

17. The involvement of the Catholic Church in the AIDS-prevention campaign led to the marginalization of the voices of sexual minorities as activists were eclipsed by the "moral authority" of the church (Owczarzak 2009). Thus political engagement was discouraged.

18. Interesting parallels can be noted between the current situation in Poland and the reproductive rights restrictions under the dictator Nicolai Ceaușescu in state socialist Romania. Similarly to what is taking place in Poland, the sociologist Gail Kligman shows (1998) that following Ceaușescu's abortion ban, Romanian women turned to clandestine abortions even under the most dire and risky of circumstances, and physicians, risking imprisonment, subverted the law by providing care. She argues (1998, 14–15) that these "structurally determined survival mechanism[s]" were in effect "duplicitous practices" that promoted political passivity and public complicity with Ceaușescu's regime.

19. Chełstowska uses the estimate of 150,000 illegal abortions per year, derived as the average from the range of 80,000 to 200,000 provided by the Federation for Women and Family Planning.

Chapter 6: The "Dying Nation" and the Postsocialist Logics of Declining Motherhood

This chapter is adapted from J. Mishtal, "Irrational Non-reproduction? The 'Dying Nation' and the Postsocialist Logics of Declining Motherhood in Poland," *Anthropology & Medicine* 19, no. 2 (2012): 153–69, and reproduced here with permission from Taylor & Francis, obtained on January 21, 2013, license number 3073651307770.

1. "Mało nas," *Polityka*, no. 46 (2376), November 16, 2002, 13. See http://archiwum.polityka.pl/art/malo-nas,428422.html, accessed March 27, 2015.

2. UN Population Division. Total fertility rate. (Eurostat data source.) http://epp.eurostat.ec.europa.eu/statistics_explained/index.php/Fertility_statistics, accessed May 27, 2014.

3. "Podstawowe informacje o rozwoju demograficznym Polski do 2013 roku" (Warsaw: Central Statistical Agency), January 30, 4. http://stat.gov.pl/obszary-tematyczne/ludnosc/ludnosc/podstawowe-informacje-o-rozwoju-demograficznym-polski-do-2013-roku-,12,4.html and http://stat.gov.pl/cps/rde/xbcr/gus/L_podst_inf_o_rozwoju_dem_pl_do_2013.pdf, accessed March 27, 2015.

4. It is not surprising that a focus on religious family values would not increase fertility as scholars have shown that a religious family ethos is linked with greater gender inequity in the family, which in turn drives women's preferences for fewer children (Castles 2003; Dey 2006; McDonald 2000).

5. "Podstawowe informacje o rozwoju demograficznym Polski do 2013 roku" (Warsaw: Central Statistical Agency), January 30, 4. http://stat.gov.pl/obszary

-tematyczne/ludnosc/ludnosc/podstawowe-informacje-o-rozwoju-demograficznym
-polski-do-2013-roku-,12,4.html and http://stat.gov.pl/cps/rde/xbcr/gus/L_podst
_inf_o_rozwoju_dem_pl_do_2013.pdf, accessed March 27, 2015.

6. The feminist scholar Anne Phillips argues (1997) that incorporating socialist principles that ensure access to education at all levels for women into liberal democratic politico-economic systems can lead to greater gender equality.

7. The postsocialist transformations included other socioeconomic complexities, including the need to reinvent one's usefulness in the new market economy, and emergent understandings of the "personhood" of the postsocialist worker in a newly privatizing environment (Burawoy and Verdery 1999; Dunn 2004).

8. For the embrace of neoliberal market changes and anti-union sentiments in Poland see also Ost and Weinstein (1999). Ost further argues (1999) that the socio-economic class stratification and the associated increase in economic hardships for the majority of Poles have led to the strengthening of the radical right, which became the main political voice bringing attention to the growing postsocialist poverty. Moreover, it is worth noting that the position of the church in Poland with regard to the poor, as evidenced through the Wałęsa administration's anti-working-class agenda stands in contrast to the liberation theology movement of Latin America where some groups within the Catholic Church explicitly positioned themselves on the side of the poor. Although liberation theology was criticized by the Vatican under Popes John Paul II and Benedict XVI, recently Pope Francis has made remarks that suggest an easing of tension between the Vatican and the liberation theology members of the Catholic Church (Carroll 2013).

9. Gini coefficients are tracked by the World Bank, although data are not always available to calculate the coefficients every year (World Bank 2007).

10. See: http://www.becikowe.com/, accessed March 27, 2015.

11. Discussions about declining fertility in Europe are prominent at the level of the European Union; however, the EU has no mandate to require particular social service provisions or any other policies aimed at stimulating births. Thus, each member of the Union devises its own work-family reconciliation policy.

12. The limited nature of the new maternity leave to only "elite" women with full work contracts was the topic of a press conference titled "When Will Young Women Begin to Give Birth?," which was held by Wanda Nowicka on May 13, 2014, in her role as the vice marshal (deputy speaker) of the Lower House of the Polish Parliament. She also expressed a serious concern that the Polish Ministry of Labor and Social Politics fails to collect any data that would indicate how many women enjoy full work contracts and would therefore be eligible for the new maternity leave. See http://www.wandanowicka.eu/wydarzenia/1054-kiedy-mlode-kobiety-zaczna-rodzic.html, accessed March 27, 2015.

13. In 2001, Prime Minister Leszek Miller of the leftist SLD party established the office of the Plenipotentiary on Equal Status of Women and Men and appointed

a well-known politician and feminist Jaruga Nowacka for this position. Ostensibly to advance gender equality in Poland, the office was mainly symbolic as the plenipotentiary had virtually no power to affect policies. Nevertheless, the existence of the office was significant in the state's acknowledgment of gender inequalities in Poland. In 2005, however, the office of the plenipotentiary was eliminated by the conservative Prime Minister Marcinkiewicz of the conservative Law and Justice party (founded by the Kaczyński twins). His move met with written protests submitted by over eighty NGOs to the Polish government as well as the European Commissioner for Employment, Social Affairs and Equal Opportunities, but with no result. Despite the protest, the office of the plenipotentiary has never been renewed.

14. Sterilization of Roma women in Eastern European nations without their full consent while undergoing cesarean sections have been documented in cases at the European Court of Human Rights.

15. See "Rodzina wielodzietna—koszt czy inwestycja?" *Religia Deon.pl*, http://www.deon.pl/religia/kosciol-i-swiat/z-zycia-kosciola/art,14205,rodzina-wielodzietna-koszt-czy-inwestycja.html, accessed March 27, 2015.

16. "Declaration on the Decrease of Fertility in the World," Pontifical Council for the Family,Vatican, February 27, 1998. See http://www.vatican.va/roman_curia/pontifical_councils/family/documents/rc_pc_family_doc_29041998_fecondita_en.html, accessed March 27, 2015.

17. The perceived threat of "Islamization" and other anti-immigrant and nationalist sentiments have intensified across the Eastern European region after the Soviet collapse. These sentiments are often expressed in the context of ethnonationalist pronatalist discourses that pitch migrants as a "problem," albeit one that is abstract and not defined (Rivkin-Fish 2010, 723).

Conclusion

1. The main institutional agent of the Polish church in campaigns that have introduced bills seeking further criminalization of abortion is the Foundation Pro, launched in 1992, which in April 2013 was collecting signatures for another such bill, known as the "Stop Abortion" initiative; however, the bill was later rejected by the Parliament. The group promises to continue these and other efforts, including campaigns to oppose sex education in schools and policies granting legal status to same-sex unions, and their activities have generally intensified in recent years. The reproductive rights activists at the Federation for Women and Family Planning have noted that Foundation Pro's graphic exhibits of fetuses (recently shown in a number of locations in Poland) constitutes a "new trend" in their campaigning against

abortion; this is believed to be a strategy imported from the United States. See www
.stopaborcji.pl, accessed May 27, 2014.

2. The term "double discourse" has also been used to describe the politics of
abortion in Mexico based on a "gentlemen's agreement" between the politicians and
the Catholic Church, according to which abortion is illegal but accessible to those
who can pay (Ortiz-Ortega 2005).

3. A growing use of ARTs has been observed and researched around the world
(e.g., Inhorn and van Balen 2002). The postponement of childbearing owing to an
inability to reconcile work and family, as well as inadequate state support for families, leads to an increase in age-related infertility and a growing use of ARTs (Chavkin
2008).

4. See http://www.nasz-bocian.pl/, accessed May 27, 2014.

5. See http://www.novum.com.pl/pl/nowosci/szansa-na-bezplatny-zabieg-in
-vitro/, accessed May 27, 2014.

6. See http://www.astra.org.pl/mission.html, accessed May 27, 2014.

7. See "Spanish Abortion Bill Set to Trigger Huge Protest in Madrid," *Eu-
ronews*, February 1, 2014, http://www.euronews.com/2014/02/01/spanish-abortion
-bill-set-to-trigger-huge-protest-in-madrid/, accessed May 27, 2014.

References

Abridged Statistical Yearbook of Poland. 2008. (May): 1–712. Warsaw: Central Statistical Agency.

Abridged Statistical Yearbook of Poland. 2014. (June): 1–727. Warsaw: Central Statistical Agency.

Abu-Lughod, L. 1990. "The Romance of Resistance: Tracing Transformations of Power through Bedouin Women." *American Ethnologist* 17 (1): 41–55.

Allen, A. 1996. "Foucault on Power: A Theory for Feminists." In *Feminist Interpretations of Foucault,* edited by S. J. Hekman, 265–81. University Park: Pennsylvania State University Press.

Alvarez, S. 1990. *Engendering Democracy in Brazil: Women's Movements in Transition Politics.* Princeton, NJ: Princeton University Press.

———. 1998. "Latin American Feminisms 'Go Global': Trends of the 1990s and Challenges for the New Millennium." In *Cultures of Politics, Politics of Cultures: Re-visioning Latin American Social Movements,* edited by S. Alvarez, E. Dagnino, and A. Escobar. Boulder, CO: Westview Press.

Baban, A. 2000. "Women's Sexuality and Reproductive Behavior in Post-Ceauşescu Romania: A Psychological Approach." In *Reproducing Gender: Politics, Publics, and Everyday Life after Socialism,* edited by S. Gal and G. Kligman, 225–55. Princeton, NJ: Princeton University Press.

Balicki, M. 2003. "List Ministra Zdrowia w sprawie obowiązku przestrzegania praw kobiet." http://www.mz.gov.pl/wwwmz/index?mr=q101&ms=&ml=pl&mi=&mx=0&mt=0&my=1&ma=01059.

Bartnik, C. 2010. "Zło pedagogiki liberalistycznej." *Nasz Dziennik.* http://www.radiomaryja.pl/artykuly.php?id=107898.

Bax, M. 1991. "Religious Regimes and State-Formation: Toward a Research Perspective." In *Religious Regimes and State-Formation,* edited by E. R. Wolf, 7–27. Albany: State University of New York Press.

Bayes, J. H., and N. Tohidi. 2001. "Conflict in Beijing." In *Globalization, Gender, and Religion: The Politics of Women's Rights in Catholic and Muslim Contexts,* edited by J. H. Bayes and N. Tohidi, 1–16. New York: Palgrave.

Bellier, I., and T. M. Wilson, eds. 2000. *An Anthropology of the European Union: Building, Imagining, and Experiencing the New Europe.* Oxford: Berg.

Bernard, H. R. 1995. *Research Methods in Anthropology.* Walnut Creek, CA: Altamira Press.

———. 2006. *Research Methods in Anthropology: Qualitative and Quantitative Approaches.* Oxford: Altamira Press.

Bernardi, L. 2007. "An Introduction to Anthropological Demography." *Max Planck Institute for Demographic Research* 031 (August): 1–19.

Bernhard, M. H. 1993. *The Origins of Democratization in Poland.* New York: Columbia University Press.

Beveridge, F., S. Nott, and K. Stephen. 2000. "Addressing Gender in National and Community Law and Policy-Making." In *Social Law and Policy in an Evolving European Union*, edited by J. Shaw, 135–56. Portland: Hart.

Boguszewski, R. 2009. "Dwie dekady przemian religijności w Polsce." Warsaw: CBOS Centrum Badania Opinii Społecznej (Public Opinion Research Center). Report number BS/120/2009, 1–28.

———. 2010. "Co jest ważne, co można, a czego nie wolno—normy i wartosci w życiu Polaków." Warsaw: CBOS—Centrum Badania Opinii Społecznej (Public Opinion Research Center). Report number BS/99/2010, 1–16.

Bongaarts, J. 2002. "The End of the Fertility Transition in the Developed World." *Population and Development Review* 28 (3): 419–43.

Borneman, J. 1998. *Subversions of International Order: Studies in the Political Anthropology of Culture.* Albany: State University of New York Press.

Brodribb, S. 1993. *Nothing Mat(t)ers: A Feminist Critique of Postmodernism.* North Melbourne: Spinifex.

Brush, L. D. 2003. *Gender and Governance.* Walnut Creek, CA: AltaMira Press.

Buchowski, M. 1996. "The Shifting Meanings of Civil and Civic Society in Poland." In *Civil Society*, edited by C. Hann and E. Dunn, 79–98. London: Routledge.

Bunda, M. 2010. "Polki za granicą." *Polityka.Pl:* 1. http://www.polityka.pl/społeczenstwo /1509174,1,polki-za-granica.read#ixzz1b269fcTT.

Bunda, M., and M. Perzanowski. 2010. "Aborcja po polsku. W trybach ochrony." *Polityka.Pl:* 1–3. http://www.polityka.pl/tygodnikpolityka/spoleczenstwo /1509126,1,aborcja-po-polsku.read.

Burawoy, M., and K. Verdery, eds. 1999. *Uncertain Transition—Ethnographics of Change in the Postsocialist World.* Lanham, MD: Rowman and Littlefield.

Butler, J. 1990. *Gender Trouble: Feminism and the Subversion of Identity.* New York: Routledge.

Byrnes, T. 1997. "The Catholic Church and Poland's Return to Europe." *East European Quarterly* 30 (January): 433–48.

Bystydzinski, J. M. 1995. "Women and Families in Poland: Pressing Problems and Possible Solutions." In *Family, Women, and Employment in Central Eastern Europe*, edited by B. Łobodzińska, 193–204. Westport, CT: Greenwood Press.

Caldwell, J. 1976. "Toward a Restatement of Demographic Transition Theory." *Population and Development Review* 2 (3/4): 321–66.

Caldwell, J., and T. Schindlmayr. 2003. "Explanations of the Fertility Crisis in Modern Societies." *Population Studies* 57 (3): 241–63.

Callahan, D. 1999. "The Social Sciences and the Task of Bioethics." *Daedalus* 128 (4): 275–94.

Carrette, J., ed. 1999. *Religion and Culture by Michel Foucault.* New York: Routledge.

———. 2000. *Foucault and Religion: Spiritual Corporality and Political Spirituality.* New York: Routledge.

Carroll, J. 2013. "Who Am I to Judge?" *New Yorker,* December 23, 80–91.

Castles, F. 2003. "The World Turned Upside Down: Below Replacement Fertility, Changing Preferences, and Family-Friendly Public Policy in 21 OECD Countries." *Journal of European Social Policy* 13 (3): 209–27.

Catechism of the Catholic Church. 1993. Vatican, Libreria Editrice Vaticana. http://www.vatican.va/archive/ENG0015/_INDEX.HTM#fonte.

Chavkin, W. 2008. "Biology and Destiny: Women, Work, Birthrates, and Assisted Reproductive Technologies." *Global Empowerment of Women: Responses to Globalization and Politicized Religions,* edited by C. Elliott, 45–56. New York: Routledge.

Chavkin, W., and E. Chesler, eds. 2005. *Where Human Rights Begin: Health, Sexuality, and Women in the New Millennium.* New Brunswick, NJ: Rutgers University Press.

Chavkin, W., L. Leitman, and K. Polin 2013. "Conscientious Objection and Refusal to Provide Reproductive Healthcare: A White Paper Examining Prevalence, Health Consequences, and Policy Responses." *International Journal of Gynecology and Obstetrics* 123 (Suppl. 3): S41–S53.

Chełstowska, A. 2011. "Stigmatisation and Commercialisation of Abortion Services in Poland: Turning Sin into Gold." *Reproductive Health Matters* 19 (37): 98–106.

Chidester, D. 1986. "Michel Foucault and the Study of Religion." *Religious Studies Review* 12 (1): 1–39.

Chimiak, G. 2003. "Bulgarian and Polish Women in the Public Sphere." *International Feminist Journal of Politics* 5 (1): 3–27.

Chołuj, B. 1997. "Bożena Chołuj, Gender Studies." In *Same o Sobie: Rozmowy z 13 Członkiniami,* edited by K. Lohman, M. Malachowska, and S. F. Nowicki, 7–21. Warsaw: Społeczny Komitet Organizacji Pozarządowych.

Chrzanowska-Kozioł, K. 2002. "Ile dać księdzu po kolędzie?" Warsaw: TVN. http://dziendobry.tvn.pl/video/ile-dac-ksiedzu-po-koledzie,1,newest,18109.html.

Ciechocinska, M. 1993. "Gender Aspects of Dismantling the Command Economy in Eastern Europe: The Case of Poland." In *Democratic Reform and the*

Position of Women in Transitional Economies, edited by V. M. Moghadam. Oxford: Oxford University Press.

Clifford, J., and G. Marcus 1986. *Writing Culture: The Poetics and Politics of Ethnography*. Berkeley: University of California Press.

Commission to Inquire into Child Abuse. 2009. "Final Report of the Commission to Inquire into Child Abuse Dated 20th May 2009." Executive Summary, 1–30.

Connell, R. W. 1990. "The State, Gender, and Sexual Politics: Theory and Appraisal." *Theory and Society* 19 (5): 507–44.

Corrin, C., ed. 1992. *Superwomen and the Double Burden: Women's Experiences of Change in Central and Eastern Europe and the Former Soviet Union*. Toronto: Second Story Press.

Coyle, A. 2003. "Fragmented Feminisms." *Gender and Development* 11 (3): 57–65.

Creed, G., and J. Wedel. 1997. "Second Thoughts from the Second World: Interpreting Aid in Post-Communist Eastern Europe." *Human Organization* 56 (3): 253–64.

Curtin, J., and W. Higgins. 1998. "Feminism and Unionism in Sweden." *Politics and Society* 26 (1): 69–93.

Czupryniak, L., and J. Loba. 2004. "Route of Corruption in Poland's Health Care System." *Lancet* 364 (9448): 1856.

Dahlerup, D. 2002. "Three Waves of Feminism in Denmark." In *Thinking Differently*, edited by G. Griffin and R. Braidotti. London: Zed Books.

Daniel, K. 1995. "The Church-State Situation in Poland after the Collapse of Communism." *Brigham Young University Law Review* 2:401–19.

David, H. P., and A. Titkow. 1994. "Abortion and Women's Rights in Poland." *Studies in Family Planning* 25 (4): 239–42.

Dean, M. 1999. *Governmentality*. London: SAGE.

Declaration on the Decrease of Fertility in the World. 1998. Vatican: Libreria Editrice Vaticana. http://vatican.va/roman_curia/pontifical_councils/family/documents/rc_pc_family_doc_29041998_fecondita_en.html.

Dembinska, A. 2012. "Bioethical Dilemmas of Assisted Reproduction in the Opinions of Polish Women in Infertility Treatment: A Research Report." *Journal of Medical Ethics* 38 (12): 731–34.

Derczyński, W. 2003. "Opinie o prawnej regulacji przerywania ciąży." Warsaw: Centrum Badania Opinii Społecznej, 1–9.

Deveaux, M. 1996. "Feminism and Empowerment: A Critical Reading of Foucault." In *Feminist Interpretations of Foucault*, edited by S. J. Hekman, 211–38. University Park: Pennsylvania State University Press.

Dey, I. 2006. "Wearing Out the Work Ethic: Population Ageing, Fertility, and Work-Life Balance." *Journal of Social Policy* 35 (4): 671–88.

De Zordo, S., and J. Mishtal. 2011. "Physicians and Abortion: Provision, Political Participation, and Conflicts on the Ground: The Cases of Brazil and Poland." *Women's Health Issues* 21 (3S): 32–36.

Diskin, H. 2001. *The Seeds of Triumph: Church and State in Gomułka's Poland.* Budapest: Central European University Press.

Dölling, I., D. Hahn, and S. Scholz. 2000. "'Birth Strike' in the New Federal States: Is Sterilization an Act of Resistance?" In *Reproducing Gender: Politics, Publics, and Everyday Life after Socialism,* edited by S. Gal and G. Kligman, 118–47. Princeton, NJ: Princeton University Press.

Domanski, H. 2002. "Is the East European 'Underclass' Feminized?" *Communist and Post-Communist Studies* 35 (4): 671–88.

Donadio, R., and L. Goodstein. 2010. "In Rare Cases, Pope Justifies Use of Condoms." *New York Times,* November 20. http://www.nytimes.com/2010/11/21/world/europe/21pope.html?pagewanted=all&_r=0.

Dunn, E. 2004. *Privatizing Poland: Baby Food, Big Business, and the Remaking of Labor.* Ithaca, NY: Cornell University Press.

ECHR (European Court of Human Rights). May 26, 2011. "'Inhuman Treatment' of Mother Denied Timely Access to an Amniocentesis Whose Baby Was Born Severely Disabled." Press Release: ECHR 020, 1–6. http://www.coe.int/t/dg3/healthbioethic/texts_and_documents/Bioethics_and_caselaw_Court_EN.pdf.

Economist. 1991. ". . . and unto Poland, What Is God's." May 25, 51.

———. 2004. "Screwing the Brand Names." September 16, 1–2. http://www.economist.com/node/3205917.

Einhorn, B., and C. Sever. 2005. "Gender, Civil Society, and Women's Movements in Central and Eastern Europe." In *Gender and Civil Society,* edited by J. Howell and D. Mulligan, 23–53. New York: Routledge.

Ekiert, G. 1997. "Rebellious Poles: Political Crises and Popular Protest under State Socialism, 1945–89." *East European Politics and Societies* 11 (Spring): 299–338.

Elias, N. 1978. *The Civilizing Process.* Vols. 1–3. New York: Pantheon Books.

Erikson, S. L. 2005. "Now It Is Completely the Other Way Around": Political Economics of Fertility in Re-unified Germany." In *Barren States,* edited by C. B. Douglass, 49–72. New York: Berg.

EU Network of Independent Experts on Fundamental Rights. December 14, 2005. *Opinion No 4-2005: The Right to Conscientious Objection and the Conclusion by EU Member States of Concordats with the Holy See.* 1–41. http://ec.europa.eu/justice/fundamental-rights/files/cfr_cdfopinion4_2005_en.pdf

Fodor, E. 1997. "Gender in Transition: Unemployment in Hungary, Poland, and Slovakia." *East European Politics and Societies* 11 (3): 470–501.

———. 2002. "Gender and the Experience of Poverty in Eastern Europe and Russia after 1989." *Communist and Post-Communist Studies* 35 (4): 369–82.

Fodor, E., C. Glass, J. Kawachi, and L. Popescu. 2002. "Family Policies and Gender in Hungary, Poland, and Romania." *Communist and Post-Communist Studies* 35 (4): 475–90.

Ford, L. 2012. "Gro Harlem Brundtland Censures Rio+20's Gender Equality Outcomes." *Guardian*, June 22. http://www.theguardian.com/global-development/2012/jun/22/gro-harlem-brundtland-rio20-gender-equality.

Foucault, M. 1977. *Discipline and Punish: Birth of the Prison.* New York: Vintage Books.

———. 1978. *The History of Sexuality.* New York: Vintage.

———. 1991a. "Governmentality." In *The Foucault Effect*, edited b. G. Burchell, C. Gordon, and P. Miller, 87–104. Chicago: University of Chicago Press.

———. 1991b. "On Religion." In *Religion and Culture by Michel Foucault*, edited by J. Carrette, 106–9. New York: Routledge.

Fraser, N. 1989. "Foucault on Modern Power: Empirical Insights and Normative Confusions." *Unruly Practices: Power, Discourse and Gender in Contemporary Social Theory*, edited by N. Fraser. Minneapolis: University of Minnesota Press.

Frątczak, E. 2004. "Family and Fertility in Poland—Changes during the Transition Period." In *PIE International Workshop on Demographic Changes and Labor Markets in Transition Economies.* Tokyo, Japan.

Freundl, G., I. Sivin, and I. Batár. 2010. "State-of-the-Art of Non-Hormonal Methods of Contraception: IV. Natural Family Planning." *European Journal of Contraception and Reproductive Health Care* 15 (2): 113–23.

Friedrich, K. 2005. "'Land without a Quisling': Patterns of Cooperation with the Nazi German Occupation Regime in Poland during World War II." *Slavic Review* 64 (4): 711–46.

Funk, N. 2004. "Feminist Critiques of Liberalism: Can They Travel East?" *Signs: Journal of Women in Culture and Society* 29 (3): 695–720.

Fuszara, M. 1991. "Legal Regulation of Abortion in Poland." *Signs: Journal of Women in Culture and Society* 17 (1): 117–28.

———. 2000a. "Feminism, the New Millennium, and Ourselves: A Polish View." In *Feminisms at a Millennium*, edited by J. A. Howard and C. Allen, 75–81. Chicago: University of Chicago Press.

———. 2000b. "New Gender Relations in Poland in the 1990s." *Reproducing Gender: Politics, Publics, and Everyday Life after Socialism*, edited by S. Gal and G. Klingman. Princeton, NJ: Prineton University Press.

Gal, S. 1994. "Gender in the Post-Socialist Transition." *East European Politics and Societies* 8 (2): 256–86.

———. 1996. "Feminism and Civil Society." Special issue, *Replika* 6:74–83. http://www.c3.hu/scripta/scriptao/replika/honlap/english/01/07fgal.htm.

Gal, S., and G. Kligman. 2000a. *The Politics of Gender After Socialism*. Princeton, NJ: Princeton University Press.

——, eds. 2000b. *Reproducing Gender: Politics, Publics, and Everyday Life after Socialism*. Princeton, NJ: Princeton University Press.

Garmany, J. 2010. "Religion and Governmentality: Understanding Governance in Urban Brazil." *Geoforum* 41 (6): 908–18.

Gautier, M. L. 1997. "Church Attendance and Religious Belief in Postcommunist Societies." *Journal for the Scientific Study of Religion* 36 (2): 289–96.

Gazeta.pl. 2002. "Co łączy ustawę aborcyjną z integracją z UE—list do Parlamentu Europejskiego." February 4, 1–2. Warsaw. www.gazeta.pl.

Gazeta Wyborcza. 2012. "Tusk karci posłów za głosowanie w sprawie aborcji: PO jest na największym zakręcie od momentu powstania." October 11, 1–2. http://m.wyborcza.pl/wyborcza/1,105402,12655365.html.

Ghodsee, K. 2004. "Feminism-by-Design: Emerging Capitalisms, Cultural Feminism, and Women's Nongovernmental Organizations in Postsocialist Eastern Europe." *Signs: Journal of Women in Culture and Society* 29 (3): 728–53.

Ginsburg, F., and R. Rapp, eds. 1989. *Contested Lives: The Abortion Debate in an American Community*. Berkeley: University of California Press.

——. 1991. "The Politics of Reproduction." *Annual Review of Anthropology* 20: 311–43.

——, eds. 1995. *Conceiving the New World Order: The Global Politics of Reproduction*. Berkeley: University of California Press.

Gipson, J., D. Becker, J. Mishtal, and A. Norris 2011. "Conducting Collaborative Abortion Research in International Settings." *Women's Health Issues* 21 (3S): 58–62.

Gołąb, T. 2006. "The Pill Is against Nature." *Sunday Guest [Gość Niedzielny]:* 2.

Goldfarb, J. 1997. "Why Is There No Feminism after Communism?" *Social Research* 64 (2): 235–57.

Goldstein, D. M. 2013. *Laughter Out of Place: Race, Class, Violence, and Sexuality in a Rio Shantytown*. With a new preface. Berkeley: University of California Press.

Goven, J. 1993. "Gender Politics in Hungary: Autonomy and Anti-Feminism." In *Gender Politics and Post-Communism: Reflections from Eastern Europe and the Former Soviet Union*, edited by N. Funk and M. Mueller, 224–40. New York: Routledge.

——. 2000. "New Parliament, Old Discourse? The Parental Leave Debate in Hungary." In *Reproducing Gender: Politics, Publics, and Everyday Life after Socialism*, edited by S. Gal and G. Kligman. Princeton, NJ: Princeton University Press.

Graff, A. 2001. *Świat bez kobiet. Płeć w polskim życiu publicznym*. Warsaw: W.A.B. Press.

Grzybowski, M. 1998. "Poland." In *The Handbook of Political Change in Eastern Europe*, edited by T. H. Sten Berglund and Frank H. Aarebrot, 157–90. Cheltenham, UK, Edward Elgar.

Haddad, L. B., and N. M. Nour. 2009. "Unsafe Abortion: Unnecessary Maternal Mortality." *Reviews in Obstetrics and Gynecology* 2 (2): 122–26.

Halliburton, M. 2011. "Resistance or Inaction? Protecting Ayurvedic Medical Knowledge and Problems of Agency." *American Ethnologist* 36 (1): 86–101.

Halsaa, B. 2002. "The History of the Women's Movement in Norway." In *Thinking Differently*, edited by G. Griffin and R. Braidotti, 351–60. London: Zed Books.

Haney, L. 1996. "Homeboys, Babies, Men in Suits: The State and the Reproduction of Male Dominance." *American Sociological Review* 61 (5): 759–78.

———. 2003. "Welfare Reform with a Familiar Face: Reconstituting State and Domestic Relations in Post-Socialist Eastern Europe." In *Familes of a New World: Gender, Politics, and State Development in a Global Context*, edited by L. Haney and L. Pollard, 159–78. Routledge, New York: Routledge.

Haney, L., and L. Pollard, eds. 2003. *Families of a New World.* New York: Routledge.

Hanley, E. 2003. "A Party of Workers or a Party of Intellectuals? Recruitment into Eastern European Communist Parties, 1945–1988." *Social Forces* 81 (4): 1073–1105.

Hann, C. 1994. "After Communism: Reflections on East European Anthropology and the Transition." *Social Anthropology* 2 (3): 229–49.

———. 1996. "Introduction: Political Society and Civil Anthropology." In *Civil Society*, edited by C. Hann and E. Dunn, 1–26. London: Routledge.

———. 1997. "The Nation-State, Religion, and Uncivil Society: Two Perspectives from the Periphery." *Daedalus* 126 (2): 27–45.

———. 2000. "Problems with the (De)privatization of Religion." *Anthropology Today* 16 (6): 14–20.

Hartmann, H. 2010. "The Unhappy Marriage of Marxism and Feminism: Towards a More Progressive Union." In *Feminist Theory Reader: Local and Global Perspectives*, edited by Carole R. McCann and Syung-kyung Kim, 206–21. New York: Routledge.

Hartsock, N. 1990. "Foucault on Power: A Theory for Women?" In *Feminism/Postmodernism*, edited by L. J. Nicholson. New York: Routledge.

Hauser, E. 1995. "Traditions of Patriotism, Questions of Gender: The Case of Poland." In *Sexual Politics and the Public Sphere*, edited by N. Funk and M. Mueller. New York: Routledge.

Hauser, E., B. Heyns, and J. Mansbridge. 1993. "Feminism in the Interstices of Politics and Culture." *Gender and Politics and Post-Communism: Reflections from Eastern Europe and the Former Soviet Union*, edited by N. Funk and M. Mueller. New York: Routledge.

Hemment, J. 2004. "Strategizing Gender and Development: Action Research and Ethnographic Responsibility in the Russian Provinces." In *Post-Soviet Women Encountering Transition: Nation Building, Economic Survival, and Civic Activism*, edited by K. Kuehnast and C. Nechemias, 313–34. Washington, DC: Woodrow Wilson Center Press.

———. 2007. *Empowering Women in Russia: Activism, Aid, and NGOs*. Bloomington, Indiana University Press.

Henzler, M. 2002. "Więcej dziadków niż wnuków." *Polityka*, December 7 (2379): 20–22. http://archiwum.polityka.pl/art/wiecej-dziadkow-niz-wnukow,376758 .html.

Hetnal, A. 1998. "The Polish Catholic Church in Pre-and Post-1989 Poland: An Evaluation." *East European Quarterly* 32 (Winter): 503–29.

Hipsz, N. 2011. "Opinie o prawnej dopuszczalności i regulacji aborcji." *Centrum Badania Opinii Społecznej*, Report number BS/102/2011, 1–12. Warsaw.

Hodorogea, S., and R. Comendant. 2010. "Prevention of Unsafe Abortion in Countries of Central Eastern Europe and Central Asia." *International Journal of Gynecology and Obstetrics* 110 (Supplement): S34–S37.

Htun, M. 2003. "Women and Democracy." In *Constructing Democratic Governance in Latin America*, edited by J. I. Dominguez and M. Shifter, 118–36. Baltimore: Johns Hopkins University Press.

Hyman, A., K. Blanchard, F. Coeytaux, D. Grossman, and A. Teixeira. 2013. "Misoprostol in Women's Hands: A Harm Reduction Strategy for Unsafe Abortions." *Contraception* 87 (2): 128–30.

Inhorn, M. C. 2006. "Defining Women's Health: A Dozen Messages from More than 150 Ethnographies." *Medical Anthropology Quarterly* 20 (3): 345–78.

Inhorn, M. C., and F. van Balen, eds. 2002. *Infertility around the Globe: New Thinking on Childlessness, Gender, and Reproductive Technologies*. Berkeley: University of California Press.

IPPFEN (International Planned Parenthood Federation—European Network). 2009. *Abortion Legislation in Europe. Updated January 2012*, 1–86. Brussels, Belgium. http://www.ippfen.org/resources/abortion-legislation-europe.

Ivanica, M. 2003. *An Overview of the Treaty of Accession of Cyprus, Czech Republic, Estonia, Hungary, Latvia, Lithuania, Malta, Poland, Slovakia, Slovenia to the European Union*. Brussels: European Institute of Public Administration.

Izdebski, Z. 2006. "Summary." In *Seksualność Polaków w dobie HIV/AIDS. Ryzykowna dekada. Studium porównawcze 1997–2001–2005*, 118–30. Zielona Góra: Wydawnictwo Uniwersytetu Zielonogórskiego (University of Zielona Góra Press).

Jackowski, J. M. 2007. "Bitwa o rodzinę." *Nasz Dziennik*, October 17, 2007, 1–4. http://www.radiomaryja.pl/artykuly.php?id=91802.

Jakubowska, L. 1990. "Political Drama in Poland." *Anthropology Today* 6 (4): 10–13.

———. 1993. "Writing about Eastern Europe. Perspectives from Ethnography and Anthropology." In *The Politics of Ethnographic Reading and Writing*, edited by H. Driessen, 143–59. Saarbrücken: Breitenbach.

———. 2001. "Morality, Rationality, and History: Dilemmas of Land Reprivatization in Poland." In *Poland beyond Communism: "Transition" in Critical Perspective*, edited by M. Bukowski, Conte, E., and C. Nagengast, 125–40. Fribourg, Switzerland: Presses Universitaires de Fribourg.

———. 2012. *Patrons of History: Nobility, Capital, and Political Transitions in Poland.* Burlington, VT: Ashgate.

Jessop, B. 2004. "The Gender Selectivities of the State: A Critical Realist Analysis." *Journal of Critical Realism* 3 (2): 207.

Jezuici, B. 1998. "Kobieta." In *Jezus Uczy i Zbawia*, edited by Z. Marek. Kraków: WAM Press.

Joffe, C. E. 1995. *Doctors of Conscience: The Struggles to Provide Abortion before and after Roe v. Wade.* Boston: Beacon Press.

Johannisson, E., et al., eds. 1997. *Assessment of Research and Service Needs in Reproductive Health in Eastern Europe—Concerns and Commitments.* New York: Parthenon.

John Paul II. 1981. Apostolic Exhortation *Familiaris Consortio* of Pope John Paul II to the Episcopate, to the Clergy, and the Faithful of the Whole Catholic Church on the Role of the Christian Family in the Modern World. Vatican, Libreria Editrice Vaticana, 1–66. http://www.vatican.va/holy_father/john_paul_ii/apost _exhortations/docucments/hf_jp-ii_exh_19811122_familiaris-consortio_en.html.

———. 1995a. Encyclical *Evangelium Vitae:* To the Bishops, Priests and Deacons, Men and Women Religious Lay Faithful and All People of Good Will on the Value and Inviolability of Human Life, 1–90. Vatican: Libreria Editrice Vaticana. http://www.vatican.va/holy_father/john_paul_ii/encyclicals/documents /hf_hf_jp-ii_let_25031995_evangelium-vitae_en.html.

———. 1995b. Letter of Pope John Paul II to Women. Vatican: Libreria Editrice Vaticana.

Jones, R. K., and K. Kooistra. 2011. "Abortion incidence and access to services in the United States, 2008." *Perspectives on Sexual and Reproductive Health* 43 (1): 41–50.

Jones, R. K., Finer, L.B., and S. Singh. 2010. *Characteristics of U.S. Abortion Patients, 2008.* New York: Guttmacher Institute.

KAI (Katolicka Agencja Informacyjna). 2002. "Unia Pracy: bp Pieronek powinien przeprosić." http://ekai.pl/wydarzenia/x1696/unia-pracy-bp-pieronek-powinien -przeprosic/.

Kenney, P. 1999. "The Gender of Resistance in Communist Poland." *American Historical Review* 104 (2): 399–425.

———. 2002. *Carnival of Revolution: Central Europe 1989*. Princeton, NJ: Princeton University Press.

Kleinman, A. 1995. "Anthropology of Bioethics." In *Writing at the Margin: Discourse between Anthropology and Medicine*, by A. Kleinman. Berkeley: University of California Press, 41–67.

Kligman, G. 1996. "Women and the Negotiation of Identity in Post-Communist Eastern Europe." In *Identities in Transition: Russia and Eastern Europe after Communism*, edited by V. Bonnell, 68–91. Berkeley: International and Area Studies.

———. 1998. *The Politics of Duplicity: Controlling Reproduction in Ceaușescu's Romania*. Berkeley: University of California Press.

Klimkowska, K. 2013. "Kłamstwo aborcyjne trwa." *Tygodnik Przegląd P.18–19*. http://www.przeglad-tygodnik.pl/pl/artykul/klamstwo-aborcyjne-trwa.

Klinger, K. 2013. "Obiecanki Arłukowicza. Projekt rozporządzenia utknął, a kobiety dalej rodzą w bólu." *Dziennik.pl*. http://zdrowie.dziennik.pl/aktualnosci/artykuly/441244,kobiety-w-szpitalach-rodza-w-bolach-i-tak-juz-zostanie .html.

Kocourkova, J. 2002. "Leave Arrangements and Childcare Services in Central Europe: Policies and Practices before and after the Transition." *Community, Work & Family* 5 (3): 301–18.

Kolchevska, N. 2005. "Gender and Slavic Studies: Overview and Goals for the Future." *NewsNet—American Association for the Advancement of Slavic Studies* 45 (5): 1–4.

Korbonski, A. 2000. "Poland Ten Years After: The Church." *Communist and Post-Communist Studies* 33 (1): 123–45.

Korzerawska, M. 1997. Nie zabijał. *Gazeta Wyborcza*, May 17, 114. http://szukaj.wyborcza.pl/archiwum/1,0,246810,19970517rp_dgw,nie_zabijal,.html.

Kostadinova, T. 2003. "Voter Turnout Dynamics in Post-Communist Europe." *European Journal of Political Research* 42 (6): 741–59.

Koster, A. 1991. "Clericals Versus Socialists: Toward the 1984 Malta School War." In *Religious Regimes and State-Formation*, edited by E. R. Wolf, 105–32. Albany: State University of New York Press.

Kozłowska, K. B. 2011. "Orzeczenie Europejskiego Trybunału Praw Człowieka w Sprawie R.R. Przeciwko Polsce." http://www.bpp.gov.pl/index.php?id=a8#kom28.

Krause, E. 2005a. *A Crisis in Births: Population Politics and Family Planning in Italy*. Belmont, CA: Wadsworth Thomson.

———. 2005b. "'Toys and Perfumes': Imploding Italy's Population Paradox and Motherly Myths." In *Barren States*, edited by C. B. Douglass, 159–82. New York: Berg.

Kubik, J. 1994. *The Power of Symbols against the Symbols of Power: The Rise of Solidarity and the Fall of State Socialism.* University Park: Pennsylvania State University Press.

———. 2001. "Rebelliousness and Civility: Strategies of Coping with the Systemic Change in Poland." In *Poland beyond Communism*, edited by E. Conte, M. Bukowski, and C. Nagengast, 141–62. Fribourg, Switzerland: Presses Universitaires de Fribourg.

Kulawik, T. 2009. "Science Policy and Public Accountability in Poland: The Case of Embryonic Stem Cell Research." *Science and Public Policy* 36 (6): 474–76.

Kulczycki, A. 1995. "Abortion Policy in Postcommunist Europe: The Conflict in Poland." *Population and Development Review* 21 (3): 471–505.

Kulish, N. 2011. "Provocateur's Strong Showing Is a Sign of a Changing Poland." *New York Times*, October 10, 1–3. http://www.nytimes.com/2011/10/11/world /europe/polands-palikot-movement-signals-a-changing-society.html ?pagewanted=all.

Laba, R. 1991. *The Roots of Solidarity.* Princeton, NJ: Princeton University Press.

Lampland, M. 1994. "Family Portraits: Gendered Images of the Nation in Nineteenth-Century Hungary." *East European Politics and Societies* 8 (2): 287–316.

———. 1995. *The Object of Labor: Commodification in Socialist Hungary.* Chicago: University of Chicago Press.

Lang, S. 1997. "The NGOization of Feminism." In *Transitions, Environments, Translations: Feminisms in International Politics*, edited by J. W. Scott, C. Kaplan, and D. Keates, 101–20. London: Routledge.

Lee, H. 2001. "Transition to Democracy in Poland." *East European Quarterly* 35 (1): 87–107.

Levada, W., and L. F. Ledaria. 2008. "Instructions Dignitas Personae on Certain Bioethical Questions." Rome, Vatican. http://www.vatican.va/roman_curia/ congregations/cfaith/documents/rc_con_cfaith_doc_20081208_dignitas -personae-en.html.

Leven, B. 1994. "The Status of Women and Poland's Transition to a Market Economy." In *Women in the Age of Economic Transformation*, edited by N. Aslanbeigui et al., 27–42. New York: Routledge.

Levitt, P., and S. Merry. 2009. "Vernacularization on the Ground: Local Uses of Global Women's Rights in Peru, China, India, and the United States." *Global Networks* 9 (4): 441–61.

Łobodzińska, B. 1995. "Equal Opportunities: Obstacles and Remedies." In *Family, Women, and Employment in Central Eastern Europe*, edited by B. Łobodzińska. Westport, CT: Greenwood Press.

Lock, M., and P. A. Kaufert. 1998. *Pragmatic Women and Body Politics.* Cambridge: Cambridge University Press.

Long, K. S. 1996. *We All Fought for Freedom: Women in Poland's Solidarity Movement.* Boulder, CO: Westview Press.

Makara-Strudzińska, M., S. Kołodziej, and R. Turek. 2005. "Nierozwiązany problem: nieletnie matki." *Annales Universitatis Mariae Curie-Skłodowska* 60 (Supplement 16): 297.

Maleck-Lewy, E., and M. M. Ferree. 2000. "Talking about Women and Wombs: The Discourse of Abortion and Reproductive Rights in the G.D.R. during and after the Wende." In *Reproducing Gender: Politics, Publics, and Everyday Life after Socialism*, edited by S. Gal and G. Kligman, 97–112. Princeton, NJ: Princeton University Press.

Marody, M. 1993. "Why Am I Not a Feminist?" *Social Research* 60 (Winter): 853–64.

Marody, M., and A. Giza-Poleszczuk. 2000. "Changing Images of Identity in Poland: From the Self-Sacrificing to the Self-Investing Woman." In *Reproducing Gender: Politics, Publics, and Everyday Life after Socialism*, edited by S. Gal and G. Kligman, 151–75. Princeton, NJ: Princeton University Press.

Matynia, E. 1995. "Finding a Voice: Women in Postcommunist Central Europe." In *The Challenge of Local Feminism*, edited by A. Basu. Boulder, CO: Westview Press.

Maziarski, W. 2008. "Terror antyaborcyjny." *Newsweek*, June 8, 2.

Mazur, P. 1981. "Contraception and Abortion in Poland." *Family Planning Perspectives* 13 (4): 195–98.

McDaniel, S. A. 1996. "Toward a Synthesis of Feminist and Demographic Perspectives on Fertility." *Sociological Quarterly* 37 (1): 83–104.

McDonald, P. 2000. "Gender Equity in Theories of Fertility Transition." *Population and Development Review* 26 (3): 427–39.

———. 2006. "Low Fertility and the State: The Efficacy of Policy." *Population and Development Review* 32 (3): 485–510.

McMahon, P. C. 2002. "International Actors and Women's NGOs in Poland and Hungary." In *The Power and Limits of NGOs: A Critical Look at Building Democracy in Eastern Europe and Eurasia*, edited by S. E. Mendelson and J. K. Glenn, 29–53. New York: Columbia University Press.

McMenamin, I., and V. Timonen. 2002. "Poland's Health Reform: Politics, Markets and Informal Payments." *Journal of Social Policy* 31 (1): 103–18.

Michaels, M. W., and L. M. Morgan, eds. 1999. *Fetal Subjects, Feminist Positions.* Philadelphia: University of Pennsylvania Press.

Michnik, A. 1993. *The Church and the Left.* Chicago: University of Chicago Press.

Milanovic, B. 1999. "Explaining the Increase in Inequality during Transition." *Economics of Transition* 7 (2): 299–341.

Mishtal, J. 2009a. "Understanding Low Fertility in Poland: Demographic Consequences of Postsocialist Neoliberal Restructuring." *Demographic Research* 21
(art. 20): 599–626.

———. 2009b. "Matters of 'Conscience': The Politics of Reproductive Health and
Rights in Poland." *Medical Anthropology Quarterly* 23 (2): 161–83.

———. 2009c. "How the Church Became the State: The Catholic Regime and Re-
productive Rights and Policies in Poland." In *Collected Volume on Women's
Lives, Gender Relations, and State Policy in Central and Eastern Europe under
State Socialism,* edited by J. Massino and S. Penn, 133–50. New York: Palgrave
Macmillan.

———. 2010. "The Challengers of Reproductive Healthcare: Neoliberal Reforms
and Privatisation in Poland." *Reproductive Health Matters* 18 (36): 56–66.

———. 2014. "Reproductive Governance in the New Europe: Competing Visions of
Morality, Sovereignty, and Supranational Policy." *Anthropological Journal of
European Cultures* 23 (1): 59–76.

Mishtal, J., and R. Dannefer. 2010. "Reconciling Religious Identity and Reproductive Practices: The Church and Contraception in Poland." *European Journal of
Contraception and Reproductive Health* 15 (4): 232–42.

Mohanty, C. T. 2003. *Feminism without Borders.* Durham, NC: Duke University
Press.

Mojzes, P. 1999. "Religious Topography of Eastern Europe." *Journal of Ecumenical
Studies* 36 (1–2): 7–42.

Molyneux, M. 1995. "Gendered Transitions in Eastern Europe." *Feminist Studies* 21
(3): 637–45.

Monticone, R. C. 1986. *The Catholic Church in Communist Poland, 1945–1985:
Forty Years of Church-State Relations.* New York: Columbia University Press.

Morgan, L. M. 2008. *Icons of Life: A Cultural History of Human Embryos.* Berkeley: University of California Press.

Morgan, L. M., and E. F. Roberts. 2012. "Reproductive Governance in Latin America." *Anthropology & Medicine* 19 (2): 241–54.

Mosse, G. 1988. *Nationalism and Sexuality: Respectability and Abnormal Sexuality
in Modern Europe.* Madison: University of Wisconsin Press.

Mucha, J. 1989. "The Status of Unbelievers as a Group in Polish Society." *Journal of
the Anthropological Society of Oxford* 20 (3): 209–18.

Mynarska, M., and L. Bernardi. 2007. "Meanings and Attitudes Attached to Cohabitation in Poland." *Max Planck Institute for Demographic Research* 006: 1–34.

Nagengast, C. 1991. *Reluctant Socialists, Rural Entrepreneurs: Class, Culture, and
the Polish State.* Boulder, CO: Westview Press.

Nemenyi, M. 1996. "The Social Construction of Women's Roles in Hungary." *Replika* 7: 83–91.

Nesterowicz, M. 2001. *Prawo medyczne*. Toruń: Dom Organizatora TNOiK.

Niemiec, K. T. 1997. "Reproductive Health and Family Planning in Poland." In *Assessment of Research and Service Needs in Reproductive Health in Eastern Europe*, edited by E. Johannisson et al. New York: Parthenon.

Noonan, J. T. J. 1986. *Contraception: A History of Its Treatment by the Catholic Theologians and Canonists*. Cambridge, MA: Harvard University Press.

Nowakowska, U., and M. Korzeniowska. 2000. "Women's Reproductive Rights." In *Polish Women in the 90s*, edited by U. Nowakowska, 219–48. Warsaw: Women's Rights Center.

Nowicka, W. 1994. "Two Steps Back: Poland's New Abortion Law." *Journal of Women's History* 5 (3): 151–55.

———. 2001. "Struggles for and against Legal Abortion in Poland." In *Advocating for Abortion Access*, edited by B. Klugman, and D. Budlender, 226–27. Johannesburg: Women's Health Project.

———. 2002. "Unia Europejska i Kobiety." *Federacja na Rzecz Kobiet i Planowania Rodziny Biuletyn* 2 (19): 1–2.

———. 2008a. "The Anti-Abortion Act in Poland—The Legal and Actual State." In *Reproductive Rights in Poland: The Effects of the Anti-Abortion Law in Poland, Report*, edited by W. Nowicka, 17–44. Warsaw: Federation for Women and Family Planning.

———. 2008b. "The Case of a Pregnant Teen from Lublin: Chronology of Events." http://federa.org.pl.

———. 2008c. "Platforma idzie tropem Giertycha." *Rzeczpospolita*, September 17, 1. http://www.rp.pl/artykul/191855.html?print=tak&p=0.

———. 2008d. "Federacja Kobiet: Kopacz chce kontrolować ciężarne panie." *Wiadomości.wp.pl.* http://wiadomosci.wp.pl/kat,1342,title,Federacja-Kobiet-Kopacz-chce-kontrolowac-ciezarne-panie,wid,10353852,wiadomosc.html ?ticaid=114913.

———. 2010. "List otwarty w sprawie znieczulenia farmakologicznego przy porodzie." November 4, 1. Warsaw: Federation for Women and Family Planning. http://www.federa.org.pl/?option=com_content&view=article&id =246:listotwartyznieczulenie&catid=21:podrzedne.

———. 2011. "Sexual and Reproductive Rights and the Human Rights Agenda: Controversial and Contested." *Reproductive Health Matters* 19 (38): 119–28.

Nowicka, W., and F. Girard. 2002. "Clear and Compelling Evidence: The Polish Tribunal on Abortion Rights." *Reproductive Health Matters* 10 (19): 22–30.

Nowicka, W., and E. Zielińska. 2000. "Medical Community's Perspectives on Abortion." In *Report of the Federation 2000*, 1–34. http//www.federa.org.pl.

OECD (Organisation for Economic Co-operation and Development). 2011. *Poland: OCED Better Life Index*. http://www.oecdbetterlifeindex.org/countries /poland/.

Okólski, M. 1983. "Abortion and Contraception in Poland." *Studies in Family Planning* 14 (11): 263–74.

Oleksy, E. H. 2000. "American Feminism and Pedagogy: The Case of Poland." *American Studies International* 38 (3): 36–46.

———. "Women's Pictures and the Politics of Resistance in Poland." *NORA* 12 (3): 162–71.

Ong, A. 1987. *Spirits of Resistance and Capitalist Discipline: Factory Women in Malaysia.* New York: State University of New York Press.

Ortiz-Ortega, A. 2005. "The Politics of Abortion in Mexico: The Paradox of Doble Discurso." In *Where Human Rights Begin: Health, Sexuality and Women in the New Millennium,* edited by E. Chesler and W. Chavkin, 154–79. New Brunswick, NJ: Rutgers University Press.

Osa, M. 1997. "Creating Solidarity: The Religious Foundations of the Polish Social Movement." *East European Politics and Societies* 11 (2): 339–65.

Ost, D. 1990. *Solidarity and the Politics of Antipolitics: Opposition and Reform in Poland since 1968.* Philadelphia: Temple University Press.

———. 1993. Introduction to *The Church and the Left,* by D. Ost, 1–29. Chicago: University of Chicago Press.

———. 1999. "The Radical Right in Poland." In *The Radical Right in Central and Eastern Europe since 1989,* edited by S. P. Ramet, 85–107. University Park: Pennsylvania State University Press.

———. 2005. *The Defeat of Solidarity: Anger and Politics in Postcommunist Europe.* Ithaca, NY: Cornell University Press.

Ost, D., and M. Weinstein. 1999. "Unionists against Unions: Toward Hierarchical Management in Post-Communist Poland." *East European Politics and Societies* 13 (1): 1–33.

O'Toole, F. 2012. "When Is an Abortion Not an Abortion?" *Irish Times,* November 17, 1–4. http://www.irishtimes.com/newspaper/weekend/2012/1117/1224326695598.html.

Owczarzak, J. 2009. "Defining Democracy and the Terms of Engagement with the Postsocialist Polish State: Insights from HIV/AIDS." *East European Politics and Societies* 23 (3): 421–45.

Paltrow, S. 1986. "Poland and the Pope: The Vatican's Relations with Poland, 1978 to the Present." *Millennium: Journal of International Studies* 15 (1): 1–26.

Pankowski, K. 2013. "Potencjał niezadowolenia społecznego—stosunek do różnych form protestu." Report number: BS/55/2013, 1–8. Warsaw: CBOS Centrum Badania Opinii Społecznej (Public Opinion Research Center) (April).

Paul VI. 1968. "The Encyclical *Humanae Vitae:* On the Regulation of Birth." Vatican: Vatican Editrice Vaticana, 1–17. http://www.vatican.va/holy_father/paul_vi/encyclicals/documents/hf_p-vi_enc_25071968_humanae-vitae_en.html.

———. 1969. "En reponse a la demande May 29, 1969." Vatican: Vatican Editrice Vaticana.

Pawlicki, J. 2005. "Europa: w poszukiwaniu utraconego sensu." *Gazeta Wyborcza,* June 23, 1–4. http://wyborcza.pl/1,75515,2783195.html.

Pease, N. 1991. "The 'Unpardonable Insult': The Wawel Incident of 1937 and Church-State Relations in Poland." *Catholic Historical Review* 77 (3): 422–36.

Penn, S. 2003. "Poland Backs Away from Liberalizing Abortion Laws. *Women's News,* February 17. http://womensenews.org/story/health/030207/county -searches-clues-breast-cancer-rates.

———. 2005. *Solidarity's Secret: The Women Who Defeated Communism in Poland.* Ann Arbor: University of Michigan Press.

Peters, E. 2005. "Quoniam abundavit iniquitas: Dominicans as Inquisitors, Inquisitors as Dominicans." *Catholic Historical Review* 91 (1): 105–21.

Petö, A. 2002. "The History of the Hungarian Women's Movement." In *Thinking Differently: A Reader in European Women's Studies,* edited by G. Griffin and R. Braidotti, 361–71. London: Zed Books.

Phillips, A. 1997. "Sexual Equality and Socialism." *Dissent* 44:28–38.

———. 2002. "Does Feminism Need a Conception of Civil Society." In *Alternative Conceptions of Civil Society,* edited by S. Chambers and W. Kymlicka, 71–89. Princeton, NJ: Princeton University Press.

Piłka, M. "Prawda, dzieci i pieniądze." *Fronda.pl,* 1–7. http://www.fronda.pl/a /prawda-dzieci-i-pieniadze,28639.html.

Pine, F. 2002. "Retreat to Household? Gendered Domains in Postsocialist Poland." In *Postsocialism: Ideals, Ideologies, and Practices in Eurasia,* edited by C. Hann, 17:95–113. New York: Routledge.

Podgórska, J. 2009. "Aborcja on-line: Świeża krew prosi o pomoc." *Polityka.Pl,* November 12, 1. http://www.polityka.pl/spoleczenstwo/artykuly/1500423,1 ,aborcja-on-line.read?backTo=http://www.polityka.pl/spoleczenstwo /artykuly/1509126,1,aborcja-po-polsku.read.

Polityka. 2002. "Mało nas." No. 46 (2376), November 16, 13. http://archiwum .polityka.pl/art/malo-nas,376412.html.

Profamily Politics of the State Program. 1999. The Magistrate for Family Affairs. Document number 1522, 1–91. November 16. Warsaw.

Rabinow, P., and N. Rose. 2006. "Biopower Today." *BioSocieties* 1:197–217.

Radić, R. 1999. "The Proselytizing Nature of Marxism-Leninism." *Journal of Ecumenical Studies* 36:80–94.

Radkowska-Walkowicz, M. 2012. "The Creation of 'Monsters': The Discourse of Opposition to in Vitro Fertilization in Poland." *Reproductive Health Matters* 20 (40): 30–37.

Rapp, R. 2001. "Gender, Body, Biomedicine: How Some Feminist Concerns Dragged Reproduction to the Center of Social Theory." *Medical Athropology Quarterly* 15 (4): 466–77.

Ratzinger, J. 2004. "Letter to the Bishops of the Catholic Church on the Cooperation of a Man and a Woman in the Church and the World. Rome, Vatican: 1–13." http://www.vatican.va/roman_curia/congregations/cfaith/documents/rc _con_cfaith_doc_20040731_collaboration_en.html.

Regulska, J. 1998. "Transition to Local Democracy." In *Women in the Politics of Post-communist Eastern Europe*, edited by M. Rueschemeyer. New York: M. E. Sharpe.

———. 1999. "NGOs and Their Vulnerabilities during the Transition: The Case of Poland." *Voluntas: International Journal of Voluntary and Nonprofit Organizations* 10 (1): 61–71.

———. 2009. "Governance or Self-Governance in Poland? Benefits and Threats 20 Years Later." *International Journal of Politics, Culture, and Society* 22:537–56.

Reher, D. 2007. "Towards Long-Term Population Decline: A Discussion of Relevant Issues." *Journal of Population* 23:189–207.

Reporters Without Borders. 2003. "Poland—Annual Report 2003." May 2, 1–2. http://en.rsf.org/article.php3?id_article=6526.

Rich, V. 1992. "Poland: Medical Ethics Code." *Lancet* 339 (8803): 1221–22.

———. 1994. "Polish Abortions." *Lancet* 343 (8905): 1090.

Rivkin-Fish, M. 2003. "Anthropology, Demography, and the Search for a Critical Analysis of Fertility: Insights from Russia." *American Anthropologist* 105 (2): 289–301.

———. 2004. "Gender and Democracy: Strategies for Engagament and Dialogue on Women's Issues after Socialism in St. Petersburg." *Post-Soviet Women Encountering Transition: Nation Building, Economic Survival, and Civic Activism*, edited by K. Kuehnast and C. Nechemias, 228–312. Washington, DC: Woodrow Wilson Center Press:.

———. 2005. *Women's Health in Post-Soviet Russia: The Politics of Intervention.* Bloomington: Indiana University Press.

———. 2010. "Pronatalism, Gender Politics, and the Renewal of Family Support in Russia: Toward a Feminist Anthropology of 'Maternity Capital.'" *Slavic Review* 69 (3): 701–724.

Rogulska, B. 2012. "Postawy Wobec Stosowania Zapłodnienia in Vitro." Warsaw: CBOS Centrum Badania Opinii Społecznej, 1–11.

Rosada, S., and J. Gwóźdź. 1955. "Church and State in Poland." In *Church and State Behind the Iron Curtain*, edited by V. Gsovski, 159–252. New York: Praeger.

Rose, N., and C. Novas. 2005. "Biological Citizenship." In *Global Assemblages: Technology, Politics, and Ethics as Anthropological Problems*, edited by A. Ong and S. J. Collier. Malden, MA: Blackwell.

Rosenberg, D. J. 1991. "Shock Therapy: GDR Women in Transition from a Socialist Welfare State to a Social Market Economy." *Signs: Journal of Women in Culture and Society* 17 (1): 129–51.

Rossilli, M. G. 1999. "The European Union's Policy on Equality of Women." *Feminist Studies* 25 (1): 171–81.

Rueschemeyer, M. 1998. *Women in the Politics of Postcommunist Eastern Europe.* London: M. E. Sharpe.

Rutkiewicz, M. 2001. "Towards a Human Rights-Based Contraceptive Policy: A Critique of the Anti-Sterilization Law in Poland." *European Journal of Health Law* 8:225–42.

Rynek Zdrowia. 2010. "Do rzecznika praw pacjenta wpłynęło 40 tys. skarg i zapytań." February 11, 1. http://www.rynekzdrowia.pl/Finanse-i-zarzadzanie/Do -rzecznika-praw-pacjenta-wplynelo-40-tys-skarg-i-zapytan,15531,1.html.

Scheper-Hughes, N. 1992. *Death without Weeping: The Violence of Everyday Life in Brazil.* Berkeley: University of California Press.

———. 1995. "The Primacy of the Ethical: Propositions for a Militant Anthropology." *Current Anthropology* 36 (3): 409–40.

Schild, V. 1998. "Market Citizenship and the 'New Democracies': The Ambiguous Legacies of Contemporary Chilean Women's Movements." *Social Politics* 5 (Summer): 232–49.

Schneider, J. C., and P. T. Schneider. 1996. *Festival of the Poor.* Tucson: University of Arizona Press.

Scott, J. 1985. *Weapons of the Weak: Everyday Forms of Peasant Resistance.* New Haven, CT: Yale University Press.

Sherif, B. 2001. "The Ambiguity of Boundaries in the Fieldwork Experience: Establishing Rapport and Negotiating Insider/Outsider Status." *Qualitative Inquiry* 7 (4): 436–47.

Sherwin, S. 2008. "Whither Bioethics? How Feminism Can Help Reorient Bioethics." *International Journal of Feminist Approaches to Bioethics* 1 (1): 7–27.

Shore, C. 2000. *Building Europe: The Cultural Politics of European Integration.* London: Routledge.

Siedlecka, E. 2013. "Komisja Europejska grozi Polsce za brak przepisów o in vitro." *Gazeta Wyborcza,* January 28, 1–3. http://wyborcza.pl/1,75248,13307058 ,Komisja_Europejska_grozi_Polsce_za_brak_przepisow.html.

———. 2014. "Chazan zwolniony—problem zostaje." *Gazeta Wyborcza,* July 10, 1–3. http://wyborcza.pl/1,75968,16299596,Chazan_zwolniony___problem _zostaje.html.

Siemińska, R. 1994. "Polish Women as the Object and Subject of Politics during and after the Communist Party." In *Women and Politics Worldwide,* edited by B. J. Nelson and N. Chowdhury, 608–24. New Haven, CT: Yale University Press.

Šiklová, J. 1993. "McDonald's, Terminators, Coca Cola Ads, and Feminism?" In *Bodies of Bread and Butter: Reconfiguring Women's Lives in Post-Communist Czech Republic*, edited by L. Busheikin. Prague: Prague Gender Center.

———. 1997. "Feminism and the Roots of Apathy in the Czech Republic." *Social Research* 64 (2): 258–80.

Simpson, P. 1994. "International Trends: An Update of the Polish Election: What Did It Mean for Women?" *Journal of Women's History* 6 (1): 67–74.

———. 1996. "The Troubled Reign of Lech Wałęsa in Poland." *Presidential Studies Quarterly* 26 (2): 317–36.

Simpson, V. L. 2009. "Pope Says Condoms Worsen HIV Problem." *Washington Post*, March 18, 1–2. http://www.washingtonpost.com/wp-dyn/content/article/2009/03/17/AR2009031703369.html.

Snitow, A. 1993. "The Church Wins, Women Lose; Poland's Abortion Law." *Nation* 256 (16): 556–60.

Sobotka, T. 2004. "Is Lowest-Low Fertility in Europe Explained by the Postponement of Childbearing." *Population and Development Review* 30 (2): 195–220.

Soper, K. 1993. "Productive Contradictions." In *Up against Foucault: Explorations of Some Tensions between Foucault and Feminism*, edited by C. Ramazanoglu, 29–50. London: Routledge.

Sporniak, A. 2003. "Contraception in the Confessional." *Tygodnik Powszechny*, June 8, 1–4. http://www2.tygodnik.com.pl/tp/2813/wiara01_print.html.

Šribar, R. 2002. "Lacking Integration: The Relationship between the Women's Movement and Gender/Women's Studies in Transitional Slovenia." In *Thinking Differently: A Reader in European Women's Studies*, edited by G. Griffin and R. Braidotti, 372–77. London: Zed Books.

Staniszkis, J. 1984. *Poland's Self-Limiting Revolution*. Princeton, NJ: Princeton University Press.

Stark, R., and L. Iannaccone. 1996. "Response to Lechner: Recent Religious Declines in Quebec, Poland, and the Netherlands: A Theory Vindicated." *Journal for the Scientific Study of Religion* 35 (September): 265–71.

Statistical Yearbook of Poland. 2007. Warsaw: GUS (Główny Urząd Statystyczny [Central Statistical Office]).

———. 2013. Wyznania Religijne. Stowarzyszenia Narodowościowe i Etniczne w Polsce 2009–2011, 1–398. Warsaw: GUS (Główny Urząd Statystyczny [Central Statistical Office]).

Stefańczyk, I. 2004. "Reproductive Health Services in Poland: Country Report, ASTRA—Central and Eastern European Women's Network for Sexual and Reproductive Health and Rights," 1–4. http://www.astra.org.pl/pdf/publications/POLAND.pdf.

Stoilkova, M. 2005. "A Quest for Belonging: The Bulgarian Demographic Crisis, Emigration, and the Postsocialist Generations," in *Barren States*, edited by C. B. Douglass, 115–36. New York: Berg.

Stopler, G. 2005. "The Liberal Bind: The Conflict between Women's Rights and Patriarchal Religion in the Liberal State." *Social Theory and Practice* 31 (2): 191–231.

Sudman, S., E. Blair, N. Bradburn, and C. Stocking 1977. "Estimates of Threatening Behavior Based on Reports of Friends." *Public Opinion Quarterly* 41:261–64.

Swatos, W. 1994. *Politics and Religion in Central and Eastern Europe*. Westport, CT: Praeger.

Szaflarski, M. 2001. "Gender, Self-reported Health, and Health-Related Lifestyles in Poland." *Health Care for Women International* 22 (3): 207–27.

Szawarski, Z. 1992. "Polish Doctors Vote to Stop Carrying out Abortions." *British Medical Journal* 304 (6820): 137.

Szelenyi, I., E. Fodor, and E. Hanley. 1997. "Left Turn in Post-Communist Politics: Bringing Class Back In?" *East European Politics and Societies* 11 (1): 190–224.

Szlachetka, M., and A. Pochrzest. 2008. "Agata z matką chcą aborcji. Szpital odmawia." *Gazeta Wyborcza*, June 6, 1–2.

Szostkiewicz, A. 1999. "Religion after Communism." *Commonweal* 126 (September): 17–19.

Szymaniak, M. 2010. "Chrześcijańskiej Europie grozi islamizacja?" *Rzeczpospolita*, January 10, 1–2. http://www.rp.pl/artykul/417184.html.

Taras, R. 1995. *Consolidating Democracy in Poland*. Boulder, CO: Westview Press.

Tarkowska, E. 2002. "Intra-household Gender Inequality: Hidden Dimensions of Poverty among Polish Women." *Communist and Post-Communist Studies* 35 (4): 411–32.

Pontifical Council for Pastoral Assistance to Health Care Workers. 1995. "The Charter for Health Care Workers." Vatican City. http://www.vatican.va /roman_curia/pontifical_councils/hlthwork/documents/rc_pc_hlthwork_doc _19950101_charter_en.html.

Titkow, A. 1998. "Polish Women in Politics: An Introduction to the Status of Women in Poland." In *Women in the Politics of Postcommunist Eastern Europe*, edited by M. Rueschemeyer. New York: M. E. Sharpe.

———. 1999. "Poland." In *From Abortion to Contraception*, edited by H. P. David, 165–90. Westport, CT: Greenwood Press.

Traynor, I. 2003. "Abortion Issue Threatens Polish Admission to EU." *Guardian*, January 30, 1–3. http://www.guardian.co.uk/world/2003/jan/30/eu.politics.

Trojan, J. 1994. "Theology and Economics in the Postcommunist Era." *Christian Century* 111 (March): 278–80.

Trujillo, A. L. 2003a. "The Family and Life in Europe." Pontifical Council for the Family. Vatican City. http://www.vatican.va/roman_curia/pontifical_councils /family/documents/rc_pc_family_doc_20030614_family-europe-trujillo_en.html.

———. 2003b. "Family Values versus Safe Sex: A Reflection by His Eminence, Alfonso Cardinal López Trujillo, President, Pontifical Council for the Family, December 1, 2003." Vatican City. http://www.vatican.va/roman_curia/pontifical_councils/family /documents/rc_pc_family_doc_20031201_family-values-safe-sex-trujillo_en.html.

Trujillo, A. L., and F. G. Hellín. 1997. "Vademecum for Confessors Concerning Some Aspects of the Morality of Conjugal Life." Pontifical Council for the Family. Vatican City, February 12. http://www.vatican.va/roman_curia/pontifical _councils/family/documents/rc_pc_family_doc_12021997_vademecum_en.html.

———. 2000. "Family, Marriage, and 'De Facto' Unions." Pontifical Council for the Family. Vatican City, July 26. http://www.vatican.va/roman_curia/pontifical _councils/family/documents/rc_pc_family_doc_20001109_de-facto-unions _en.html.

Tumiłowicz, B. 2005. "Na czym powinna polegać racjonalna polityka prorodzinna?" *Przegląd*, 46. http://www.przeglad-tygodnik.pl/pl/artykul/na-czym -powinna-polegac-racjonalna-polityka-prorodzinna.

UN (United Nations). 2010. "Total Fertility Rate." In *World Population Prospects: The 2010 Revision.* http://data.un.org/data/aspx?d-popdiv&f=variableID %3a54#popdiv.

———. 2012. "Committee Concerned about 'Baby Boxes' in Europe." UN News & Media, United Nations Radio, June 11, 1. http://www.unmultimedia.org /radio/english/2012/06/un-committee-concerned-with-baby-boxes-in-europe/.

Tymowska, K. 2001. "Health Care under Transformation in Poland." *Health Policy* 56 (2): 85–98.

van Heesch, M. M., G. J. Bonsel, J. C. Dumoulin, J. L. Evers, M. A. van der Hoeven, and J. L. Severens. 2010. "Long-Term Costs and Effects of Reducing the Number of Twin Pregnancies in IVF by Single Embryo Transfer: The TwinSing Study." *BMC Pediatrics* 10:75.

Verdery, K. 1991. *National Ideology under Socialism: Identity and Cultural Politics in Ceauşescu's Romania.* Berkeley: University of California Press.

———. 1993. "Nationalism and National Sentiment in Post-Socialist Romania." *Slavic Review* 52 (2): 179–203.

———. 1996. *What Was Socialism and What Comes Next?* Princeton, NJ: Princeton University Press.

Vogel-Polsky, E. 2000. "Parity Democracy—Laws and Europe. In *Gender Policies in the European Union*, edited by M. G. Rossilli, 61–85. New York: Peter Lang.

Volkogonov, D. 1996. Trotsky: The Eternal Revolutionary. New York: Free Press.

Walczewska, S. 2000. *Damy, rycerze i feministki: Kobiecy dyskurs emancypacyjny w Polsce.* Kraków: Wydawnictwo eFKa.

Wasilewski, J., and E. Wnuk-Lipiński .1995. "Poland: Winding Road from the Communist to the Postsocialist-Solidarity Elite." *Theory and Society* 24 (5): 669–96.

Watson, P. 1993. "Eastern Europe's Silent Revolution." *Sociology* 27 (3): 471–87.

———. 1996. "The Rise of Masculinism in Eastern Europe. In *Mapping the Women's Movement*, edited by M. Threlfall, 216–31. New York: Verso.

Wciórka, B. 2000. *Społeczeństwa obywatelskie? Między aktywnością społeczną a biernością*. Warsaw: CBOS Centrum Badania Opinii Społecznej (Public Opinion Research Center).

Wedel, J. 1986. *The Private Poland*. New York: Facts on File Publication.

———, ed. 1992. *The Unplanned Society: Poland During and After Communism*. New York: Columbia University Press.

———. 1998. *Collision and Collusion: The Strange Case of Western Aid to Eastern Europe, 1989–1998*. New York: St. Martin's Press.

Weigel, G. 1992. *The Final Revolution: The Resistance Church and the Collapse of Communism*. New York: Oxford University Press.

WHO. 2006. *The World Health Report 2006*, Annex Table 2: Health Expenditures, Poland, 179–85. Geneva: WHO (World Health Organization).

———. 2012a. *Safe Abortion: Technical and Policy Guidance for Health Systems*, 1–134. Geneva: WHO (World Health Organization).

———. 2012b. *Trends in Maternal Mortality: 1990 to 2010*. WHO, UNICEF, UNFPA and The World Bank estimates, 1–72. Geneva: WHO (World Health Organization).

Wiśniewska, K. 2012. "Okna życia: ratują czy szkodzą porzuconym dzieciom." *Gazeta Wyborcza*, 1–2. http://wyborcza.pl/1,75478,12976976,Okna_zycia__ratuja_czy _szkodza_porzuconym_dzieciom.html.

Wolf, E. R. 1991. Introduction to *Religious Regimes and State-Formation*, by E. Wolf, 5–6. Albany: State University of New York Press.

World Bank. 2007. "Distribution of Income or Consumption." In *World Development Indicators*, 66–69. http://wdi.worldbank.org/table/2.9 and http://data .worldbank.org/indicator/SI.POV.GINI

Wróblewska, W. 2002. "Women's Health Status in Poland in the Transition to a Market Economy." *Social Science and Medicine* 54 (5): 707–26.

Zajicek, A., and T. Calasanti. 1995. "The Impact of Socioeconomic Restructuring on Polish Women." In *Family Women and Employment in Central Eastern Europe*, edited by B. Łobodzińska. Westport, CT: Greenwood Press.

Zielińska, E. 2000. "Between Ideology, Politics, and Common Sense: The Discourse of Reproductive Rights in Poland." In *Reproducing Gender: Politics, Publics, and Everyday Life after Socialism*, edited by S. Gal and G. Kligman, 23–57. Princeton, NJ: Princeton University Press.

Guide to Pronunciation

The following key provides a guide to the pronunciation of Polish words and names.

a is pronounced as in *father*
c as ts, as in *cats*
ch as guttural h, as in German BACH
cz as hard ch, as in *church*
g (always hard), as in *get*
i as ee, as in *meet*
j as y, as in *yellow*
rz as hard zh, as in French *jardin*
sz as hard sh, as in *ship*
szcz as hard shch, as in *fresh cheese*
u as oo, as in *boot*
w as v, as in *vat*
ć as soft ch, as in *cheap*
ś as soft sh, as in *sheep*
ż as hard zh, as in French *jardin*
ź as soft zh, as in *seizure*
ó as oo, as in *boot*
ą as a nasal, as in French *on*
ę as a nasal, as in French *en*
ł as w, as in *way*
ń as ny, as in *canyon*

The accent in Polish words always falls on the penultimate syllable.

Index

abortion, 1, 2; bans, 15, 18, 37, 40–42, 43, 44, 58–63, 71–73, 103, 140, 158, 186–87, 189, 193, 195; conscience clause law, 45–52, 64–65; decriminalization, 22, 218n3; EU on, 193; feminism on, 15, 70–73, 74, 78–81; foreign clinics, 150–54; and human rights, 194; illegal, 15, 41, 67–68, 143–50, 155–56, 158, 161, 185, 197; legal, access to, 41–42, 46, 51, 58, 59, 67–68, 140, 143, 154–57; lost language of, 81–82; medications for, 146, 152–53, 219n14; methods, 144–46; moratorium, 47–50; opposition to ban, 58, 71–73, 98–99, 107, 110, 156–57, 197; political passivity toward ban, 155–59, 186; public apathy toward, 71–72, 74, 78; under state socialism, 5, 6, 26; statistics, 143; strategies to circumvent laws, 14, 156, 159, 186; for women's health, 36
absolution, 15; after confession, 115–16, 118–19, 120, 122, 134, 180; denial of, 120–23
abstinence, sexual, 53, 91, 95, 123, 134, 216n35
Accession Treaty of Poland, 62–63, 102, 158
adoption, 154
Agata (legal case): abortion request/denial, 59; case background, 95–97, 158; legal victory of, 101–3
agency and power, 11–12, 14, 156, 159, 186
AIDS, 43, 216n35, 220n17
Alvarez, Sonia, 76

anti-Semitism, 24–25
Arłukowicz, Bartosz, 167–68
ARTs. *See* Assisted Reproductive Technologies
Assisted Reproductive Technologies (ARTs), 190–92
Association for State Neutrality (Neutrum), 70, 199
ASTRA Network, 70, 187, 194
AWS. *See* Solidarity Election Action

baby boxes, 154
Balicki, Marek, 59–60, 61
bans/prohibitions: abortion, 15, 18, 37, 40–42, 43, 44, 58–63, 71–73, 103, 140, 158, 186–87, 193; contraception, 43, 134–35, 179; opposition to, 58, 71–73, 98–99, 107, 110, 156–57; political passivity toward, 155–59
baptism, 124–25, 134
Bax, Mart, 34
becikowe (baby bonus), 174–75
Benedict XVI (pope), 2, 43, 86, 216n35, 221n8
Billings Ovulation Method, 135
bioethics, religious, 42–44, 49
biopolitics, Foucauldian, 14, 164; state socialist/postsocialist, 183; unofficial, 14, 156, 159, 185
biopower, 164, 182–83
birth control. *See* abstinence, sexual; calendar method of birth control; condoms; contraception; family planning; IUDs, pills, contraceptive; reproductive rights; withdrawal method of birth control

JOANNA MISHTAL is an associate professor of anthropology at the University of Central Florida. She researches the politics of gender, focusing on reproductive rights, health, and social policies in Poland, her native country.